# The
# Student Edition
# of MATLAB®

*Student*
*User Guide*

The MATLAB®
Curriculum Series

*PRENTICE HALL, Englewood Cliffs, NJ 07632*

Library of Congress Cataloging-in-Publication Data

The Student edition of MATLAB student user guide.
    p.   cm. -- (The MATLAB curriculum series)
  Includes index.
  ISBN 0-13-856006-4
  1. MATLAB (Computer program)  2. Numerical analysis--Data
processing.   I. Prentice-Hall, inc.  II. Series.
QA297.S8434   1992
519.4'0285'5369--dc20                                    91-38049
                                                         CIP

Acquisitions Editor: *Pete Janzow*
Production Editor: *Joe Scordato*
Copy Editor: *Kathleen Schiaparelli*
Cover Designer: *Bruce Kenselaar*
Prepress Buyer: *Linda Behrens*
Manufacturing Buyer: *Dave Dickey*
Supplements Editor: *Alice Dworkin*
Editorial Assistant: *Phyllis Morgan*

© 1992 by The MathWorks, Inc.
Published by Prentice-Hall, Inc.
A Paramount Communications Company
Englewood Cliffs, New Jersey 07632

Printed in the United States of America

10  9  8  7  6

ISBN 0-13-856006-4

Apollo and Domain are trademarks of Apollo Computer Inc.
Apple, the Apple logo, ImageWriter, LaserWriter, Macintosh, and
    MacWrite MPW are trademarks of Apple Computer Corporation.
DEC, VAX, VMS, MicroVax, and VT are trademarks of Digital
    Equipment Corporation.
HERCULES is a trademark of Hercules Computer Technology.
IBM and IBM-PC are trademarks of IBM.
INTEL is a trademark of Intel Corporation.
Language Systems FORTRAN is a trademark of Language Systems
    Corporation.
LaserJet is a trademark of Hewlett-Packard.
MacFortran is a trademark of Absoft Corporation.
MacNosy is a trademark of Jasik Designs.
MATLAB and PC-MATLAB are trademarks of The MathWorks, Inc.
Microsoft is a trademark of Microsoft Corporation.
MS-DOS and Excel are trademarks of Microsoft Corporation.
PostScript is a trademark of Adobe Systems, Inc.
SideKick is a trademark of Borland International.
SUN is a trademark of Sun Microsystems.
Tektronix is a trademark of Tektronix, Inc.
THINK C is a trademark of Symantec Corporation.
UNIX is a trademark of AT&T Bell Laboratories.
X Window System is a trademark of M.I.T.

Prentice-Hall International (UK) Limited, *London*
Prentice-Hall of Australia Pty. Limited, *Sydney*
Prentice-Hall Canada Inc., *Toronto*
Prentice-Hall Hispanoamericana, S.A., *Mexico*
Prentice-Hall of India Private Limited, *New Delhi*
Prentice-Hall of Japan, Inc., *Tokyo*
Simon & Schuster Asia Pte. Ltd., *Singapore*
Editora Prentice-Hall do Brasil, Ltda., *Rio de Janeiro*

**The MathWorks, Inc.**
Cochituate Place
24 Prime Park Way
Natick, Massachusetts 01760

# Contents

The
t Edition
MATLAB

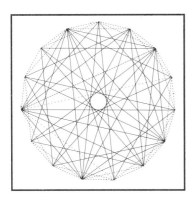

# Preface to the Instructor

In tens of thousands of industrial, government, and academic settings, MATLAB® has become the premier software package for interactive numeric computation, data analysis, and graphics, spanning a broad range of engineering and scientific applications. Now students can affordably use this powerful software product in their undergraduate and graduate studies, while getting acquainted with a tool that will prove invaluable throughout their careers.

As computers have become indispensable for creative work in science and engineering, academic institutions are increasingly aware of the importance of computer use and promoting software "literacy." However, the high cost of commercial-quality software and the challenge of integrating it into the curriculum have made it difficult to turn that awareness into positive results.

In response, we created *The Student Edition of MATLAB* and this *User Guide* so students can be introduced to this powerful tool early in their academic careers. *The Student Edition of MATLAB* encapsulates algorithmic mathematics in a form that can be easily applied to a wide range of disciplines, in courses such as Digital Signal Processing, Control Theory, Linear Algebra, Signals and Systems, Numerical Methods, Applied Mathematics, and Advanced Engineering Mathematics. By itself or when coupled with the *MATLAB Curriculum Series* texts, MATLAB can be incorporated effectively into the curriculum to enhance the understanding of both fundamental and advanced topics, while enabling the student actively to put theory into practice.

We are pleased and somewhat surprised to see how quickly this movement is already happening. As we visit many colleges and universities from Stanford to MIT and travel on to the leading institutions throughout Europe and the Pacific rim, we are consistently rewarded by the sight of students using MATLAB, not simply to get the answers, but rather to understand *how* to get the answers. It is happening across departments at schools, large and small, around the world. We sincerely hope that you enjoy taking part.

## Organization of the User's Guide

The book is divided into five major parts. *Part One: Getting Started* introduces the student to MATLAB's purpose, capabilities, and user instructions. *Part Two: Tutorial* highlights the capabilities of the package. *Part Three: The Signals and Systems Toolbox* builds on the foundation of the *The Student Edition of MATLAB*, to provide functions specialized for signal processing and control systems. *Part Four: Reference* lists the functions included in the *Student Edition of MATLAB*. Finally, *Appendices* highlights additional information on the use of MATLAB on the Macintosh and the use of advanced features.

## The MATLAB Curriculum Series

The MATLAB Curriculum Series is a selection of supplemental texts for use with *The Student Edition of MATLAB* and features MATLAB-based exercises and problem sets. These are designed to supplement standard texts for the following courses: Digital Signal Processing, Control Theory, Linear Algebra, Signals and Systems, Linear Systems, Numerical Methods, Applied Mathematics, and Advanced Engineering Mathematics. Additional texts in other course areas are anticipated.

# Instructor Support Policy

Prentice Hall and The MathWorks provide telephone and email support to registered instructors who have adopted *The Student Edition of MATLAB* for use in their courses. If you encounter difficulty using the Student Edition software:

1. Read the relevant section of this manual containing tutorial and/or reference information on the commands or the procedures you are trying to execute.

2. Use the software's online help facility by typing `help command` at the MATLAB prompt (where `"command"` is the name of the function about which you would like information).

3. Contact Prentice Hall by phone or email at:
   Phone: **1-201-592-3096**
   Email: **matlab@prenhall.com**

Prentice Hall will answer your technical questions and will handle any problems with defective disks, etc. If a glitch in the software is confirmed by us, we will attempt to provide a workaround until a fix is available.

*Important Reminder to Instructors: Take a moment right now, to complete and return to us the registration card at the front of the book.*

# Using MATLAB in the Classroom

A free professor's supplement, *Using MATLAB in the Classroom* is available upon request from Prentice Hall. This booklet is a compendium of exercises, projects, and teaching ideas contributed by professors in a variety of disciplines at universities nationwide. We hope you will find it useful. Additional ideas, projects and contributions are highlighted in *The Student Edition*, Prentice Hall's MATLAB newsletter for university users. Drop us a note if you'd like to be on our mailing list.

# Acknowledgments

Many people at The MathWorks and Prentice Hall contributed to the development of *The Student Edition of MATLAB*. However, particular thanks go to Peter Janzow at Prentice Hall and Elizabeth Callanan of The MathWorks, whose organizational skills and tireless efforts made it happen. They managed to keep everyone focused on the goal of delivering the product and kept the project on a demanding schedule.

Other key contributors at Prentice Hall to *The Student Edition of MATLAB* included Phyllis Morgan, Joe Scordato and Kathleen Schiaparelli, whose patience and production pace were exemplary.

Other key contributors at The MathWorks to *The Student Edition of MATLAB* who worked on the software or documentation, or acted as reviewers, included Jim Boyles, Cheryl Checkoway, Julie Forgaard, J. Michael Hammond, Jason Kinchen, John N. Little, Loren Shure, Josh Tillotson, and Jim Tung.

We also wish to thank the MATLAB Student Edition focus group who met at The MathWorks in May 1991 and to all those who generously volunteered at beta sites.

Finally, we wish to thank all of our friends and collegues in the academic community who have supported MATLAB during its first decade of development and who have continually urged The MathWorks to make a low cost, but high powered, version available to students. We are very pleased to be able to make this response to that prodding.

Cleve Moler
Natick, Massachusetts

# The
# Student Edition
# of MATLAB

# Part One

# Getting Started

# 1
# To the Student

*The Student Edition of MATLAB* brings us back to our roots. The very first version of MATLAB, written at the University of New Mexico and Stanford University in the late 1970s, was intended for use in courses in matrix theory, linear algebra, and numerical analysis. We had been involved in the development of LINPACK and EISPACK, which were Fortran subroutine packages for matrix manipulation, and we wanted our students to be able to use these packages without writing Fortran programs.

Today, MATLAB's capabilities extend far beyond the original "Matrix Laboratory" MATLAB is an interactive system and programming language for general scientific and technical computation. Its basic data element is a matrix that does not require dimensioning. This allows solution of many numeric problems in a fraction of the time it would take to write a program in a language such as Fortran, Basic, or C. Furthermore, problem solutions are expressed in MATLAB almost exactly as they are written mathematically.

We've continued to maintain close ties to the academic community and have offered academic discounts and classroom licensing arrangements. We have been pleased with the popularity of MATLAB in the computer labs on campus. *The Student Edition* makes it practical for students to use MATLAB on their personal computers in their homes, dorms, or wherever they work and study.

Mathematics is the common language of much of science and engineering. Matrices, differential equations, arrays of data, plots, and graphs are the basic building blocks of both applied mathematics and MATLAB. It is the underlying mathematical base that makes MATLAB accessible and powerful. One professor, who is a big MATLAB fan, told us, "The reason why MATLAB is so useful for signal processing is that it wasn't designed specifically for signal processing, but for mathematics."

MATLAB has been used in many different fields.

- A physics grad student analyzing data from her experiments with magnetic fields of superconductors.

- An internationally-known amusement park modeling the control systems for their water rides.

- A large food company analyzing how microwave ovens cook pizzas.

- A cable television company investigating digital TV.

- A sports equipment manufacturer modeling golf swings.

- A third grader learning her multiplication tables.

In all these cases, and thousands more, MATLAB's mathematical foundation made it useful in places and applications far beyond those we contemplated originally.

## 1.1 About the Cover

The cover on this guide and other MathWorks publications depicts various solutions to a problem that has played a small but interesting role in the history of numerical methods during the last 30 years. The problem involves finding the modes of vibration of a membrane supported by an L-shaped domain consisting of three unit squares. The non-convex corner in the domain generates singularities in the solutions, thereby providing challenges for both the underlying mathematical theory and the computational algorithms. There are important applications, including wave guides, structures, and semiconductors.

When we first looked at this problem in the 1960s, typical computer runs took up to half an hour of dedicated computer time on what were then Stanford University's primary computers, an IBM 7090 and a Burroughs B5000. Today, MATLAB allows us to express the entire algorithm in a few dozen lines, to compute the solution with great accuracy in a few minutes on a computer at home, and to readily manipulate three-dimensional displays of the results. We have included our MATLAB program, `membrane.m`, with the M-files supplied along with MATLAB.

## 1.2 The Student Edition of MATLAB vs. Professional MATLAB

*The Student Edition* is available for MS-DOS compatible personal computers and Macintoshes. It is identical to the professional version 3.5 of MATLAB except for four features:

- Each vector or matrix is limited to 1024 elements (that's a 32-by-32 matrix).

- The metafile and graphics postprocessor feature for graphics hardcopy is not available.

- A math coprocessor is not required, but will be used if it's available.

- A *Signals and Systems Toolbox* is included for student use.

The same professional version of MATLAB 3.5 is also available on workstations, mainframes, and supercomputers. The list of machines includes Sun, DEC VAX, DEC RISC, Hewlett Packard/Apollo, Silicon Graphics, IBM RS/6000, Convex, Alliant, and Cray. Using MATLAB on a Mac is just like using it on a Cray, except the Cray doesn't have a mouse, but it runs faster if there aren't too many other users.

## 1.3 How to Upgrade to Professional MATLAB

You can obtain a professional version of MATLAB for Macintosh and DOS personal computers, a number of UNIX and VMS workstations, and two supercomputers. For product information or to place an order, call or write to your educational account representative at The MathWorks at:

Mail: The MathWorks, Inc.
University Sales Department
Cochituate Place
24 Prime Park Way
Natick, MA 01760-1520

Telephone: (508) 653-1415

Fax: (508) 653-2997

Email: info@mathworks.com

## 1.4 Technical Support

### 1.4.1 Student Support Policy

Neither Prentice Hall, Inc. nor The MathWorks, Inc. provides technical support to student users of *The Student Edition of MATLAB*.†

If you encounter difficulty while using the Student Edition software:

1. Read the relevant section of this Student User Guide containing tutorial and/or reference information on the commands or procedures you are trying to execute.

2. Use the software's online `help` facility by typing `>>help command` at the MATLAB prompt (where `"command"` is the name of the function you are executing).

3. Write down the sequence of procedures you were executing so that you can explain to your instructor the nature of the problem. Be certain to note the exact error message you encountered.

### 1.4.2 Student User Registration

At the back of this book is a perforated card allowing you to register as a user of *The Student Edition of MATLAB*. Take a moment *now* to complete and return this card to us. Registered student users:

- Are entitled to replace defective disks at no charge.
- Qualify for a discount on upgrades to professional versions of MATLAB®.
- Become active members of the worldwide MATLAB® user community.

**It is VERY important that you return this card and also notify us of any changes of address using the change of address card (also at back of book). Otherwise you will not be on our mailing list and you will not qualify for student upgrades and other promotions.**

---

† Registered instructors adopting *The Student Edition* for student use in their courses are entitled to technical support (see *Preface* for details).

### 1.4.3 Defective Disk Replacement

Contact Prentice Hall at (201) 592-3096 for disk replacement. You must send us your damaged or defective disk, and we will provide you with a new one.

### 1.4.4 Limited Warranty

No warranties, express or implied, are made by The MathWorks, Inc. that the program or documentation is free of error. Further, The MathWorks, Inc. does not warrant the program for correctness, accuracy, or fitness for a task. *You rely on the results of the program solely at your own risk.* The program should not be relied on as the sole basis to solve a problem whose incorrect solution could result in injury to person or property. If the program is employed in such a manner, it is at the user's own risk, and The MathWorks, Inc. disclaims all liability for such misuse. Neither The MathWorks, Inc. nor anyone else who has been involved in the creation, production, or delivery of this program shall be liable for any direct or indirect damages.

# 1.5 Toolboxes and Professional MATLAB

Because MATLAB is an interactive environment, scientists and engineers are able to analyze and develop algorithms with exceptional improvements in productivity and creativity. As a result of the new algorithms with application-specific uses, The MathWorks offers a series of *application toolboxes* that contain sets of MATLAB functions designed for specific applications.

These toolboxes add specific functionality for applications such as digital signal processing, automatic control system design, nonlinear simulation, parametric modeling, optimization, spline analysis, and analytical chemistry. One toolbox, the *Signals and Systems Toolbox*, has been specifically designed for use and inclusion with *The Student Edition of MATLAB*.

The MathWorks family of products includes the following:

## MATLAB

### Professional version

Linear algebra, high-speed computational kernel, extensive mathematical functionality, data analysis, 2-D and 3-D graphics, rapid algorithm development, matrix based programming environment.

## Education Version

This is the professional version but priced at a lower rate for academic use.

## SIMULAB

Block diagram and differential equation models; simulation, linearization, and trim; linear and nonlinear models; continuous and discrete (digital) models; mouse-driven and highly interactive, X Windows/Motif and Macintosh windowing systems.

## Optimization Toolbox

General minimization of nonlinear functions, including function minimization and maximization, constrained and unconstrained problems, nonlinear least-squares, semi-infinite and multi-objective techniques.

## Control System Toolbox

Modern and classical techniques; state-space and transfer function models; root-locus; pole placement and LQC; Bode, Nyquist, Nichols and SVD frequency response plots; impulse, step and general time response plots, bookkeeping and system interconnection; transformations between models, and model reduction.

## System Identification Toolbox

Find transfer function models from input/output data; MA, AR, ARMA, Box-Jenkins modeling; parametric and nonparametric modeling; spectral analysis; recursive and batch techniques; model validation and goodness of fit; automatic and manual order selection; model-based signal processing.

## MMLE3 State-Space Identification Toolbox

Implementation of NASA MMLE3 algorithm.

## Mu-Analysis and Synthesis Toolbox

System computations, frequency responses, and time simulations of multivariable linear systems, structured singular value analysis for computing robust stability and performance characterization of uncertain systems. H-infinity and H2 optimal control design.

## Signal Processing Toolbox

Digital and analog filter design; spectrum analysis; convolution, correlation, and FFT analysis; 1-D and 2-D signal processing.

## Robust Control Toolbox

LQG-based optimal control synthesis using loop transfer recovery and frequency-weighted methods, H2 and H-infinity optimal control synthesis, singular-value based model reduction, and spectral factorization and model building.

## Spline Toolbox

Piecewise polynomials and B-spline; spline construction and manipulation; datafitting and smoothing; function differentiation, integration and evaluation.

## Chemometrics Toolbox

Calibration matrix development and evaluation; quantitative analysis methods development; multiple linear regression; principal component regression; partial least squares.

For more information regarding any of the MathWorks products contact The MathWorks, Inc. (see Section 1.3).

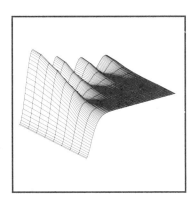

# 2

# If You Insist on Not Reading Instructions

## 2.1 MS-DOS Quick Start

If you are one of those experts who wants to see something from MATLAB *right now* and would rather read the instructions later, this page is for you. Here is an abbreviated set of instructions for installing MATLAB on a PC equipped with a hard disk:

1. Boot your system, if it is not already.

2. Create a subdirectory called \MATLAB on the hard disk and make it the current directory:

   ```
   MKDIR \MATLAB
   CD \MATLAB
   ```

3. Insert the MATLAB Diskette 1 in floppy drive A.

4. Make sure \MATLAB is the current directory on the hard disk, and execute A:INSTALL. This executes a batch file that copies and decompresses the files from *Disk 1* onto the hard disk. It will then prompt you to insert any additional diskettes required (*Disk 2, Disk 3, etc.*), from which all files are copied to the hard disk.

5. Remove the last disk from drive A and return all disks to the plastic sleeve at the back of the guide.

6. Check to make sure that a minimum of `FILES=20` is set in your `CONFIG.SYS` file and add `\MATLAB\BIN` to your `PATH` setting.

7. Execute MATLAB (by typing `MATLAB`) and try it out for a while. Type `demo` at the MATLAB prompt to see some demonstrations.

8. Go read the instructions.

Although attempts have been made to provide the most complete and up-to-date information in this manual, some information may have changed while it was being printed. Please check the `README` file for the latest release notes.

## 2.2 Macintosh Quick Start

If you are one of those experts who wants to see something from MATLAB *right now* and would rather read the instructions later, this section is for you. Here is an abbreviated set of instructions for installing *The Student Edition of MATLAB* on your Mac equipped with a hard disk:

1. Insert the disk labeled "The Student Edition of MATLAB for the Macintosh" into your 800K drive, and double-click on it to open it.

2. Drag the `Student MATLAB.sea` file onto your hard disk.

3. Eject the disk.

4. *The Student Edition of MATLAB* is shipped in compressed form and must be decompressed before it can be used. To decompress the software, simply double-click on the `Student MATLAB.sea` file (on your hard disk). An open file dialog will appear, with the prompt "Select Destination Folder..." If you wish to install *The Student Edition of MATLAB* on your hard disk, click on the **Extract** button. If you wish to install *The Student Edition of MATLAB* elsewhere you can navigate there, then click on the **Extract** button.

5. A dialog box will appear, showing the decompression progress. When the dialog box disappears, you should find a Student MATLAB folder on your hard disk.

6. Delete the `Student MATLAB.sea` from you hard disk.

Your Student MATLAB installation is complete. Store your original disk as a backup.

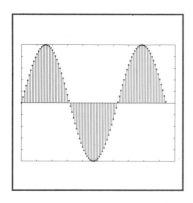

# 3
# About this Guide

---

## 3.1 Organization

*The Student Edition of MATLAB User Guide* is divided into five main parts:

**Getting Started**

The first section describes how to install and start MATLAB on the PC or Macintosh. This includes installation instructions, explaining the mechanics of making backup copies, configuring the system, and invoking the program.

**Tutorial**

The *Tutorial* is an introduction to using MATLAB. The basic features - including matrix manipulation, graphics, language features, and M-files - are described. Many examples are given.

**Signals and Systems Toolbox**

This toolbox, designed specifically for use with *The Student Edition*, contains some of the most frequently used functions from the professional versions of both the Signal Processing and Control Systems Toolboxes.

**Reference**

The *Reference* section contains a comprehensive description of each MATLAB function, including syntax, usage, and information about the algorithms used.

**Appendices**

*Appendix A* describes features specific to the Macintosh version of MATLAB. *Appendix B* discusses how to write MAT-files which allow you to transfer data files between MATLAB and other programs. *Appendix C* describes the printing capabilities of the professional version of MATLAB on the PC. *Appendix D* lists references used in this manual.

---

## 3.2  Conventions Used in this Guide

The following conventions are used throughout this manual:

| | |
|---|---|
| **Bold Initial Caps** | Key names, menu names, and items that can be selected from menus; for example, **Edit** menu. |
| `Constant Width` | User input, function names, commands, and screen displays. |
| *Italics* | Book titles, names of sections of this book, MATLAB toolbox names, mathematical notation, and for the introduction of new terms; for example, *Tutorial*. |
| ALL CAPS | File names; for example, MATLAB.BAT. |

**Note:** Commands and user input entered in MATLAB are case sensitive, so be certain to enter these exactly as shown in this guide.

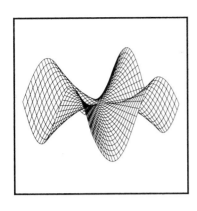

# 4
# MATLAB
# on MS-DOS PCs

## 4.1 System Requirements

*The Student Edition of MATLAB* for the PC requires:

- IBM PC/XT, PC/AT, PS/2, or compatible MS-DOS computer.

- At least 320K of memory.

- MS-DOS or PC-DOS version 3.1 or higher.

- A hard disk with at least 3M bytes of free space.

- A 360K byte 5¼", 720K byte 3½", 1.2M byte 5¼", or 1.44M byte 3½" floppy disk drive.

- Color Graphics Adapter (CGA), Enhanced Graphics Adapter (EGA), Hercules Monochrome Graphics Card (HGC), Video Graphics Array card (VGA), AT&T 6300 Graphics card (ATT), or compatible. Color graphics are available on systems with a VGA or an EGA (the EGA must have 256K bytes of video memory, however).

## 4.2 Disk Contents

MATLAB is distributed in compressed format on three or more 360K byte 5¼" diskettes, on two 720K byte 3½" diskettes, or just one 1.2M byte high-density diskette. The installation procedure moves the files on these diskettes to your hard disk and decompresses them.

After installation, your \MATLAB directory will contain the following subdirectories that themselves contain the various components of the MATLAB system:

| | |
|---|---|
| \BIN | Executable images and batch files for the MATLAB system. |
| \MATLAB | *MATLAB Toolbox* M-files. |
| \DEMO | Demonstration M-files. |
| \SIGSYS | *Signals and Systems Toolbox* M-files. |
| \LOADSAVE | Subroutines for reading and writing MAT-files from Fortran, C, and Pascal programs. |

The \MATLAB\BIN directory contains the batch files and executable images for MATLAB:

| | |
|---|---|
| MATLAB.BAT | Batch file to invoke MATLAB. |
| PCMATLAB.EXE | MATLAB executable binary program image. |
| EGAEPSON.COM | EGA and VGA screen-dump utility for Epson compatible printers. |
| EGALASER.COM | EGA and VGA screen-dump utility for Hewlett- Packard LaserJet compatible printers. |
| *.DRV | Graphics device drivers. |

The \MATLAB\MATLAB directory contains the *MATLAB Toolbox* files:

| | |
|---|---|
| README.M | A file you should read that lists new M-files that were added after this guide was printed. |
| *.M | Many M-files. |
| MATLAB.HLP | The file used by the help facility. |

The `MATLAB\LOADSAVE` directory contains subroutines for reading and writing MAT-files from Fortran, C, and Pascal programs. See *Subroutines to Read and Write MAT-Files* for more information on these files.

| | |
|---|---|
| `*.C` | Some subroutines and sample programs to interface C programs to MATLAB data files. |
| `*.FOR` | Some subroutines and sample programs to help interface Fortran programs to MATLAB data files. |
| `TESTLS.PAS` | An example program that shows how to interface Pascal programs to MATLAB data files. |
| `FLOADXX.FOR` | Fortran program calling C file I/O routines. |
| `FSAVEXX.FOR` | Fortran program calling C file I/O routines. |
| `FLOADSAV.C` | C subroutines for file I/O. |
| `FLOADSAV.OBJ` | Compiled object module. Included for convenience. |

# 4.3 Installation and Configuration

## 4.3.1 Overview

This section of the *User Guide* contains instructions that are specific to the MS-DOS Personal Computer implementation of MATLAB. These include:

- Installation instructions, explaining the mechanics of installing and configuring the software on your system, and

- Operational instructions for using PC-specific features of *The Student Edition of MATLAB* like editing, graphics, and hardcopy operations.

## 4.3.2 Installing MATLAB

*The Student Edition of MATLAB* is distributed in compressed format on two 360K byte 5¼" diskettes or one 720K bytes 3½" diskettes. The files on these diskettes will be moved to your hard disk and decompressed.

MATLAB is copyrighted and licensed for use on a single computer only. You are *not* allowed to give the program to friends or to install the program on multiple computers. *Do not proceed with these instructions if you will violate the license or copyright laws.*

*Doing so makes you liable for criminal prosecution.* See your site license for more detailed licensing information.

The following instructions assume drive A is a floppy disk drive and drive C is the hard disk. If this is not the case, substitute the correct drive designation when following the instructions. All commands given are MS-DOS commands; if you are using a PC for the first time, we suggest that you enlist the help of a knowledgeable user.

1. Create a subdirectory on the hard disk called \MATLAB and set it to the current directory:

   ```
   C> C:
   C> MKDIR \MATLAB
   C> CD \MATLAB
   ```

2. Insert the MATLAB diskette labeled *Disk 1* in drive A and execute:

   ```
   C> A:INSTALL
   ```

   This runs a program that copies and decompresses the files on the distribution diskettes to the current directory on the hard disk. If MATLAB has been distributed to you on more than one diskette, you will be prompted to insert the other diskettes (*Disk 2*, etc.).

3. Remove the last disk from drive A and return all disks to the plastic sleeve at the back of the guide.

4. Add \MATLAB\BIN to the MS-DOS search path. Update the PATH setting in your AUTOEXEC.BAT file so that MS-DOS will run MATLAB regardless of the hard disk directory you're in. If you don't have a PATH command in your AUTOEXEC.BAT file, here is one you can use:

   ```
   PATH=C:\;C:\MATLAB\BIN
   ```

   See the PATH section in *Environment Parameters* for more information on setting your PATH.

5. Check your CONFIG.SYS file. Each time MS-DOS is started, it searches the root directory of the boot disk for a special configuration file named CONFIG.SYS. If the file is found, the commands within it are used to configure MS-DOS. There are several commands that must be present in order for MATLAB to operate correctly:

   ```
   FILES=20
   BUFFERS=20
   BREAK=ON
   ```

If you already have a CONFIG.SYS file, check that these commands are in it. If you do not have a CONFIG.SYS, then create one. For more information, see an MS-DOS manual.

This completes the program installation. You're now ready to start MATLAB. To invoke MATLAB execute the command MATLAB.

### 4.3.3 Getting Started

After a moment, the MATLAB banner will appear, and you should see a prompt that looks like ">>". The MATLAB interpreter is awaiting commands from you. To enter a small matrix, put brackets around the data and separate the rows with semicolons:

```
A = [1 2 3;4 5 6;7 8 10]
```

MATLAB will respond with:

```
A =
       1       2       3
       4       5       6
       7       8      10
```

To invert this matrix, enter:

```
B = inv(A)
```

MATLAB will respond with the result. If you are new to MATLAB and have never used it before on another system, you should turn now to the *Tutorial* (Chapter 2) for an introduction to the MATLAB language. You may also want to start by executing demo, which brings up a set of demonstrations you can run.

At the heart of MATLAB is a new language that you'll have to learn before you can fully exploit its power. Don't be intimidated - you can pick up the basics of MATLAB in just a few minutes and mastery comes after only a few hours of use.

You'll be rewarded with high-productivity, high-creativity computing power that users say "changes their lives."

### 4.3.4 Configuring MATLAB

This section discusses how to configure MATLAB to make best use of the resources available on your PC. Topics include:

- Graphics card specification
- Using a mouse for ginput

- Program stack size specification

- Speeding up overlay operations

## Graphics Card Specification

MATLAB includes drivers for five different graphics cards:

| Graphics drivers | |
|---|---|
| Color Graphics Adapter | CGA |
| Enhanced Graphics Adapter | EGA |
| Video Graphics Array | VGA |
| Hercules Monochrome Graphics Card | HGC |
| AT&T 6300, Olivetti M24, Compaq flat-display | ATT |

When MATLAB is invoked, it automatically detects the type of graphics card present in your system and uses the appropriate driver. If this is not satisfactory, a command line argument to the batch file MATLAB.BAT can be used to override the default automatic selection.

MATLAB is usually invoked through MATLAB.BAT, which invokes PCMATLAB.EXE. To override for, say, EGA operation, edit the file MATLAB.BAT and replace the command PCMATLAB with the command PCMATLAB CGA. You can also invoke MATLAB with MATLAB CGA. Command line arguments for the other graphics cards are given by the abbreviations shown in the table above. They are not case sensitive.

Graphics will appear in color on systems with a VGA or an EGA (the EGA needs to have 256K bytes of video memory, however). Color is *not* available on the CGA or on EGAs with fewer than 256K bytes of video memory.

Hercules monochrome graphics cards have video memory that can store two screens worth of graphics. The two memory regions are known as Screen 0 and Screen 1. MATLAB runs in the so-called "full mode" and uses Screen 0 for the Command screen and Screen 1 for the Graph screen. This may be important if you are trying to use a **Shift-PrtSc** screen dump utility. For example, if you have the screen dump program hprint loaded, use **Shift PrtSc-1** to obtain a hardcopy of the Graph screen. This hprint program is provided along with official Hercules cards.

Some of the VGA clones in use, including Compaq and Dell VGAs, have a ROM bug that occasionally causes glitches to appear on the screen when switched from alphanumeric mode to VGA high-resolution graphics mode. In MATLAB this is manifested by a spurious line at the top of a graph.

If you find the glitch too distracting, you may prefer to use your VGA in EGA mode by overriding the automatic VGA selection (see above). Some VGA clones have problems using print-screen dump utilities when in VGA mode. The dump utilities often work if MATLAB is started in EGA mode.

## Mouse and ginput

The `ginput` function provides a means of picking off (selecting) points from the graph window using a mouse or the arrow keys.

`[x,y] = ginput(n)` displays the graph window, puts up a crosshair, and gets n points in data coordinates from the graph window, returning them in column vectors x and y. The crosshair can be positioned with a mouse or by the arrow keys on the numeric keypad. Data points are entered by pressing a mouse button or any key on the keyboard. See the reference section for complete information on how to use `ginput`.

`ginput` supports Microsoft and Microsoft-compatible mouses. In order for it to operate correctly, the Microsoft Mouse device driver must be installed in the `CONFIG.SYS` file in the usual way; consult the mouse user's guide for more information.

In the absence of a mouse, the arrow keys on the numeric keypad can be used to move the crosshair. The keys on the diagonals of the keypad move the crosshair diagonally, and the + and - keys control the speed of movement, making it faster and slower, respectively.

## Stack Specification

The MATLAB program stack size is set to 16,384 or 3EFCh bytes. It is possible to exceed this stack size by using highly recursive or nested M-files. This results in the error message:

```
R6006: Stack overflow
```

and a return to the DOS prompt. Stack size can be changed by using the `EXEMOD.EXE` program that is provided with most of Microsoft's language products (C, Fortran, Pascal). To change the stack size to the maximum possible, 7000 Hex bytes (28,672 bytes) use:

```
EXEMOD PCMATLAB /STACK 7000
```

Any increase in program stack size decreases the amount of memory available in the MATLAB workspace.

## Overlay Operations

To keep the workspace as large as possible within the 640K byte confines of DOS, portions of the PC-MATLAB program are stored in an "overlay" within the PC-MATLAB executable. The main part of the program is always memory resident. When a nonmemory resident portion of the program is needed for a computation, PC-MATLAB "swaps" parts of the overlay file into memory. It remains there until a different nonmemory resident portion is needed.

You can tell if an overlay swap is in progress by watching the hard disk in-use light. If it comes on after the initial M-file compilation stage while PC-MATLAB is working, and there are no load/save operations underway, then it is due to an overlay operation. Ordinarily, the overlay process does not cause any significant performance degradation.

If you insist on eliminating entirely the disk access overhead from overlays, there are two choices:

- Install a disk cache program. Disk caches save the most recently used portion of the hard disk in memory, so that subsequent disk requests are likely to find what they need in memory rather than having to go to the disk.

- Install the PCMATLAB.EXE onto a ramdisk. (This makes sense, however, only if you are using a ramdisk with EMS, whose extra memory is not used by PC-MATLAB.)

  AT-MATLAB does not use overlays; all of the program is resident in extended memory.

  There is little advantage to putting the M-files on a ramdisk; they are small files that are rapidly accessed on the hard disk.

# 4.4 Using MATLAB on the PC

This section discusses how to use DOS-specific features of MATLAB. Topics covered include:

- Invoking MATLAB

- Command-line editing and recall

- Editors and external programs

- MATLABPATH and environment variables.

## 4.4.1 Invoking **MATLAB**

The command `MATLAB` invokes MATLAB. MATLAB automatically senses the type of graphics card your system has. If the computer fails to properly set the graphics mode or blanks the screen inappropriately, please see *Graphics Card Specification* on page 20 for more information.

## 4.4.2 Command Line Editor

The **arrow** keys on the keypad can be used to edit mistyped commands or to recall previous command lines. For example, suppose you enter:

```
log(sqt(atan2(3+4)))
```

You have misspelled `sqrt`. MATLAB responds with the error message:

```
Undefined variable or function.
Symbol in question sqt.
```

Instead of retyping the entire line, simply hit the **Up-Arrow** key. The incorrect line will be displayed again and you can move the cursor over using the **Left-Arrow** key until you can insert the missing `r`:

```
log(sqrt(atan2(3+4)))
ans =
0.2026
```

The **arrow** keys on the keypad work on copies of the previous input lines, which have been saved in a moderately sized input buffer. Here is a brief description of their functions:

| Last-line Editing and Recall Keys ||
| --- | --- |
| Up Arrow | Recall previous line. |
| Down Arrow | Recall next line. |
| Left Arrow | Move left one character. |
| Right Arrow | Move right one character. |
| Ctrl-Left Arrow | Move left one word. |
| Ctrl-Right Arrow | Move right one word. |
| Home | Move to beginning of line. |
| End | Move to end of line. |
| Esc | Cancel current line. |
| Ins | Toggle between insert and overtype mode. |
| Del | Delete character at cursor. |
| Backspace | Delete character left of cursor. |

### 4.4.3 Editors and External Programs

The exclamation point character (!) is used within MATLAB to indicate that the rest of an input line should be issued as a command to the DOS operating system. This is quite useful for invoking DOS utilities or for running other programs without quitting MATLAB. For example:

```
!date
```

runs the MS-DOS utility that shows the date, and:

```
!edlin darwin.m
```

invokes the `edlin` editor on a file named `darwin.m`. After these programs complete, control is returned to MATLAB.

In MATLAB, the amount of memory available for an external program is limited to the unused portion of the memory available in the MATLAB workspace. The `who` command shows how much free memory is left, and external programs must fit into this space. If you get a message saying there is not enough memory, you can try using the MATLAB `pack` command or you can clear unneccessary variables.

As you become more proficient with MATLAB, you will find yourself working with M-files more and more. M-files are created and modified using an editor or word processor. By design, MATLAB does not have a built-in editor. The choice of editors and word processors is a matter of personal preference. Instead of forcing you to learn a new editor, MATLAB lets you use whichever editor you are already accustomed to.

There are several ways in which you can intermingle the use of your editor with the use of MATLAB. The most obvious way is to terminate the MATLAB session and to start up the editor. When finished editing, the editor can be terminated and MATLAB reinvoked. Unfortunately, the process of creating and debugging M-files usually involves repeated MATLAB to EDIT to MATLAB cycles, and this slow, manual sequence quickly becomes cumbersome.

The best method of using an editor with MATLAB is accomplished without terminating MATLAB. The exclamation point character (!), introduced in the first part of this section, allows programs to be run directly from MATLAB, without terminating the program. It requires, however, that you have enough free memory in your workspace to fit your editor. Small programming editors work well using this method.

A less desirable method of working with an editor is to use a simple MS-DOS batch file to automate the cycle. The file `MATLAB.BAT`, used to invoke MATLAB, contains a loop that cycles between the MATLAB program and an editor program. To install your favorite editor, edit `MATLAB.BAT` and put the command that invokes your editor in the designated area.

If you are running MATLAB and you want to edit a file, simply type `edit`. This will save your variables in a file, quit MATLAB, and invoke the editor that you specified. When you exit from your editor, control is automatically returned to MATLAB and the variables reloaded. For more information, type `help edit` in MATLAB or see `MATLAB.BAT`.

Which method should you use? It depends. Most people who have lots of memory, a small editor, and usually work with small variables will find the ! method is best. If you have limited memory, a large editor, or full workspaces, you may prefer to use the batch file cycling method.

A final note: If your word processor has two ways of writing files, *a document mode* and a *nondocument mode*, choose the nondocument mode for editing MATLAB M-files. The other file type may contain strange control characters, perhaps disagreeable to MATLAB.

## 4.4.4 Environment Parameters

MATLAB has a number of configuration parameters that it obtains from MS-DOS environment variables. The *environment* is a special global "message-board" area used by the MS-DOS operating system to hold customization information that various programs might want. The MS-DOS operating system prompt you see on your screen is one example of an environment parameter. Two other environment parameters are important to MATLAB, `PATH` and `MATLABPATH`.

## PATH

The MS-DOS `PATH` command allows programs to be run from hard disk subdirectories or disk drives other than the current directory. Without a `PATH` setting, the current directory has to be changed to the directory containing a program before the program can be invoked. `PATH` gives MS-DOS a *search path* to use when looking for commands. Normally, if you input the name of something to MS-DOS, for example by typing `IHTFP`, the MS-DOS interpreter:

1. Searches the current directory for `IHTFP`.

2. Searches the directories specified by the environment symbol `PATH` for `IHTFP`.

If MS-DOS finds `IHTFP`, it will try to execute it. The search path is set by listing the directories separated by semicolons. For example:

```
C> PATH=A:\;B:\;C:\BIN;C:\MATLAB\BIN
```

causes MS-DOS to search on drive A, drive B, and then in directories `C:\BIN` and `C:\MATLAB\BIN` for commands. The `PATH` setting is normally put in the `AUTOEXEC.BAT` file.

## MATLABPATH

Like MS-DOS, MATLAB has a search path. The MS-DOS search path is specified with PATH; MATLAB's search path is specified with MATLABPATH. If you input the name of something to MATLAB, for example by typing `test`, the MATLAB interpreter:

1. Looks to see if `test` is a variable.

2. Checks if `test` is a built-in function.

3. Searches the directories specified by the environment symbol MATLABPATH for `test.M`. MATLAB will use the first occurrence it finds along the path. This is important if there is more than one version of a file stored with the same name, but in different places on the search path.

MATLABPATH is defined in the file MATLAB.BAT. It contains a semicolon separated list of the full pathnames to the M-file directories. The list should include standard M-file collections. A typical list might include:

```
\MATLAB\MATLAB
\MATLAB\DEMO
\MATLAB\SIGNAL
```

You can find out what MATLABPATH is set to on your system by executing `help` from inside MATLAB.

If you examine MATLAB.BAT, you'll see something like:

```
SET MATLABPATH=\MATLAB\MATLAB;\MATLAB\DEMO
```

The MS-DOS SET command is used to specify environment symbols, and here it is used to set MATLABPATH.

If you want, you can add a new directory to MATLABPATH. This allows you to organize your own libraries of M-files. Suppose a geophysicist has written a set of M-files for analyzing geophysical data and puts them in a directory called \MATLAB\GEO and then changes the SET command in MATLAB.BAT to:

```
SET MATLABPATH=\MATLAB\MATLAB;\MATLAB\DEMO;\MATLABGEO
```

This geophysicist can maintain her own private library of M-files. MATLAB will respond to them in the normal way and they won't be mixed in with all the system M-files in \MATLAB\MATLAB.

It is also possible to remove the MATLABPATH definition from MATLAB.BAT and to place it into your AUTOEXEC.BAT file.

If a pathname doesn't exist or is misspelled, DOS or MATLAB will return the error message, `Path not found`.

## Increasing Environment Space

If you see the message `Out of environment space` briefly on the screen when MATLAB is invoked, you'll have to take special action before MATLAB will respond to `MATLABPATH` correctly. This message means that you have exceeded the 128 bytes in the DOS environment table and that the `MATLABPATH` you set has been truncated.

If you issue the `SET` command from DOS, you'll see the various strings currently in the environment table. There may be a long `PATH` statement or something else using up a lot of space. To remedy the problem, you could clear some strings out of the table by shortening the path or by removing other items from the environment, but you'll probably prefer to enlarge the table instead.

To increase the size of the environment table under DOS 3.0 or 3.1, put:

```
SHELL=C:\COMMAND.COM C:\ /P /E:30
```

in your `CONFIG.SYS` file. This reserves 30 x 16 = 480 bytes in the table. Make sure you put spaces before `/P` and `/E`. The `C:\` is the path to `COMMAND.COM`. Under DOS 3.2 and above, the meaning of the number after the `/E:` was changed to specify the environment size in bytes, instead of bytes/16 (pages). So, to reserve 480 bytes under these versions of DOS, use instead:

```
SHELL=C:\COMMAND.COM C:\ /P /E:480
```

In addition to the limitation on the overall size of the environment table, DOS limits each individual environment setting to 128 bytes. Unfortunately, there is no way around this limitation. If you hit this limit the only choice is to shorten the directory names into which MATLAB is installed, or to use MATLAB's built in `matlabpath` command. Type `help matlabpath` for more information.

## 4.4.5  Printing with Screen Dumps

The graphics screen on your PC can be dumped to dot-matrix or laser printers using the normal PC technique of pressing the **Shift-PrtSc** keys, *provided* that you have an appropriate driver loaded into memory. The MATLAB command `prtsc` does the same thing and allows screen dumps to be triggered under program control.

DOS comes with a driver called GRAPHICS.COM that is appropriate for dumping CGA graphics to Epson dot-matrix printers. It is loaded into memory by executing the command `GRAPHICS` from the DOS prompt. It must be loaded prior to invoking MATLAB and is usually placed in the `AUTOEXEC.BAT` file so that it is loaded automatically each time your system is booted.

Hercules graphics cards come with a diskette that contains a driver called `HPRINT.COM` that is appropriate for dumping Hercules graphics to Epson dot-matrix printers. Using this driver, the key sequence **Shift-PrtSc-1** triggers a dump of the graph screen.

Two drivers are provided along with MATLAB for systems with EGA or VGA cards and Epson or Hewlett-Packard LaserJet printers. They can be found in the `\MATLAB\BIN` directory:

`EGAEPSON.COM`    Dump EGA and VGA graphics to Epson compatible printers.

`EGALASER.COM`    Dump EGA and VGA graphics to HP LaserJet compatible printers.

Some VGA clones won't work properly with these dump utilities when in VGA mode. If you encounter such problems, try starting MATLAB in EGA mode. They are loaded by executing them in the usual way (like `GRAPHICS.COM`).

Due to a bug in MS-DOS, the second plot you send to an Epson printer using `prtsc` may have a one inch form-feed gap in it. To prevent this, in between sending plots to the printer, hit the button on the printer to take it offline, hit the form-feed button on the printer, and then hit the online button again. Alternatively, the command `prtsc('ff')` does a `prtsc` command with a form-feed patch added automatically.

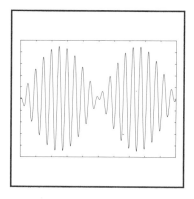

# 5
# MATLAB
# on Macintosh
# Computers

*Appendix A* contains more information about the Macintosh version of *The Student Edition of MATLAB*.

## 5.1 System Requirements

*The Student Edition of MATLAB* for the Macintosh requires:

- Any Macintosh.
- At least 1 MB of memory.
- System software version 6.0 or higher.
- A single 800K disk drive and a hard disk, or two 800K drives.
- Monaco 12 point font.

## 5.2 Installation

MATLAB is shipped on a single 800K floppy disk. The disk contains two versions of MATLAB for the Macintosh: **Student MATLAB** is for use on a Macintosh without a math coprocessor. **Student MATLAB/fpu** is for use on a Macintosh equipped with a math coprocessor.

Note that these two versions are licensed as a single copy. You may not install each version on a different computer.

### 5.2.1 On a Hard Disk System

To install *The Student Edition of MATLAB* on a hard disk, perform the following steps.

1. Insert the disk labeled "The Student Edition of MATLAB for the Macintosh" into your 800K drive, and double-click on it to open it.

2. Drag the `Student MATLAB.sea` file onto your hard disk.

3. Eject the disk.

4. *The Student Edition of MATLAB* is shipped in a compressed form and must be decompressed before it can be used. To decompress the software, simply double-click on the `Student MATLAB.sea` file (on your hard disk). An open file dialog will appear, with the prompt "Select Destination Folder..." If you wish to install *The Student Edition of MATLAB* on your hard disk, click on the **Extract** button. If you wish to install *The Student Edition of MATLAB* elsewhere you can navigate there, then click on the **Extract** button.

5. A dialog box will appear, showing the decompression progress. When the dialog box disappears, you should find a Student MATLAB folder on your hard disk.

6. Delete the `Student MATLAB.sea` file from your hard disk.

Your Student MATLAB installation is complete. Store your original disk as a backup.

## 5.2.2  On a Floppy Disk System

The Student MATLAB system is large enough that we do not recommend running it from a single 800K floppy disk. If you want to try, you'll have to pick and choose a subset of MATLAB files and functions that fit on a single 800K diskette.

The newer Macintoshes have 1.4MB high-density disk drives, which require special high-density disks. These disks are identified by an "HD" on the case or an extra, square cutout opposite the disk-lock tab. The entire Student MATLAB system can fit on these high-density disks. Please refer to your system documentation to determine whether your Macintosh has a high-density disk-drive.

## 5.2.3  On an 800K Floppy Disk

To install *The Student Edition of MATLAB* on an 800K floppy disk, perform the following steps. In the procedure below, we suggest that you remove particular files. This is one possible subset of Student MATLAB that fits on a single 800K diskette. Feel free to pick and choose a subset of Student MATLAB that is more appropriate for your needs.

1. Find a computer with a hard disk and install Student MATLAB temporarily. Follow the instructions in the section *On a Hard Disk System*.

2. Double-click on the `Student MATLAB` folder (on the hard disk) to open it. Delete the `Demonstrations` folder.

3. Double-click on the `MATLAB_Toolbox` folder (in the `Student MATLAB` folder on the hard disk) to open it. Delete the `LOAD SAVE` folder and `matlab.hlp` file.

4. If you have a Macintosh without a math coprocessor, delete the application STUDENT-MATLAB/fpu. If you have a Macintosh with a math coprocessor, delete the application STUDENT-MATLAB.

5. Drag the `Student MATLAB` folder onto your floppy disk. We suggest that you use a disk that has been recently formatted.

6. Delete the `Student MATLAB` folder from the hard disk.

Your Student MATLAB installation is complete. Store your original disk as a backup.

## 5.2.4  On a 1.4MB Floppy Disk

To install *The Student Edition of MATLAB* on a 1.4MB floppy disk, perform the following steps.

1. Find a computer with a hard disk and install Student MATLAB temporarily. Follow the instructions in the section *On a Hard Disk System*.

2. Drag the `Student MATLAB` folder onto your floppy disk.

3. Delete the `Student MATLAB` folder from the hard disk.

Your Student MATLAB installation is complete. Store your original disk as a backup.

### 5.2.5 Running Student MATLAB

If you have a Macintosh without a math coprocessor, you should run STUDENT-MATLAB. If you have a Macintosh with a coprocessor, you should run STUDENT-MATLAB/fpu to take advantage of the math coprocessor.

## 5.3 Files in the MATLAB Folder

The `MATLAB` folder contains the `MATLAB` program as well as other folders.

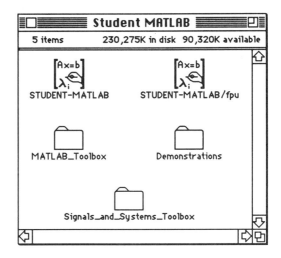

The main MATLAB system includes:

| | |
|---|---|
| `MATLAB_Toolbox` | Contains kernel MATLAB functions and the Help file. |
| `Demonstrations` | Contains a set of demonstrations that can be run from MATLAB. |

| | |
|---|---|
| Signals and Systems | Contains functions for signal processing. |
| README | A file containing the latest release notes. |

## 5.4 Macintosh File Types

The file folders in the MATLAB folder contain MATLAB script files, function files, and data files. The icons for each of these file types are:

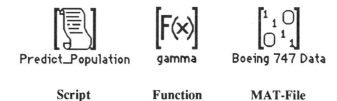

**Script**      **Function**      **MAT-File**

This manual refers to script files and function files collectively as *M-files*. Data files are called *MAT-files*. On hardware platforms other than the Macintosh, M-files end with a filename extension of .m, and MAT-files end with .mat. On the Macintosh, this is permitted but not necessary, because different file types are distinguished by different icons.

MATLAB can create ASCII text files. The icon of this file type is:

**Text File**

In addition to M-files and MAT-files, professional MATLAB provides MEX- files, which allow you to call C or Fortran functions from MATLAB. The icon of this file type is:

**MEX-File**

After you run MATLAB for the first time, a MATLAB Settings file is created in the MATLAB folder. The icon of a settings file is:

MATLAB Settings

**Settings File**

The MATLAB Settings file saves user preferences, such as print dialog information and default window sizes, as well as the MATLAB search path, which is discussed in greater detail in in the section on *Configuration* (Section 5.6).

The help text for MATLAB is contained in a help file. The icon of this file type is:

matlab.hlp

**Help File**

## 5.5 MATLAB File Types

*The Student Edition of MATLAB* works with three different types of files:

- scripts

- functions

- MAT-files

Scripts and functions contain ASCII text, while MAT-files contain binary data. All three file types can be imported from and exported to the outside world.

### 5.5.1 Conversion from Text to M-File

Under the **File** menu are the **M-File to TEXT** and **TEXT to M-File** items. These items open dialog boxes that allow you to select M-files for conversion from the special MATLAB file type to standard text files that can be transferred to other programs or computers. In addition, MATLAB can edit and run scripts or functions created by your favorite editor or word processing program, as long as the M-file is a standard text file with a .m extension.

## 5.5.2 Importing ASCII (TEXT) Flat File Data

There are three ways to import data into MATLAB:

**Clipboard**    Copy the data into the **Clipboard** from another application and paste it into a MATLAB Edit window. See the example in the *Using the Clipboard* section found in *Appendix A*.

**Load**    **Load**, from the **Workspace** menu, reads both MAT-files and TEXT flat files. A flat file is an ordinary ASCII file that contains newline-separated rows and space-separated or tab-separated columns of numbers.

**Program**    Use the example C or Fortran code provided to write a routine that converts your data into the MAT-file format. See `load` in the *Reference* section and C and Fortran files in the `LOAD SAVE` folder in the `MATLAB_Toolbox` folder.

See the *Tutorial* section on importing and exporting data. The C and Fortran code that reads and writes MAT-files is discussed in Appendix B: *Reading and Writing MAT-Files*.

## 5.5.3 Exporting ASCII (TEXT) Flat File Data

There are two ways to export data from MATLAB:

**Save**    The command `save fname X /ascii` exports the variable X in 8-digit ASCII form to the file named `fname`. See `load` and `save` in the *Reference* section for more information.

**Program**    Use the example C or Fortran code provided to write a routine that converts data from the MAT-file format into a file with the format of your choice. See `load` in the *Reference* section and the C and Fortran files in the `LOAD SAVE` folder in the `MATLAB_Toolbox` folder.

    See the *Tutorial* section on importing and exporting data. The C and Fortran code that reads and writes MAT-files is discussed in Appendix B: *Reading and Writing MAT-Files*.

# 5.6 Configuration

A very important MATLAB feature is the search path. The search path is the set of folders in which the MATLAB interpreter looks for M-files when you issue a command. On the Macintosh, the search path is set by selecting **Set Path** from the **M-File** menu.

If you give MATLAB some input, for example `Hobbs`, the MATLAB interpreter searches for `Hobbs` in the following order:

1. Check if `Hobbs` is a variable.

2. Check if `Hobbs` is a built-in function.

3. Check the current folder for an M-file named `Hobbs`.

4. Search the folders in the order specified by the MATLAB search path. Within each folder, MATLAB checks for an M-file named `Hobbs`.

By default, the search path includes all of the folders within the folder where the MATLAB program resides on your hard disk. The essential contents are:

| | |
|---|---|
| `MATLAB_Toolbox` | A folder containing over 100 M-file functions that are part of the main MATLAB system. |
| `Demonstrations` | A folder containing demonstration scripts. |
| `Signals and Systems Toolbox` | A folder containing functions for signal processing. |

Any other folders in the `MATLAB` folder will be included in the search path as well.

The MATLAB interpreter also consults the MATLAB search path when loading data files (both ASCII and MAT-files) from disk. When you try to load a file, for example, when you enter `load foo`, the MATLAB interpreter searches for `foo` in the following order:

1. Check the current folder for the file `foo`, which can be an ASCII file or a MAT-file.

2. Check the current folder for a MAT-file named `foo.mat`. (Note that if you type `load foo.mat`, the MATLAB interpreter skips the first step.)

3. Search the folders in the order specified by the MATLAB search path. Within each folder, MATLAB first checks for the file `foo`, and then checks for `foo.mat`.

### 5.6.1 Setting MATLAB's Search Path

To change the search path, select **Set Path** from the **M-File** menu. A dialog box lists the current search path. By default, MATLAB searches all folders within the MATLAB core folder.

To specify a search path manually, enter the desired path in the path window, and press the **Save** button. Whenever you press the **Save** button, the search path is written to the MATLAB Settings file and takes effect each time you run MATLAB. We recommend that you do not use the manual path specification.

To temporarily change your search path to all the folders immediately within the MATLAB folder, press the **Auto Set** button.

To have MATLAB automatically set a search path that includes all folders within the MATLAB folder each time you run MATLAB, delete all the text in the dialog box, and press the **Save** button. You need to restart MATLAB for the change to take effect.

### 5.6.2 Organizing Libraries of M-Files

MATLAB's path searching allows you to organize your own libraries of functions and scripts. Suppose a geophysicist has written her own set of M-files for analyzing geophysical data. If she puts them in a folder called Geo within the MATLAB folder, she can maintain her own private library of M-files. MATLAB responds to them in the normal way, and it won't be necessary to copy these files into every folder in which she might want to run MATLAB.

## 5.7 Using MATLAB on the Macintosh

### 5.7.1 Getting Started

Once you have successfully installed MATLAB, you can run the program. If you are using a hard disk and your MATLAB folder is not already open, double-click on it on your hard disk. If you are using a floppy disk system, double click on the folder on your floppy disk.

## 5.7.2 Invoking MATLAB

To invoke MATLAB, double-click on the MATLAB program icon. After a moment, the MATLAB Command window appears. You also see a Graph window partially hidden behind it.

In the Command window is a prompt that looks like >>. The MATLAB interpreter is awaiting instructions from you. To enter a small sample matrix, put brackets around the data and separate the rows with semicolons:

```
A = [1 2 3;4 5 6;7 8 10]
```

MATLAB responds with

```
A =
        1       2       3
        4       5       6
        7       8       10
```

To invert this matrix, enter

```
B = inv(A)
```

MATLAB responds with the result. If you are new to MATLAB and have never used it before on another system, turn now to the *Tutorial* for an introduction to the MATLAB language.

MATLAB is different from other Macintosh applications you may have used before in that it is a *language*. Since MATLAB is a language, you need to learn it before you can fully exploit its power. Don't be intimidated - you can pick up the basics of MATLAB in just a few minutes and master MATLAB after only a few hours of use. You will soon be rewarded with high-productivity, high-creativity computing power.

To run one of the demonstration scripts provided with MATLAB, do the following:

1. Select **About MATLAB** from the  menu.

2. Click on the **Demos** button.

3. Select one of the demonstration scripts, perhaps "An Introduction."

4. Click on the **Run** button.

5. Press any key during pauses in the demo.

If you have used MATLAB before on another computer system, continue reading this section to find out more about Macintosh-specific features.

### 5.7.3 Invoking MATLAB from Other Folders

You can invoke MATLAB by double-clicking on the program file, an M-file, a MAT-file, or a settings file. If you double-click on an M-file, MATLAB opens an Edit window on the designated M-file after starting. If you double-click on a MAT-file, MATLAB loads the data into the workspace after starting.

If you double-click on a settings file, MATLAB loads the user preferences and MATLAB's search path stored in that file. It is possible, therefore, to vary user preferences and MATLAB's search path by having several settings files, one for each configuration.

We recommend that you work in a folder on your Macintosh other than the main `MATLAB` folder. The `MATLAB` folder and related subfolders contain many files that are part of the MATLAB system and we encourage you to keep your own files separate. We suggest that you

- create a folder called `Work` in the `MATLAB` folder, or
- use your own folders elsewhere in your file system.

When working in several folders on the Macintosh, the problem of how to invoke programs that are located elsewhere, without maintaining duplicate copies of programs, arises. With MATLAB this is especially true because in normal use the MATLAB program file remains where it resides in the `MATLAB` folder. MATLAB expects to find its M-file folders beneath the folder in which it resides.

To invoke MATLAB from another folder, copy a small M-file, MAT-file, or settings file to the places from which you need to invoke MATLAB. Double-clicking on this file automatically starts MATLAB.

### 5.7.4 Printing

MATLAB allows you to make hard copy in the normal Macintosh way. Under the **File** menu are the usual two items for printing:

| | |
|---|---|
| **Page Setup** | Select page orientation, reduction, etc. |
| **Print** | Print current window. |

Selecting **Print** sends to the printer the contents of the currently active window. If you're in a Command or Edit window and you have made a selection, your selection is sent to the printer. Otherwise the entire window is sent to the printer. If a Graph window is active, the graph is printed.

The dialog boxes that appear when you print contain options for number of copies to print, page range, paper size, paper orientation, etc. The specific choices depend upon whether you have a LaserWriter, ImageWriter, or other printer connected to your system.

The dialog box that appears if you are printing a graph to a LaserWriter or other laser printer, contains a choice of **Best/Fixed Size** or **Draft/Resizable** radio buttons at the bottom of the dialog box. The first option sends PostScript directly to the printer for the highest quality plot. Unfortunately, the dimensions of the Graph window are not captured by this option. The second option uses QuickDraw and reflects the plot in the Graph window, but produces lower quality output than option one.

To print a graph under program control from an M-file, use the MATLAB command `prtsc`, which is short for Print Screen. `prtsc` makes the Graph window active and triggers a **Print** using the current page setup and job setup options.

The `meta`, `GPP`, and `print` commands, described in the *Reference* section, are not used in the Macintosh version of MATLAB.


## Saving the Graph in Encapsulated PostScript File (EPSF) Format

When the Graph window is active, **Save As** from the **File** menu saves the file on disk in either PICT or Encapsulated PostScript File (EPSF) format.


## Save Screen as a MacPaint Document

Hold down the **Command** and **Shift** keys while typing the number **3** to create a MacPaint document named "Screen 0" that contains a picture of the screen. MacPaint stores objects in a bit-map representation.

## Capture Document as a PostScript File

When you print to a LaserWriter, the output is converted by the Macintosh LaserWriter driver into PostScript, a page description language, and then sent to the LaserWriter. It is possible to intercept the PostScript and to save it as a file on disk rather than letting it go to the printer. Select **Print** from the **File** menu to get the standard LaserWriter dialog box. Immediately after clicking the **OK** button, press **Command-F**. This creates in the current directory a TEXT file named "Postscript0" that contains the actual ASCII file that would be sent to the printer. **Command-K** does the same but adds the LaserPrep information as well.

Note that these PostScript capture options do not work while running background printing under MultiFinder.

# Part Two

# Tutorial

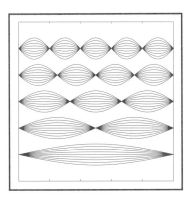

# 6
# Fundamentals

MATLAB works with essentially only one kind of object, a rectangular numerical matrix with possibly complex elements. In some situations, special meaning is attached to 1-by-1 matrices, which are scalars, and to matrices with only one row or column, which are vectors. Operations and commands in MATLAB are intended to be natural, in a matrix sense, not unlike how they might be indicated on paper.

Let's begin by looking at how matrices can be entered into MATLAB. If you're a "never-ever" user, you may find it useful to invoke MATLAB at this time and follow along.

## 6.1 Entering Simple Matrices

Matrices can be introduced into MATLAB in several different ways:

- Entered by an explicit list of elements,
- Generated by built-in statements and functions,
- Created in M-files,
- Loaded from external data files.

The MATLAB language contains no dimension statements or type declarations. Storage is allocated automatically, up to the amount available on any particular computer.

The easiest method of entering small matrices is to use an explicit list. The explicit list of elements is separated by blanks or commas, is surrounded by brackets, [ and ], and uses the semicolon ; to indicate the ends of the rows. For example, entering the statement

```
A = [1 2 3; 4 5 6; 7 8 9]
```

results in the output

```
A =
     1     2     3
     4     5     6
     7     8     9
```

The matrix A is saved for later use.

Large matrices can be spread across several input lines, with carriage returns replacing the semicolons. Although hardly necessary for a matrix of this size, the above matrix could also have been produced by three lines of input,

```
A = [ 1 2 3
      4 5 6
      7 8 9 ]
```

Matrices can be entered from disk files with names ending in ".m". If a file named gena.m contains three lines of text,

```
A = [ 1 2 3
      4 5 6
      7 8 9 ]
```

then the statement gena reads the file and generates A.

The load command can read matrices generated by earlier MATLAB sessions or matrices in ASCII form exported from other programs. More on this later.

## 6.2 Matrix Elements

Matrix elements can be any MATLAB expressions; for example,

```
x = [ -1.3  sqrt(3)  (1+2+3)*4/5 ]
```

results in

```
x =
    -1.3000    1.7321    4.8000
```

Individual matrix elements can be referenced with indices inside parentheses, ( and ). Continuing our example,

```
x(5) = abs(x(1))
```

produces

```
x =
   -1.3000    1.7321    4.8000    0.0000    1.3000
```

Notice that the size of x is automatically increased to accommodate the new element and that the undefined intervening elements are set to zero.

Big matrices can be constructed using little matrices as elements. For example, we could attach another row to our matrix A with

```
r = [10 11 12];
A = [A; r]
```

which results in

```
A =
        1        2        3
        4        5        6
        7        8        9
       10       11       12
```

Little matrices can be extracted from big matrices using :. For example,

```
A = A(1:3, :);
```

takes the first three rows and all the columns of the current A to give us back the original A. (More on : later.)

# 6.3 Statements and Variables

MATLAB is an *expression* language. Expressions typed by the user are interpreted and evaluated by the MATLAB system. MATLAB statements are frequently of the form

*variable = expression*

or simply

*expression*

Expressions are composed from operators and other special characters, from functions, and from variable names. Evaluation of the expression produces a matrix, which is then displayed on the screen and assigned to the variable for future use. If the variable name and the = sign are omitted, a variable with the name `ans`, which stands for "answer," is automatically created. For example, typing the expression

```
1900/81
```

produces

```
ans =
   23.4568
```

A statement is normally terminated with the carriage return or enter key. However, if the last character of a statement is a semicolon, `;`, the printing is suppressed, but the assignment is still carried out. This is useful in M-files (more later) and in situations where the result is large enough to make the individual numbers uninteresting. For example,

```
p = conv(r,r);
```

convolves the numbers in `r` with themselves, but does not display the result.

If the expression is so complicated that the statement will not fit on one line, an ellipsis consisting of three or more periods, `. . .`, followed by the carriage return, can be used to indicate that the statement continues on the next line. For example,

```
s = 1 - 1/2 + 1/3 - 1/4 + 1/5 - 1/6 + 1/7  ...
        - 1/8 + 1/9 - 1/10 + 1/11 - 1/12;
```

evaluates the partial sum of the series, assigns the sum to the variable `s`, but does not print anything. The blank spaces around the =, +, and - signs are optional, but are included here to improve readability.

Variable and function names are formed by a letter, followed by any number of letters and digits (or underscores). Only the first 19 characters of a name are remembered.

MATLAB is case-sensitive; it normally distinguishes between upper- and lower-case letters, so `a` and `A` are *not* the same variable. All the function names must be in lower case; `inv(A)` would invert `A`, but `INV(A)` references an undefined function. However, the command `casesen` makes MATLAB insensitive to the case of letters. In this mode, `a` and `A` refer to the same matrix, and `INV(a)` inverts it.

## 6.4 Getting Workspace Information

The example statements entered up to this point have created variables that are stored in the MATLAB *workspace*. Executing

```
who
```

lists the variables in the workspace:

```
Your variables are:
A          ans        p          r          s          x
leaving 291636 bytes of memory free.
```

This shows that six variables have been generated by our examples, including ans. More detailed information showing the size of each of the current variables is obtained with whos which, for our example so far, produces

```
Name      Size      Total    Complex

A         3 by 3    9           No
ans       1 by 1    1           No
p         1 by 5    5           No
r         1 by 3    3           No
s         1 by 1    1           No
x         1 by 5    5           No

Grand total is (24 * 8) = 192 bytes,

leaving 291636 bytes of memory free.
```

Each element of a real matrix requires 8 bytes of memory, so our 3-by-3 matrix A uses 72 bytes and all of our variables use a total of 192 bytes. The amount of remaining free memory depends upon the total amount available in the system and will vary from computer to computer. On computers with virtual memory, an unlimited amount may be available.

The variable ans, along with an unlisted variable eps, have special meaning to MATLAB. They are *permanent* variables that cannot be cleared.

The variable eps is a tolerance for determining such things as near singularity and rank. Its initial value is the distance from 1.0 to the next largest floating point number. For the IEEE arithmetic used on many personal computers and workstations,

$$eps \ = \ 2^{-52}$$

which is approximately $2.22 \times 10^{-16}$. eps may be reset to any other value, including zero.

## 6.5 Numbers and Arithmetic Expressions

Conventional decimal notation, with optional decimal point and leading minus sign, is used for numbers. A power-of-ten scale factor can be included as a suffix. Here are some examples of legal numbers:

```
3            -99           0.0001
9.6397238    1.60210E-20   6.02252e23
```

On computers using IEEE floating point arithmetic, the relative accuracy of numbers is eps, which is approximately 16 significant decimal digits. The range is roughly $10^{-308}$ to $10^{308}$.

Expressions can be built up using the usual arithmetic operators and precedence rules:

| | |
|---|---|
| + | addition |
| − | subtraction |
| * | multiplication |
| / | right division |
| \ | left division |
| ^ | power |

The operations on matrices described later make it convenient to have the two symbols for division. The scalar expressions 1/4 and 4\1 have the same numerical value, namely 0.25. Parentheses are used in the standard way to alter the usual precedence of arithmetic operations.

Most ordinary elementary mathematical functions found on a good scientific calculator are built-in functions, for example, `abs`, `sqrt`, `log`, and `sin`. More can be added easily with M-files. A later section has a complete list of functions.

A number of built-in functions simply return commonly used special values. The function `pi` returns $\pi$, precalculated by the program as `4*atan(1)`. A more provocative way to generate $\pi$ is

```
imag(log(-1))
```

The function `Inf`, which stands for infinity, is found in very few calculator systems or computer languages. On some computers, it is made possible by the IEEE arithmetic implemented in a math coprocessor. On other computers, floating point software is used to simulate a coprocessor. One way to generate the value returned by `Inf` is

```
s = 1/0
```

which results in

```
s =

    ∞


Warning: Divide by Zero.
```

On machines with IEEE arithmetic, division by zero does *not* lead to an error condition or termination of execution. It does produce a warning message and a special value that can behave in a sensible manner in subsequent computation.

The variable `NaN` is an IEEE number related to `Inf` but has different properties. It stands for "Not a Number" and is produced by calculations such as `Inf/Inf` or `0/0`.

## 6.6 Complex Numbers and Matrices

Complex numbers are allowed in all operations and functions in MATLAB. Complex numbers are entered using the special functions `i` and `j`. Some of us might use

```
z = 3 + 4*i
```

while others might prefer

```
z = 3 + 4*j
```

Another example is

```
w = r*exp(i*theta)
```

There are at least two convenient ways to enter complex matrices. They are illustrated by the statements

```
A = [1 2; 3 4] + i*[5 6; 7 8]
```

and

```
A = [1+5*i   2+6*i;   3+7*i   4+8*i]
```

which produce the same result. When complex numbers are entered as matrix elements within brackets, it is important to avoid any blank spaces, because an expression like 1 + 5*i, with blanks surrounding the + sign, represents two separate numbers. (The same is true of real numbers; a blank before the exponent part in 1.23 e-4 causes an error.)

A built-in function name may be used as variable name, in which case the original built-in function becomes unavailable within the current workspace (or local M-file function) until the variable is cleared. If you use i and j as variables, and overwrite their values, a new complex unit can be generated and used in the usual way:

```
ii = sqrt(-1)
z = 3 + 4*ii
```

## 6.7 Output Format

The result of any MATLAB assignment statement is displayed on the screen, as well as assigned to the specified variable or to ans if no variable is given. The numeric display format can be controlled using the format command. format affects only how matrices are displayed, not how they are computed or saved (MATLAB performs all computation in double precision).

If all the elements of a matrix are exact integers, the matrix is displayed in a format without any decimal points. For example,

```
x = [ -1 0 1 ]
```

always results in

```
x =
     -1      0      1
```

If at least one of the elements of a matrix is not an exact integer, there are several possible output formats. The default format, called the `short` format, shows approximately 5 significant decimal digits. The other formats show more significant digits or use scientific notation. As an example, suppose

```
x = [ 4/3  1.2345e-6 ]
```

The formats, and the resulting output for this vector, are:

```
format short

   1.3333     0.0000

format short e

   1.3333E+000   1.2345E-006

format long

   1.333333333333338    0.000001234500000

format long e

    1.333333333333338E+000   1.234500000000003E-006

format hex

    3FF5555555555555    3EB4B6231ABFD271

format +
```

```
++
```

For the long formats, the last significant digit may appear to be incorrect, but the output is actually an accurate decimal representation of the binary number stored in the computer.

With the short and long formats, if the largest element of a matrix is larger than 1000 or smaller than 0.001, a common scale factor is applied to the entire matrix when it is displayed. For example,

```
x = 1.e20*x
```

multiplies x by $10^{20}$ and results in the display

```
x =

  1.0E+020 *

    1.3333    0.0000
```

The + format is a compact way of displaying large matrices. The symbols +, −, and blank are displayed for positive, negative, and zero elements.

One final command, `format compact`, suppresses many of the line-feeds that appear between matrix displays and allows more information to be shown on the screen.

## 6.8 The HELP Facility

A HELP facility is available, providing online information on most MATLAB topics. To get a list of HELP topics, type

```
help
```

To get HELP on a specific topic, type `help` *topic*. For example,

```
help eig
```

provides HELP information on the use of the eigenvalue function,

```
help[
```

tells how to use brackets to enter matrices, and

```
help help
```

is self-referential, but works just fine.

## 6.9 Quitting and Saving the Workspace

To quit MATLAB, type `quit` or `exit`. Termination of a MATLAB session causes the variables in the workspace to be lost. Before quitting, the workspace may be saved for later use by typing

```
save
```

This saves all variables in a file on disk named `matlab.mat`. The next time MATLAB is invoked, the workspace may be restored from `matlab.mat` by executing

```
load
```

`save` and `load` may be used with other file names, or to save only selected variables. The command `save temp` stores the current variables in the file named `temp.mat`. The command

```
save temp X
```

saves only variable X, while

```
save temp X Y Z
```

saves X, Y, and Z.

`load temp` retrieves all the variables from the file named `temp.mat`. `load` and `save` are also capable of importing and exporting ASCII data files; see the *Reference* section for details.

## 6.10 Functions

Much of MATLAB's power is derived from its extensive set of functions. MATLAB has a large number of functions, well over 200 at the time of this writing. Some of the functions are intrinsic, or "built-in" to the MATLAB processor itself. Others are available in the library of external M-files distributed with MATLAB (the *MATLAB Toolbox*). And some have been added by individual users, or groups of users, for more specialized applications. It is transparent to the user whether a function is intrinsic or contained in an M-file. This is an important feature of MATLAB; a user can create his own new functions, and they act just like the intrinsic functions built into MATLAB. More on M-files in a later section.

The general categories of mathematical functions available in MATLAB include:

> Elementary mathematical
> Special functions
> Elementary matrix
> Special matrices
> Matrix decompositions and factorizations
> Data analysis
> Polynomial
> Differential equation solution
> Nonlinear equations and optimization
> Numerical integration
> Signal processing

Subsequent sections introduce these different categories of analytic functions. In the *Tutorial* we will not go into details on all the individual functions; this is done online by the HELP facility and in the *Reference* section.

Up until now, we have only seen functions with one input argument and one output argument. MATLAB functions can also be used with multiple arguments. For example,

```
x = sqrt(log(z))
```

shows the nested use of two simple functions. There are MATLAB functions that use two or more input arguments. For example,

```
theta = atan2(y, x)
```

Of course, each one of the arguments could have been an expression.

Some functions *return* two or more output values. The output values are surrounded by brackets, [ and ], and separated by commas:

```
[V,D] = eig(A)
[y,i] = max(X)
```

The first function here returns two matrices, V and D, the eigenvectors and eigenvalues, respectively, of matrix A. The second example, using max, returns the maximum value y and the index i of the maximum value in vector X.

Functions that permit multiple output arguments can return fewer output arguments. For example, max with one output argument,

```
max(X)
```

returns just the maximum value.

The input or right-hand arguments to a function are *never* modified by MATLAB. The outputs, if any, of a function are always returned in left-hand arguments.

# 7

# Matrix Operations

Matrix operations are fundamental to MATLAB; wherever possible they are indicated the way they would be in a textbook or on paper, subject only to the character set limitations of the computer.

## 7.1 Transpose

The special character prime ' (apostrophe) denotes the transpose of a matrix. The statements

```
A = [ 1 2 3; 4 5 6; 7 8 0 ]
B = A'
```

result in

```
A =
        1       2       3
        4       5       6
        7       8       0

B =
        1       4       7
        2       5       8
        3       6       0
```

and

```
x = [ -1  0  2 ]'
```

produces

```
x =
        -1
         0
         2
```

The prime ' transposes in a formal matrix sense; if Z is a complex matrix, then Z' is its complex conjugate transpose. This can sometimes lead to unexpected results if used carelessly with complex data. For an unconjugated transpose, use Z.' or conj(Z').

## 7.2 Addition and Subtraction

Addition and subtraction of matrices are denoted by + and −. The operations are defined whenever the matrices have the same dimensions. For example, with the above matrices, A + x is not correct because A is 3-by-3 and x is 3-by-1. However,

```
C = A + B
```

is acceptable, and results in

```
C =
         2     6    10
         6    10    14
        10    14     0
```

Addition and subtraction are also defined if one of the operands is a scalar, that is a 1-by-1 matrix. In this case, the scalar is added to or subtracted from all the elements of the other operand. For example

```
y = x - 1
```

gives

```
y =
        -2
        -1
         1
```

## 7.3 Matrix Multiplication

Multiplication of matrices is denoted by $*$. The operation is defined whenever the "inner" dimensions of the two operands are the same; that is $X*Y$ is permitted if the second dimension of $X$ is the same as the first dimension of $Y$. For example, the above $x$ and $y$ are both 3-by-1, so the expression $x*y$ is NOT defined and results in an error message. However, several other vector products are defined, and are very useful. The most common is the inner product, also called the dot product or scalar product. This is

```
x'*y
```

which results in

```
ans =
        4
```

Of course, $y'*x$ would give the same result. There are two outer products, which are transposes of each other.

```
x*y'  =
        2      1     -1
        0      0      0
       -4     -2      2

y*x'  =
        2      0     -4
        1      0     -2
       -1      0      2
```

An element-by-element product is described in the next section. (There is no special provision in MATLAB for computing vector cross products. However, anyone needing cross products can easily write an M-file to compute them.)

Matrix-vector products are special cases of general matrix-matrix products. For our example $A$ and $x$,

```
b = A*x
```

is allowed and results in the output

```
b =
        5
        8
       -7
```

Naturally, a scalar can multiply, or be multiplied by, any matrix.

```
pi*x

    ans =
        -3.1416
         0.0000
         6.2832
```

## 7.4 Matrix Division

There are two "matrix division" symbols in MATLAB, \ and /. If A is a nonsingular square matrix, then A\B and B/A correspond formally to left and right multiplication of B by the inverse of A , that is inv(A)*B and B*inv(A), but the result is obtained directly without the computation of the inverse. In general,

    X = A\B     is a solution to     A*X = B

    X = B/A     is a solution to     X*A = B

Left division, A\B, is defined whenever B has as many rows as A. If A is square, it is factored using Gaussian elimination. The factors are used to solve the equations A*X(:,j) = B(:,j) where B(:,j) denotes the $j$-th column of B. The result is a matrix X with the same dimensions as B. If A is nearly singular (according to the LINPACK condition estimator, RCOND), a warning message is displayed.

If A is not square, it is factored using Householder orthogonalization with column pivoting. The factors are used to solve the under- or overdetermined equations in a least squares sense. The result is an $m$-by-$n$ matrix X where $m$ is the number of columns of A and $n$ is the number of columns of B . Each column of X has at most $k$ nonzero components, where $k$ is the effective rank of A.

Right division, B/A, is defined in terms of left division by B/A = (A'\B')'.

For example, since our vector b was computed as A*x, the statement

```
z = A\b
```

results in

```
z =
        -1
         0
         2
```

Sometimes, the use of \ and / to compute least squares solutions to over- or underdetermined systems of equations can cause surprises. It is possible to "divide" one vector by another. For example, with the above vectors x and y,

```
s = x\y
```

produces

```
s =
         0.8000
```

This is because $s = 0.8$ is the value of the scalar which solves the overdetermined equation $xs = y$ in a least squares sense. We invite the reader to explain why

```
S = y/x
```

gives

```
S =
         0.0000     0.0000    -1.0000
         0.0000     0.0000    -0.5000
         0.0000     0.0000     0.5000
```

# 7.5 Matrix Powers

The expression A^p raises A to the p-th power and is defined if A is a square matrix and p is a scalar. If p is an integer greater than one, the power is computed by repeated multiplication. For other values of p, the calculation involves eigenvalues and eigenvectors, such that if [V,D] = eig(A), then

```
A^p = V*D.^p/V
```

If P is a matrix, and a a scalar, a^P is a raised to the matrix power P using eigenvalues and eigenvectors. X^P, where both X and P are matrices, is an error.

## 7.6 Elementary Matrix Functions

In MATLAB, expressions like `exp(A)` and `sqrt(A)` are regarded as array operations, defined on the individual elements of `A`. MATLAB can also calculate matrix transcendental functions, such as the matrix exponential and matrix logarithm. These special functions are defined only for square matrices, are rather difficult and expensive to compute, and sometimes have subtle mathematical properties.

A transcendental mathematical function is interpreted as a matrix function if an "m" is appended to the function name, as in `expm(A)` and `sqrtm(A)`. As MATLAB is distributed, three of these functions are defined:

| Transcendental Matrix Functions | |
| --- | --- |
| expm | matrix exponential |
| logm | matrix logarithm |
| sqrtm | matrix square root |

However, the list can be extended by adding more M-files, or using `funm`. See the M-files `sqrtm`, `logm`, and `funm` in the *MATLAB Toolbox*, and `expm` and `funm` in the *Reference* section.

Other elementary matrix functions include:

| Elementary Matrix Functions | |
| --- | --- |
| poly | characteristic polynomial |
| det | determinant |
| trace | trace |
| kron | Kronecker tensor product |

See the *Reference* section for details.

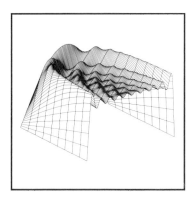

# 8

# Array Operations

We use the term *array operations* to refer to element-by-element arithmetic operations, instead of the usual linear algebraic matrix operations denoted by the symbols $*$ $/$ $\backslash$ $\hat{}$ $'$ . Preceding an operator with a period . indicates an array or element-by-element operation.

## 8.1  Array Addition and Subtraction

For addition and subtraction, the array operations and the matrix operations are the same, so + and − can be regarded as either matrix or array operations.

## 8.2  Array Multiplication and Division

Array, or element-by-element, multiplication is denoted by $.*$ . If A and B have the same dimensions, then A $.*$ B denotes the array whose elements are simply the products of the individual elements of A and B. For example, if

```
x = [ 1   2   3 ];   y = [ 4   5   6 ];
```

then

```
z = x .* y
```

results in

```
z =
      4      10      18
```

The expressions `A ./ B` and `A .\ B` give the quotients of the individual elements. So,

```
z = x ./ y
```

results in

```
z =
    0.25      0.40      0.50
```

## 8.3 Array Powers

Element-by-element powers are denoted by `.^`. Here are several examples, using the above vectors $x$ and $y$. Typing

```
z = x .^ y
```

results in

```
z =
      1      32      729
```

The exponent can be a scalar.

```
z = x .^ 2
```

```
z =
      1      4      9
```

Or, the base can be a scalar.

```
z = 2 .^ [x y]
```

```
z =
      2      4      8      16      32      64
```

*Array Operations  Chap. 8*

This last example illustrates one of MATLAB's syntactic subtleties. Although it is difficult to see, the space between the digit 2 and the period . is important. If it was not there, the period would be interpreted as a decimal point associated with the 2. MATLAB would then see only the isolated ^ and would attempt to calculate a matrix power, which in this case would result in an error message because the exponent matrix is nonsquare. An alternative to the space is to use parentheses, forcing the correct precedence.

## 8.4 Relational Operations

There are six relational operators for comparing two matrices of equal dimensions.

| Relational Operators | |
|---|---|
| < | less than |
| <= | less than or equal |
| > | greater than |
| >= | greater than or equal |
| == | equal |
| ~= | not equal |

The comparison is done between the pairs of corresponding elements; the result is a matrix of ones and zeros, with one representing TRUE and zero FALSE. For example,

```
2+2 = 4
```

is simply 0.

Relational operators can show the patterns of matrix elements satisfying various conditions. For example, here is the magic square of order 6.

```
A = magic(6)

A =
    35     1     6    26    19    24
     3    32     7    21    23    25
    31     9     2    22    27    20
     8    28    33    17    10    15
    30     5    34    12    14    16
     4    36    29    13    18    11
```

A magic square of order $n$ is an $n$-by-$n$ matrix constructed from the integers from 1 through $n^2$ with equal row and column sums. If you stare at this particular matrix long enough, you might notice that the elements that are divisible by 3 occur on every third diagonal. To display this curiosity, we type

```
P = (rem(A,3) == 0)
```

The double $=$ is the test-for-equality operator, `rem(A,3)` is a matrix of remainders, 0 is expanded to a matrix of zeros, and P becomes a matrix of ones and zeros.

```
P =
        0       0       1       0       0       1
        1       0       0       1       0       0
        0       1       0       0       1       0
        0       0       1       0       0       1
        1       0       0       1       0       0
        0       1       0       0       1       0
```

To see the pattern a little more clearly, `format +` prints matrices in a compact form, with a $+$ where there is a positive element, a $-$ where there is a negative element, and a blank space for zeros.

```
format +
P


    +   +
+   +
  +   +
    +   +
+   +
  +   +
```

The function `find` is helpful with relational operators, finding nonzero elements in a 0-1 matrix, and hence the data elements that satisfy some relational condition. For example, if Y is a vector, `find(Y < 3.0)` returns a vector containing the indices of the elements in Y that are less than 3.0.

The statements

```
i = find(Y > 3.0);
Y(i) = 10*ones(i);
```

replace with 10.0 all elements in Y greater than 3.0. It will work even if Y is a matrix, because a matrix can be referenced as a long column vector with a single subscript.

The relation `X==NaN` returns `NaN`s everywhere, since, according to the IEEE arithmetic specifications, any operation with a `NaN` results in `NaN`. But it is sometimes necessary to test for `NaN`s. So a function `isnan(X)` is provided that returns ones where the elements of `X` are `NaN`s and zeros elsewhere. Also useful is `finite(x)`, which returns ones for $-\infty < x < \infty$.

# 8.5 Logical Operations

There are three logical operators that work elementwise and are usually used on 0-1 matrices.

| Logical Operators | |
|---|---|
| & | AND |
| \| | OR |
| ~ | NOT |

The `&` and `|` operators compare two scalars, or two matrices of equal dimensions. For matrices, they work elementwise; if `A` and `B` are 0-1 matrices, then `A & B` is another 0-1 matrix representing the logical AND of the corresponding elements of `A` and `B`. The logical operators regard anything nonzero as TRUE. They return ones where TRUE and zeros where FALSE.

NOT, or logical complement, is a unary operator. The expression `~A` returns zeros where `A` is nonzero and ones where `A` is zero. Thus the two expressions

```
P | (~P)
P & (~P)
```

return all ones and all zeros, respectively.

The functions `any` and `all` are useful in conjunction with logical operators. If `x` is a 0-1 vector, `any(x)` returns 1 if *any* of the elements of `x` are nonzero, and returns 0 otherwise. The function `all(x)` returns a 1 only if *all* of the elements of `x` are non-zero. These functions are particularly useful in `if` statements,

```
if all(A < .5)
        do something
end
```

because an `if` wants to respond to a single condition, not a vector of possibly conflicting suggestions.

For matrix arguments, `any` and `all` work columnwise to return a row vector with the result for each column. Applying the function twice, as in `any(any(A))`, always reduces the matrix to a scalar condition.

Here is a summary of the relational and logical functions in MATLAB:

| Relational and Logical Functions | |
|---|---|
| any | logical conditions |
| all | logical conditions |
| find | find array indices of logical values |
| exist | check if variables exist |
| isnan | detect NaNs |
| finite | detect infinities |
| isempty | detect empty matrices |
| isstr | detect string variables |
| strcmp | compare string variables |

## 8.6 Elementary Math Functions

A set of elementary mathematical functions is applied on an element-by-element basis to arrays. For example,

```
A = [1 2 3; 4 5 6]
B = fix(pi*A)
C = cos(pi*B)
```

produces

```
A =
      1       2       3
      4       5       6

B =
      3       6       9
     12      15      18

C =
     -1       1      -1
      1      -1       1
```

Available functions include the trigonometric functions:

| Trigonometric Functions | |
|---|---|
| sin | sine |
| cos | cosine |
| tan | tangent |
| asin | arcsine |
| acos | arccosine |
| atan | arctangent |
| atan2 | four quadrant arctangent |
| sinh | hyperbolic sine |
| cosh | hyperbolic cosine |
| tanh | hyperbolic tangent |
| asinh | hyperbolic arcsine |
| acosh | hyperbolic arccosine |
| atanh | hyperbolic arctangent |

and the usual elementary functions:

| Elementary Math Functions | |
|---|---|
| abs | absolute value or complex magnitude |
| angle | phase angle |
| sqrt | square root |
| real | real part |
| imag | imaginary part |
| conj | complex conjugate |
| round | round to nearest integer |
| fix | round towards zero |
| floor | round towards $-\infty$ |
| ceil | round towards $\infty$ |
| sign | signum function |
| rem | remainder or modulus |
| exp | exponential base e |
| log | natural logarithm |
| log10 | log base 10 |

## 8.7 Special Math Functions

A number of special functions provide more advanced capabilities:

| Special Functions | |
|---|---|
| bessel | Bessel function |
| gamma | complete and incomplete gamma functions |
| rat | rational approximation |
| erf | error function |
| inverf | inverse error function |
| ellipk | complete elliptic integral of the first kind |
| ellipj | Jacobian elliptic functions |

Like the elementary functions, they operate element-by-element when given matrix inputs. See the *Reference* section for more information.

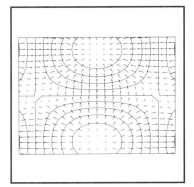

# 9
# Vectors
# and Matrix
# Manipulation

The *subscripting* abilities of MATLAB allow manipulation of rows, columns, individual elements, and subportions of matrices. Central to subscripting are vectors, which are generated using "Colon Notation." Vectors and subscripting are common MATLAB operations and make it possible to achieve fairly complex data manipulation effects.

## 9.1 Generating Vectors

The colon, :, is an important character in MATLAB. The statement

```
x = 1:5
```

generates a row vector containing the numbers from 1 to 5 with unit increment. It produces

```
x =
      1     2     3     4     5
```

Increments other than one can be used.

```
y = 0: pi/4: pi
```

results in

```
y =
    0.0000    0.7854    1.5708    2.3562    3.1416
```

Negative increments are possible.

```
z = 6:-1:1
```

gives

```
z =
    6    5    4    3    2    1
```

The colon notation allows the easy generation of tables. To get a vertical tabular form, transpose the row vector obtained from the colon notation, compute a column of function values, then form a matrix from the two columns. For example

```
x = (0.0: 0.2: 3.0)';
y = exp(-x) .* sin(x);
[x y]
```

produces

```
ans =
    0.0000    0.0000
    0.2000    0.1627
    0.4000    0.2610
    0.6000    0.3099
    0.8000    0.3223
    1.0000    0.3096
    1.2000    0.2807
    1.4000    0.2430
    1.6000    0.2018
    1.8000    0.1610
    2.0000    0.1231
    2.2000    0.0896
    2.4000    0.0613
    2.6000    0.0383
    2.8000    0.0204
    3.0000    0.0070
```

Other vector generation functions include linspace, which allows the number of points rather than the increment, to be specified,

```
k = linspace(-pi,pi,4)

k =
   -3.1416  -1.0472   1.0472   3.1416
```

and logspace, which generates logarithmically evenly spaced vectors.

## 9.2 Subscripting

Individual matrix elements may be referenced by enclosing their subscripts in parentheses. An expression used as a subscript is rounded to the nearest integer. For example, given a matrix A:

```
A   =
        1       2       3
        4       5       6
        7       8       9
```

the statement

```
A(3,3)  =  A(1,3)  +  A(3,1)
```

results in

```
A   =
        1       2       3
        4       5       6
        7       8       10
```

A subscript can be a vector. If X and V are vectors, then X(V) is [X(V(1)), X(V(2)),...,  X(V(n))]. For matrices, vector subscripts allow access to contiguous and noncontiguous submatrices. For example, suppose that A is a 10-by-10 matrix. Then

```
A(1:5,3)
```

specifies the 5-by-1 submatrix, or column vector, that consists of the first five elements in the third column of A. Similarly,

```
A(1:5,7:10)
```

is the 5-by-4 submatrix of elements from the first five rows and the last four columns.

Using the colon by itself in place of a subscript denotes *all* of the corresponding row or column. For example,

```
A(:,3)
```

is the third column and

```
A(1:5,:)
```

is the first five rows.

Fairly sophisticated effects are obtained using submatrix referencing on both sides of an assignment statement. For example,

```
A(:,[3 5 10]) = B(:,1:3)
```

replaces the third, fifth, and tenth columns of A with the first three columns of B.

In general, if v and w are vectors with integer components, then

```
A(v,w)
```

is the matrix obtained by taking the elements of A with row subscripts from v and column subscripts from w. So

```
A(:,n:-1:1)
```

reverses the columns of A and

```
v = 2:2:n;
w = [3 1 4 1 6];
A(v,w)
```

is legal, but probably of questionable utility.

One more feature in this vein is useful in advanced fiddling, A(:). On the right-hand side of an assignment statement, A(:) denotes all the elements of A strung out in a long column vector. So

```
A = [1 2; 3 4; 5 6]
b = A(:)
```

results in

```
A =
        1       2
        3       4
        5       6

b =
        1
        3
        5
        2
        4
        6
```

On the left-hand side of an assignment statement, A(:) can be used to *reshape* or *resize* a matrix. To do this, A must already exist. Then A(:) denotes a matrix with the same dimensions as A, but with new contents from the right-hand side. For example, the above A has three rows and two columns, so

```
A(:)  =  11:16
```

reshapes the six-element row vector into a 3-by-2 matrix,

```
A =
        11      14
        12      15
        13      16
```

## 9.3 Subscripting with 0-1 Vectors

The 0-1 vectors usually created from relational operations can be used to reference submatrices. Suppose A is an *m*-by-*n* matrix and L is a length *m* vector of zeros and ones. Then

```
A(L,:)
```

specifies the rows of A where the elements of L are nonzero.

Here is how outliers, those elements greater than 3 standard deviations, could be removed from a vector:

```
x  =  x(x  <=  3*std(x));
```

Similarly,

```
L  =  X(:,3)  >  100;
X  =  X(L,:);
```

replaces X with those rows of X whose third column is greater than 100.

## 9.4 Empty Matrices

The statement

```
x = [ ]
```

assigns a matrix of dimension zero-by-zero to $x$. Subsequent use of this matrix will NOT lead to an error condition; it will propagate empty matrices. This is different from the statement

```
clear x
```

which removes $x$ from the list of current variables. Empty matrices *do* exist in the workspace; they just have zero size. The function `exist` can be used to test for the existence of a matrix (or a file for that matter), while `isempty` indicates if a matrix is empty.

It is possible to generate empty vectors. If $n$ is less than 1, then `1:n` contains no elements and so

```
x = 1:n
```

is a complicated way of creating an empty $x$.

More importantly, an efficient way of removing rows and columns of a matrix is to assign them to an empty matrix. So

```
A(:,[2 4]) = [ ]
```

deletes columns 2 and 4 of $A$.

Certain matrix functions will return mathematically plausible values if given empty matrices. These include `det`, `cond`, `prod`, `sum`, and possibly others. For example, `prod`, `det`, and `sum` return 1, 1, and 0, respectively, when given null matrix arguments.

# 9.5 Special Matrices

A collection of functions generates special matrices that arise in linear algebra and signal processing.

| Special Matrices | |
| --- | --- |
| compan | companion |
| diag | diagonal |
| gallery | esoteric |
| hadamard | Hadamard |
| hankel | Hankel |
| hilb | Hilbert |
| invhilb | inverse Hilbert |
| magic | magic square |
| pascal | Pascal's triangle |
| toeplitz | Toeplitz |
| vander | Vandermonde |

For example, generate a companion matrix associated with the polynomial $x^3 - 7x + 6$.

```
p = [1 0 -7 6]
a = compan(p)

a =
        0       7      -6
        1       0       0
        0       1       0
```

The eigenvalues of a are the roots of the polynomial.

```
eig(a) =
     -3.0000
      2.0000
      1.0000
```

A Toeplitz matrix with diagonal disagreement is

```
c = [1     2     3     4     5];
r = [1.5   2.5   3.5   4.5   5.5];
t = toeplitz(c,r)

t =
  1.000   2.500   3.500   4.500   5.500
  2.000   1.000   2.500   3.500   4.500
  3.000   2.000   1.000   2.500   3.500
  4.000   3.000   2.000   1.000   2.500
  5.000   4.000   3.000   2.000   1.000
```

Other functions generate less interesting, but more useful, utility matrices.

| Utility Matrices | |
|---|---|
| zeros | zero |
| ones | constant |
| rand | random elements |
| eye | identity |
| linspace | linearly spaced vectors |
| logspace | logarithmically spaced vectors |
| meshdom | domain for mesh plots |

These functions include `eye(A)`, which returns an identity matrix of the same size as A. The catchy name is used because I and i are often used as subscripts or as `sqrt(-1)`.

The group also includes `zeros` and `ones`, which generate constant matrices of various sizes, and `rand`, which generates matrices of uniformly or normally distributed random elements. For example, to generate a random 4-by-3 matrix

```
A = rand(4,3)

A =
   0.2113   0.8096   0.4832
   0.0824   0.8474   0.6135
   0.7599   0.4524   0.2749
   0.0087   0.8075   0.8807
```

## 9.6  Building Larger Matrices

Large matrices can be formed from small matrices by surrounding the small matrices with brackets, [ and ]. For example,

```
C = [A  eye(4); ones(A)  A^2]
```

creates one such larger matrix, assuming that A has four rows. The smaller matrices in this type of construction must be dimensionally consistent or an error message results.

## 9.7  Matrix Manipulation

Several functions will rotate, flip, reshape, or extract portions of a matrix.

| Matrix manipulation | |
| --- | --- |
| rot90 | rotation |
| fliplr | flip matrix left-to-right |
| flipud | flip matrix up-and-down |
| diag | extract or create diagonal |
| tril | lower triangular part |
| triu | upper triangular part |
| reshape | reshape |
| .' | transposition |
| : | general rearrangement |

For example, to reshape a 3-by-4 matrix into a 2-by-6 matrix:

```
a =
     1    4    7   10
     2    5    8   11
     3    6    9   12

b = reshape(a,2,6)

b =
     1    3    5    7    9   11
     2    4    6    8   10   12
```

The three functions `diag`, `triu`, and `tril` provide access to diagonal, upper triangular, and lower triangular portions of matrices. For example,

```
tril(rand(4,3))
```

produces

```
ans =
     0.2113          0          0
     0.0824     0.8474          0
     0.7599     0.4524     0.2749
     0.0087     0.8075     0.8807
```

Also very useful are `size` and `length`. The function `size` returns a two-element vector containing the row and column dimensions of a matrix. If a variable is known to be a vector, `length` returns the length of the vector, or `max(size(V))`.

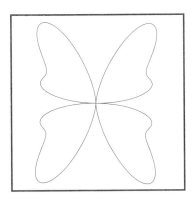

# 10
# Data Analysis

Tutorial

This section presents an introduction to data analysis using MATLAB and describes some elementary statistical tools. More powerful techniques are available using the linear algebra and signal processing functions covered in later sections.

## 10.1 Column-oriented Analysis

Matrices are, of course, used to hold all data, but this leaves a choice of orientation for multivariate data. By convention, the different variables in a set of data are put in columns, allowing observations to vary down through the rows. A data set consisting of 50 samples of 13 variables would be stored in a matrix of size 50-by-13.

Starting an example, the ever-present Longley econometric data consist of the variables

1.  GNP deflator

2.  GNP

3.  Unemployment

4.  Armed Forces

5.  Population

6.  Year

7.  Employment

In general, there are several methods for getting data into MATLAB; these are covered in detail in a later section. Assuming that the data are not already in a machine-readable form, the easiest way to enter the data is using a text editor or word processor. If we create a file called `longley.m` that contains the assignment statement

```
ldata = [
  83.0  234.289  235.6  159.0  107.608  1947  60.323
  88.5  259.426  232.5  145.6  108.632  1948  61.122
  88.2  258.054  368.2  161.6  109.773  1949  60.171
  89.5  284.599  335.1  165.0  110.929  1950  61.187
  96.2  328.975  209.9  309.9  112.075  1951  63.221
  98.1  346.999  193.2  359.4  113.270  1952  63.639
  99.0  365.385  187.0  354.7  115.094  1953  64.989
 100.0  363.112  357.8  335.0  116.219  1954  63.761
 101.2  397.469  290.4  304.8  117.388  1955  66.019
 104.6  419.180  282.2  285.7  118.734  1956  67.857
 108.4  442.769  293.6  279.8  120.445  1957  68.169
 110.8  444.546  468.1  263.7  121.950  1958  66.513
 112.6  482.704  381.3  255.2  123.366  1959  68.655
 114.2  502.601  393.1  251.4  125.368  1960  69.564
 115.7  518.173  480.6  257.2  127.852  1961  69.331
 116.9  554.894  400.7  282.7  130.081  1962  70.551];
```

we can execute the command `longley`. This accesses `longley.m` and creates the matrix called `ldata` (or any other name of your choice) in the workspace. You could try entering this matrix interactively, but the chances are remote that you would get it correct the first time. If you were to make a mistake resulting in an error message, there would be no way to correct it without starting over. (Unless your version of MATLAB has provisions for editing previous lines - see the computer-specific section).

If there are more observations than will fit across the screen, rows can be continued to the next line using the ellipsis . . . consisting of three periods. The matrix could also be entered in blocks of columns and the whole thing pieced together at the end.

For the Longley data there are 16 observations of 7 variables. This is revealed by

```
[n,p] = size(ldata)

n =
     16
p =
      7
```

For data entered in this columnwise fashion, a group of functions provides basic data analysis capabilities:

| Columnwise Data Analysis | |
|---|---|
| max | maximum value |
| min | minimum value |
| mean | mean value |
| median | median value |
| std | standard deviation |
| sort | sorting |
| sum | sum of elements |
| prod | product of elements |
| cumsum | cumulative sum of elements |
| cumprod | cumulative product of elements |
| diff | approximate derivatives |
| hist | histogram |
| corrcoef | correlation coefficients |
| cov | covariance matrix |
| cplxpair | reorder into complex pairs |

For vector arguments, these functions don't care whether the vectors are oriented in a row or column direction. For array arguments, the functions operate in a *column-oriented* fashion on the data in the arrays. This means, for example, that if max is applied to an array, the result is a row vector containing the maximum values over each column.

Thus, if

```
A =
        9       8       4
        1       6       5
        3       2       7
```

then

```
m  = max(A)
mv = mean(A)
s  = sort(A)
```

results in

```
m    =
     9        8        7

mv   =
     4.3333      5.3333      5.3333

s    =
     1        2        4
     3        6        5
     9        8        7
```

Or for the Longley data

```
m = median(ldata)

m    =
  1.0E+003 *


  0.1012   0.3975   0.3351   0.2798   0.1174   1.9550   0.0660
```

We can subtract the mean from each column of ldata using an outer product:

```
lmean = ldata - ones(n,1)*m;
```

More functions can be added to this list using M-files, but when doing so, *care must be exercised to handle the row vector case.* If you are writing your own column-oriented M-files, you should look at how this is accomplished in other M-files, for example mean.m and diff.m.

# 10.2  Missing Values

The special value, NaN, stands for *Not-a-Number* in MATLAB. Normally, it is produced by undefined expressions like 0/0, in place of an error message, thanks to conventions established by the IEEE floating point arithmetic standard. For statistics purposes, NaNs can be used to represent missing values or NAs, data that are *not available*.

The "correct" handling of NAs is a difficult problem and often varies in different situations. MATLAB, however, is uniform and rigorous in its treatment of NaNs; they propagate naturally through to the final result in any calculation. Thus if a NaN is used in any intermediate computation, the final result will be a NaN, unless the final result does not depend on the value of the NaN, were it to have one.

What this means, practically, is that NaNs should be removed from the data before statistical computions are performed. The NaNs in a vector $x$ are located at:

```
i = find(isnan(x));
```

so

```
x = x(find(~isnan(x)))
```

returns the data in $x$ with the NaNs removed. Two other ways of doing the same thing are

```
x = x(~isnan(x));
x(isnan(x)) = [ ];
```

of which the second is perhaps the most straightforward. We have been using the special function isnan to find NaNs because we *cannot* use

```
x(x == NaN) = [ ];
```

NaNs return NaN as the result of all operations, including relational ones.

If, instead of a vector, the data are in the columns of a matrix, and any *rows* of the matrix with NaNs are to be removed, we could use instead,

```
X(any(isnan(X)'),:) = [ ];
```

which is a particularly nasty, but effective statement. If you object that you will have a hard time remembering this, you are completely justified. If you frequently need to remove NaNs, the solution is to write a short M-file, for example

```
function X = excise(X)
X(any(isnan(X)'),:) = [ ];
```

Now, typing

```
X = excise(X);
```

accomplishes the same thing. More on M-files later.

## 10.3 Removing Outliers

Outliers in a data set are removed in much the same manner as NaNs. For the Longley data, the mean and standard deviations of each column of data are:

```
mv    = mean(ldata)
sigma = std(ldata)

mv  =
  1.0E+003 *

 0.101  0.387  0.319  0.260  0.117  1.954  0.065

sigma =

 10.448  96.238  90.479  67.382  6.735  4.609  3.400
```

The number of rows with outliers greater than 3 standard deviations is:

```
[n,p] = size(ldata);
e = ones(n,1);
dist = abs(ldata - e*mv);
outliers = dist > 3*e*sigma;
nout = sum(any(outliers'))

nout =
      0
```

There are none. If there were, they could be removed with

```
X(any(outliers'),:) = [ ];
```

## 10.4 Regression and Curve Fitting

Before attempting to fit a curve to data, the data should be normalized. Normalization can improve the accuracy of the final results. Still working with our Longley data, one way to normalize is to remove the mean

```
X = X - e*mean(X);
```

and to normalize to unit standard deviation

```
X = X ./ (e*std(X));
```

We can regress unemployment (the last column) on the earlier columns, using in this case our raw data,

```
y = ldata(:,7);
A = [ldata(:,1:6) ones(y)];
coef = A\y
```

which results in

```
coef =

   1.0E+003 *

    0.00001506187227
   -0.00003581917929
   -0.00002020229804
   -0.00001033226867
   -0.00005110410565
    0.00182915146461
   -3.48225863459802
```

Tutorial

The Longley data are known to be highly correlated, which we see by looking at the correlation coefficients.

```
corr(X)

ans =

   1.0000   0.9916   0.6206   0.4647   0.9792   0.9911   0.9709
   0.9916   1.0000   0.6043   0.4464   0.9911   0.9953   0.9836
   0.6206   0.6043   1.0000  -0.1774   0.6866   0.6683   0.5025
   0.4647   0.4464  -0.1774   1.0000   0.3644   0.4172   0.4573
   0.9792   0.9911   0.6866   0.3644   1.0000   0.9940   0.9604
   0.9911   0.9953   0.6683   0.4172   0.9940   1.0000   0.9713
   0.9709   0.9836   0.5025   0.4573   0.9604   0.9713   1.0000
```

Often it is useful to fit a polynomial to data. In general, a polynomial fit to data in vectors $x$ and $y$ is a function, $p$, of the form:

$$p(x) = c_1 x^d + c_2 x^{d-1} + \cdots + c_n$$

The degree is $d$ and the number of coefficients is $n = d+1$. The coefficients $c_1, c_2, \cdots c_n$ are determined by solving a system of simultaneous linear equations:

$$Ac = y$$

The columns of $A$ are successive powers of the $x$ vector. Here is one way to create $A$

```
for j=1:n
        A(:,j) = x.^(n-j);
end
```

The solution to the system of simultaneous linear equations $Ac = y$ is obtained with MATLAB's matrix division operator:

```
c = A\y
```

The function `polyfit.m` in the *MATLAB Toolbox* automates this procedure.

In the *regression* problem, other functions, usually multivariate functions of the columns of the data matrix, are fit to the data by forming the appropriate $A$ matrix. For example, using the Longley data,

```
A = [ldata(:,1)   ldata(:,2).^2   sin(ldata(:,3))   ones(n,1)];
coef = A\y;
```

finds the regression coefficients for a more complicated function.

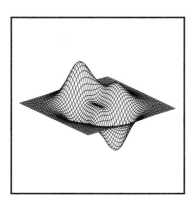

# 11
# Matrix Functions

Much of MATLAB's mathematical power is derived from its matrix functions. Some of the functions are "built-in" to the MATLAB processor itself. Others are available in the library of external M-files distributed with MATLAB. And some have been added by individual users, or groups of users, for more specialized applications. We will not go into details about the individual functions here; that is done in the *Help* facility and the *Reference* section. Further information is also available in the User's Guides for the LINPACK and EISPACK software packages, which provide the algorithmic foundation for MATLAB. In this section we will just give an overview of the available functions by grouping according to the underlying factorization and decompositions. There are four such groups:

- Triangular factorization

- Orthogonal factorization

- Eigenvalue decomposition

- Singular value decomposition

## 11.1 Triangular Factorization

The most basic factorization expresses any square matrix as the product of two essentially triangular matrices, one of them a permutation of a lower triangular matrix and the other an upper triangular matrix. The factorization is often called the "LU," or sometimes the "LR," factorization. Most of the algorithms for computing it are variants of Gaussian elimination.

The factors themselves are available from the `lu` function. The factorization is used to obtain the inverse with `inv` and the determinant with `det`. It is also the basis for the linear equation solution or "matrix division" obtained with \ and / for square matrices. For example, start with

```
A =
        1       2       3
        4       5       6
        7       8       0
```

To see the LU factorization, we use MATLAB's double assignment statement.

```
[L,U]  =  lu(A)
```

which gives

```
L =
        0.1429      1.0000      0
        0.5714      0.5000      1.0000
        1.0000      0           0


U =
        7.0000      8.0000      0.0000
        0           0.8571      3.0000
        0           0           4.5000
```

Notice that L is a permutation of a lower triangular matrix that has ones on the permuted diagonal, and that U is upper triangular. To check that the factorization does its job, we can compute the product

```
L*U
```

which should give us back the original A. It does.

```
ans =
        1       2       3
        4       5       6
        7       8       0
```

The inverse of the example matrix is obtained with

```
X  =  inv(A)
```

The inverse is actually computed from the inverses of the triangular factors

```
X  =  inv(U)*inv(L)
```

The determinant of the example matrix is obtained with

```
d = det(A)
```

which gives

```
d =
    27
```

It is computed from the determinants of the triangular factors

```
d = det(L)*det(U)
```

which produce

```
d =
    27.0000
```

Why do the two ds print in different formats? When MATLAB is asked to compute det(A) it makes note of the fact that all the elements of A are integers, so it forces the determinant to be an integer. But in calculating the second d, the elements of U are not integers, so MATLAB does not produce an exact integer result.

As an example of a system of simultaneous linear equations, take

```
b =
    1
    3
    5
```

The solution to the equation $Ax = b$ is obtained with the MATLAB matrix division operation

```
x = A\b
```

which produces

```
x =
    0.3333
    0.3333
    0.0000
```

The solution is actually computed by solving two triangular systems,

```
y = L\b,  x = U\y
```

The intermediate solution is

```
y =
    5.0000
    0.2857
    0.0000
```

Triangular factorization is also used by a specialized function, rcond. This is a quantity produced by several of the LINPACK subroutines that is an estimate of the reciprocal condition number of a square matrix.

Two other functions, chol and rref, can be included in this group because the underlying algorithms are closely related to LU factorization. The function chol produces the Cholesky factorization of a symmetric, positive definite matrix. The reduced row echelon form of a rectangular matrix, rref, is of some interest in theoretical linear algebra, although it has little computational value. It is included in MATLAB for pedagogical reasons.

## 11.2 Orthogonal Factorization

The QR factorization is useful for both square and rectangular matrices. It expresses the matrix as the product of an orthonormal matrix and an upper triangular matrix. For example, take

```
A =
      1       2       3
      4       5       6
      7       8       9
     10      11      12
```

We have chosen a rank-deficient matrix; the middle column is the average of the other two columns. The rank deficiency is revealed by the factorization.

```
[Q,R] = qr(A)
```

gives

```
Q =
   -0.0776   -0.8331    0.5444    0.0605
   -0.3105   -0.4512   -0.7709    0.3251
   -0.5433   -0.0694   -0.0913   -0.8317
   -0.7762    0.3124    0.3178    0.4461

R =
  -12.8841  -14.5916  -16.2992
        0    -1.0413   -2.0826
        0         0     0.0000
        0         0          0
```

We could check that the product Q*R produces the original A, but let's not bother. The triangular structure of R gives it zeros below the diagonal; the zero on the diagonal in R(3,3) implies that R and consequently A do not have full rank.

The QR factorization is used in solving linear systems with more equations than unknowns. For example

```
b =
    1
    3
    5
    7
```

The linear system $Ax = b$ is four equations in only three unknowns. The best solution in a least squares sense is computed by

```
x = A\b
```

which produces

```
Warning: Rank deficient, rank = 2   tol = 1.4594E-014

x =
    0.5000
    0.0000
    0.1667
```

We are warned about the rank deficiency. The quantity tol is a tolerance used in deciding that a diagonal element of R is negligible. The solution x was computed using the factorization and the two steps

```
y = Q'*b;
x = R\y
```

If we were to check the computed solution by forming A*x, we would find that it equals b to within roundoff error. This tells us that even though the simultaneous equations $Ax = b$ are overdetermined and rank-deficient, they happen to be consistent. There are infinitely many solution vectors x; the QR factorization has found just one of them.

This factorization is also the basis for the functions null and orth, which generate orthonormal bases for the null space and range of a given rectangular matrix.

## 11.3 Singular Value Decomposition

We will not attempt to explain the singular value decomposition here; we have to be content with claiming that it is a powerful tool for analysis of problems involving matrices. See the *LINPACK User's Guide* or the book by Golub and VanLoan for some justification of this claim. In MATLAB, the triple assignment

```
[U,S,V] = svd(A)
```

produces the three factors in the singular value decomposition,

```
A = U*S*V'
```

The matrices U and V are orthogonal and the matrix S is diagonal. By itself, the function svd(A) returns just the diagonal elements of S, which are the singular values of A.

The singular value decomposition is used by several other functions, including the pseudoinverse, pinv(A); the rank, rank(A); the Euclidean matrix norm, norm(A,2); and the condition number, cond(A).

## 11.4 Eigenvalues

If $A$ is an $n$-by-$n$ matrix, the $n$ numbers $\lambda$ that satisfy $Ax = \lambda x$ are the *eigenvalues* of A. They are found using

```
eig(A)
```

which returns the eigenvalues in a column vector. If A is real and symmetric, the eigenvalues will be real. But if A is not symmetric, the eigenvalues are frequently complex numbers. For example, with

```
A =
       0      1
      -1      0
```

The statement eig(A) produces

```
ans =
    0.0000 + 1.0000i
    0.0000 - 1.0000i
```

Eigenvalues and eigenvectors are obtained with a double assignment statement,

```
[X,D] = eig(A)
```

in which case the diagonal elements of D are the eigenvalues and the columns of X are the corresponding eigenvectors such that A*X = X*D.

Two intermediate results used in computing eigenvalues are the Hessenberg form, hess(A), and the Schur form, schur(A). The Schur form is used to compute transcendental mathematical functions of matrices, such as sqrtm(A) and logm(A).

If A and B are square matrices, the function eig(A,B) returns a vector containing the *generalized eigenvalues* solving the equation

$$Ax = \lambda Bx$$

The double assignment is used to obtain eigenvectors

```
[X,D] = eig(A,B)
```

producing a diagonal matrix D of generalized eigenvalues and a full matrix X whose columns are the corresponding eigenvectors so that A*X = B*X*D. The intermediate results involved in the solution of this generalized eigenvalue problem are available from qz(A,B).

## 11.5 Rank and Condition

The functions in MATLAB associated with rank and conditioning include:

| Matrix Condition | |
|---|---|
| cond | condition number in 2-norm |
| norm | 1-norm, 2-norm, F-norm, ∞-norm |
| rank | rank |
| rcond | condition estimate |

There are several different places in MATLAB where the rank of a matrix is computed implicitly: in rref(A), in A\B for nonsquare A, in orth(A) and null(A), and in the pseudoinverse pinv(A). Three different algorithms with three different criteria for negligibility are used and so it is possible that three different values could be produced for the same matrix.

With `rref(A)`, the rank of A is the number of nonzero rows. The elimination algorithm for `rref` is the fastest of the three rank-determining algorithms, but it is the least sophisticated numerically and the least reliable.

With `A\B`, `orth(A)`, and `null(A)`, the QR factorization is used as described in chapter 9 of the LINPACK guide.

With `pinv(A)`, the algorithm is based on the singular value decomposition and is described in chapter 11 of the LINPACK guide. The `pinv` algorithm is the most time-consuming, but the most reliable and is therefore also used for the explicit rank computation, `rank(A)`.

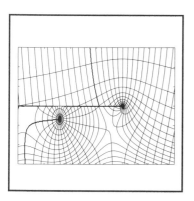

# 12
# Polynomials
# and Signal
# Processing

MATLAB has functions for working with polynomials and for digital signal processing. These functions operate primarily on vectors.

## 12.1 Polynomials

Polynomials are represented in MATLAB as row vectors containing the coefficients ordered by descending powers. For example, the characteristic equation of the matrix

```
A   =
      1       2       3
      4       5       6
      7       8       0
```

is computed with

```
p = poly(A)

p   =
      1      -6      -72      -27
```

This is the MATLAB representation of the polynomial $s^3 - 6s^2 - 72s - 27$. The roots of this equation are:

```
r = roots(p)

r =
    12.1229
    -5.7345
    -0.3884
```

which are, of course, the same as the eigenvalues of matrix A. These may be reassembled back into the original polynomial with `poly`,

```
p2 = poly(r)

p2 =
    1      -6      -72      -27
```

Consider the polynomials $a(s) = s^2 + 2s + 3$ and $b(s) = 4s^2 + 5s + 6$. The product of the polynomials is the convolution of the coefficients:

```
a = [1 2 3]; b = [4 5 6]
c = conv(a,b)

c =
    4     13     28     27     18
```

Use deconvolution to divide a back out,

```
[q,r] = deconv(c,a)

q =
    4      5      6
r =
    0      0      0      0      0
```

A complete list of polynomial functions includes:

| Polynomials | |
|---|---|
| poly | characteristic polynomial |
| roots | polynomial roots - companion matrix method |
| roots1 | polynomial roots - Laguerre's method |
| polyval | polynomial evaluation |
| polyvalm | matrix polynomial evaluation |
| conv | multiplication |
| deconv | division |
| residue | partial-fraction expansion |
| polyfit | polynomial curve fitting |

## 12.2 Signal Processing

Vectors are used to hold sampled-data signals, or sequences, for signal processing. For multi-input systems, each row corresponds to a sample point, with the observations spread across the columns of the matrix. A few signal processing functions are included with the main MATLAB system:

| Signal Processing | |
|---|---|
| abs | complex magnitude |
| angle | phase angle |
| conv | convolution |
| cov | covariance |
| deconv | deconvolution |
| fft | fast Fourier transform |
| ifft | inverse fast Fourier transform |
| fftshift | swap quadrants of matrices |

Some of these have 2-dimensional counterparts, in which case the "signal" is actually a matrix:

| 2-D Signal Processing | |
|---|---|
| fft2 | two-dimensional FFT |
| ifft2 | inverse 2-D FFT |
| fftshift | rearrange FFT results |
| conv2 | 2-D convolution |

There are many additional signal processing functions available in the *Signal Processing Toolbox*. This section is intended to be a brief introduction to the signal processing capabilities of MATLAB; see the *Additional Signal Processing Functions* section in this guide for more information.

## 12.2.1  Filtering

In the *Signal Processing Toolbox*, the function

```
y = filter(b, a, x)
```

filters the data in vector $x$ with the filter described by vectors $a$ and $b$, creating filtered data $y$. The filter structure is the general tapped delay-line filter described by the difference equation:

$$y(n) = b(1)x(n) + b(2)x(n-1) + \cdots + b(nb)x(n-nb+1)$$
$$- a(2)y(n-1) - \cdots - a(na)y(n-na+1)$$

or equivalently, the Z-transform:

$$H(z) = \frac{Y(z)}{X(z)} = \frac{b(1) + b(2)z^{-1} + \cdots + b(nb)z^{-(nb-1)}}{1 + a(2)z^{-1} + \cdots + a(na)z^{-(na-1)}}$$

For example, to find and plot the *n*-point unit impulse response of a digital filter:

```
x = [1 zeros(1,n-1)];
y = filter(b,a,x);
plot(y,'o')
```

The function `freqz` returns the complex frequency response of digital filters. The frequency response is $H(z)$ evaluated around the unit circle in the complex plane, $z = e^{j\omega}$. To use `freqz` to find and plot an *n*-point frequency response:

```
[h,w] = freqz(b,a,n);
mag = abs(h);
phase = angle(h);
semilogy(w,mag), plot(w,phase)
```

Numerous functions are available in the *Signal Processing Toolbox* for designing digital filters. We will have to be content here to claim that with some knowledge of filter design techniques, many methods are possible. For example, MATLAB's built-in complex arithmetic allows techniques like bilinear transformation and pole-zero mapping to convert *s-domain* prototypes into the *z-domain*. Also, FIR filters are designed easily using windowing techniques.

## 12.2.2 FFT

It is fair to say that the FFT algorithm for computing the discrete Fourier transform of a sequence is the workhorse of digital signal processing. Its uses range from filtering, convolution, computation of frequency response and group delay, to applications in power spectrum estimation.

`fft(x)` is the discrete Fourier transform of vector x, computed with a radix-2 fast Fourier transform if the length of x is a power of two, and with a mixed radix algorithm if the length is not a power of two. If X is a matrix, `fft(X)` is the fast Fourier transform of each column of X.

`fft(x,n)` is the n-point FFT. If the length of x is less than n, x is padded with trailing zeros to length n. If the length of x is greater than n, the sequence x is truncated. When x is a matrix, the length of the columns is adjusted the same way.

`ifft(x)` is the inverse fast Fourier transform of vector x. `ifft(x,n)` is the n-point inverse FFT.

The two functions implement the transform - inverse transform pair given by:

$$X(k+1) = \sum_{n=0}^{N-1} x(n+1) \, W_N^{kn}$$

$$x(n+1) = 1/N \sum_{k=0}^{N-1} X(k+1) \, W_N^{-kn}$$

where $W_N = e^{-j(2\pi/N)}$ and $N = length(x)$. Note that the series is written in an unorthodox way, running over $n+1$ and $k+1$ instead of the usual $n$ and $k$ because MATLAB vectors run from 1 to $N$ instead of from 0 to $N-1$.

Suppose an even-length sequence of $N$ points has a sample frequency of $f_s$. Then, for up to the Nyquist frequency, or point $n = N/2+1$, the relationship between the bin number and the actual frequency is:

$$f = (bin\_number - 1) * f_s / N$$

The fast Fourier transform (FFT) of a column vector x

```
x = [4 3 7 -9 1 0 0 0]';
```

is found with

```
y = fft(x)
```

which results in

```
y =
   6.0000
  11.4853 -  2.7574i
  -2.0000 -12.0000i
  -5.4853 +11.2426i
  18.0000
  -5.4853 -11.2426i
  -2.0000 +12.0000i
  11.4853 +  2.7574i
```

Notice that although the sequence x is real, y is complex. The first component of the transformed data is the DC contribution and the fifth element corresponds to the Nyquist frequency. The last three values of y correspond to negative frequencies and, for the real sequence x, they are complex conjugates of y(4), y(3), and y(2).

For more information, see the *Reference* section. If you do lots of signal processing, see the *Additional Signal Processing Functions* section in this guide.

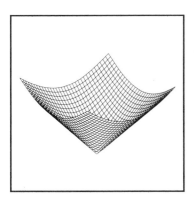

# 13
# Function Functions

A class of functions in MATLAB works not with numerical matrices, but with mathematical functions. These *function functions* include:

- Numerical integration

- Nonlinear equations and optimization

- Differential equation solution

Mathematical functions are represented in MATLAB by function M-files. For example, the function

$$humps(x) = \frac{1}{(x - .3)^2 + .01} + \frac{1}{(x - .9)^2 + .04} - 6$$

is made available to MATLAB by creating an M-file called humps.m:

```
function y = humps(x)
y = 1 ./ ((x-.3).^2 + .01) + 1 ./ ((x-.9).^2 + .04) - 6;
```

A graph of the function is:

```
x = -1:.01:2;
plot(x,humps(x))
```

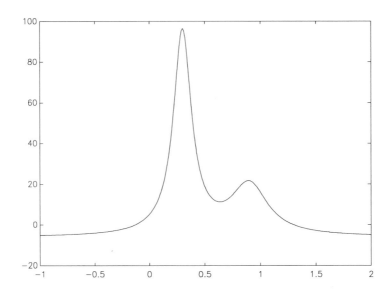

## 13.1 Numerical Integration

The area beneath *humps*(*x*) can be determined by numerically integrating *humps*(*x*), a process referred to as *quadrature*. To integrate *humps* from 0 to 1:

```
q = quad('humps',0,1)

q =
    29.8583
```

The two MATLAB functions for quadrature are:

| Numerical Integration | |
|---|---|
| quad | adaptive recursive Simpson's rule |
| quad8 | Newton Cotes 8 panel rule |

Notice that the first argument to quad is a quoted string containing the name of a function. This is why we call quad a *function function* - it is a function that operates on other functions.

# 13.2 Nonlinear Equations and Optimization

The function functions for nonlinear equations and optimization include:

| Nonlinear Equations and Optimization | |
|---|---|
| fmin | minimum of a function of one variable |
| fmins | minimum of a multivariable function (unconstrained nonlinear optimization) |
| fsolve | solution to a system of nonlinear equations (zeros of a multivariable function) |
| fzero | zero of a function of one variable |

Continuing our example, the location of the minimum of *humps*$(x)$ in the region from 0.5 to 1 is computed with fmin:

```
xm = fmin('humps',.5,1)

xm =
    0.6370
```

Its value at the minimum is:

```
y = humps(xm)

y =
   11.2528
```

From looking at the graph, it is apparent that *humps* has two zeros. The location of the zero near $x = 0$ is:

```
xz1 = fzero('humps',0)

xz1 =
    -0.1316
```

The zero near $x = 1$ is at:

```
xz2 = fzero('humps',1)

xz2 =
    1.2995
```

## 13.3 Differential Equation Solution

MATLAB's functions for solving ordinary differential equations are:

| Differential Equation Solution | |
|---|---|
| ode23 | 2nd/3rd order Runge-Kutta method |
| ode45 | 4th/5th order Runge-Kutta-Fehlberg method |

Consider the second order differential equation known as the Van der Pol equation

$$\ddot{x} + (x^2 - 1)\dot{x} + x = 0$$

We can rewrite this as a system of coupled first order differential equations

$$\dot{x}_1 = x_1(1 - x_2^2) - x_2$$
$$\dot{x}_2 = x_1$$

The first step towards simulating this system is to create a function M-file containing these differential equations. We can call it `vdpol.m`:

```
function xdot = vdpol(t,x)
xdot = zeros(2,1);
xdot(1) = x(1) .* (1 - x(2).^2) - x(2);
xdot(2) = x(1);
```

To simulate the differential equation defined in `vdpol` over the interval $0 \le t \le 20$, invoke `ode23`

```
t0 = 0; tf = 20;
x0 = [0  0.25]';   % Initial conditions
[t,x] = ode23('vdpol',t0,tf,x0);
plot(t,x)
```

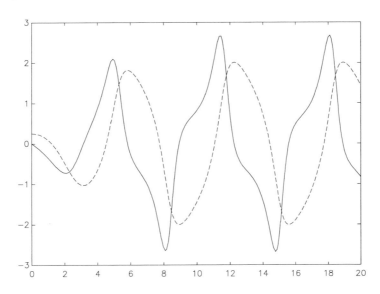

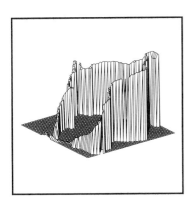

Scientific and engineering data are examined graphically in MATLAB using "graph paper" commands to create plots on the screen. There are many different types of "graph paper" from which to choose:

| Graph Paper | |
|---|---|
| plot | linear x-y plot |
| loglog | loglog x-y plot |
| semilogx | semi-log x-y plot (x-axis logarithmic) |
| semilogy | semi-log x-y plot (y-axis logarithmic) |
| polar | polar plot |
| mesh | 3-dimensional mesh surface |
| contour | contour plot |
| bar | bar chart |
| stairs | stairstep graph |

Once a graph is on the screen, the graph may be labeled, titled, or have grid lines drawn in:

| | |
|---|---|
| title | graph title |
| xlabel | x-axis label |
| ylabel | y-axis label |
| text | arbitrarily positioned text |
| gtext | mouse-positioned text |
| grid | grid lines |

There are commands for manual axis scaling and graph control:

| | |
|---|---|
| axis | manual axis scaling |
| hold | hold the plot on the screen |
| shg | show graph screen |
| clg | clear graph screen |
| subplot | break graph screen into subwindows |
| ginput | cross-hair input from mouse |

And there are commands for sending hardcopy to a printer:

| | |
|---|---|
| print | send graph to printer |
| prtsc | screen dump hardcopy |
| meta | graphics metafile |

## 14.1  X-Y Plots

The plot command creates linear x-y plots. Once plot is mastered, logarithmic and polar plots are created by substituting the words loglog, semilogx, semilogy, or polar for plot. All five commands are used the same way; they only affect how the axis is scaled and how the data are displayed.

## 14.2  Basic Form

If Y is a vector, plot(Y) produces a linear plot of the elements of Y versus the index of the elements of Y. For example, to plot the numbers {0., .48, .84, 1., .91, .6, .14}, enter them into a vector and execute plot:

```
Y = [0.   .48   .84   1.   .91   .6   .14];
plot(Y)
```

This results in a graph on your screen:

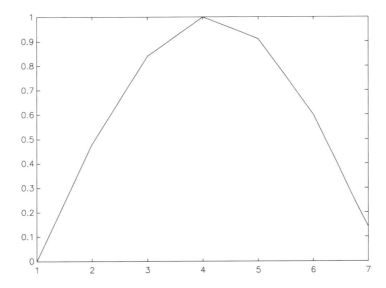

Notice that the data are auto-scaled and that X- and Y-axes are drawn.

At this point, depending upon the exact hardware you are using, the screen full of commands that you have typed in may have vanished to make way for the graph display. MATLAB has two displays, a graph display and a command display. Some hardware configurations allow both to be seen simultaneously, while others allow only one to be seen at a time. If the command display is no longer there, it can be brought back by pressing any key on the keyboard.

Once the command display has been brought back, a graph title, X and Y labels, and grid lines can be put on the plot by successively entering the commands

```
title('My first plot')
xlabel('fortnights')
ylabel('furlongs')
grid
```

This results in:

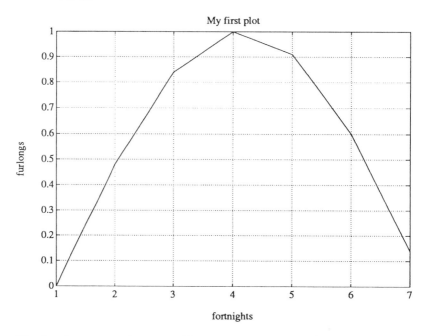

The function gtext ( '*text*' ) allows a mouse or arrow keys to position a cross-hair on the graph, at which point the text will be placed when any key is pressed.

If X and Y are vectors of the same length, the command plot (X,Y) draws an x-y plot of the elements of X versus the elements of Y. For example,

```
t = 0:.05:4*pi;
y = sin(t);
plot(t,y)
```

results in

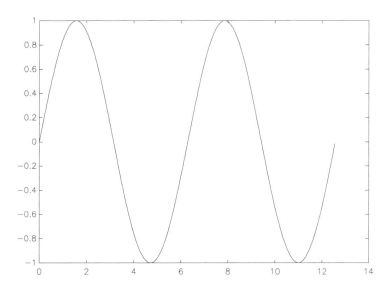

---

## 14.3  Multiple Lines

There are two ways to plot multiple lines on a single graph.  The first is to give `plot` two arguments, as in `plot(X,Y)`, where either `X`, `Y`, or both, are matrices.  Then:

1. If `Y` is a matrix, and `X` a vector, `plot(X,Y)` successively plots the rows or columns of `Y` versus the vector `X`, using a different line type for each. The row or column "direction" of `Y` is selected that has the same number of elements as vector `X`. If `Y` is a square matrix, the column direction is arbitrarily used.

2. If `X` is a matrix, and `Y` a vector, then the above rules are applied except the family of lines from `X` are plotted versus vector `Y`.

3. If `X` and `Y` are both matrices of the same size, `plot(X,Y)` plots the columns of `X` versus the columns of `Y`.

4. If no `X` is specified, as in `plot(Y)`, where `Y` is a matrix, then lines are plotted for each column of `Y` versus the row index.

The second, and easier, way to plot multiple lines on a single graph is to use `plot` with multiple arguments:

```
plot(X1,Y1,X2,Y2,...,Xn,Yn)
```

The variables `X1,Y1,X2,Y2`, etc. are pairs of vectors. Each x-y pair is graphed, generating multiple lines on the plot. Multiple arguments have the benefit of allowing vectors of differing lengths to be displayed on the same graph. As before, each pair uses a different line type.

## 14.4  Line and Mark Styles

### 14.4.1  Type

The linetypes used on a graph may be controlled if the defaults are not satisfactory. Point plots using various symbols may also be selected. For example,

```
plot(X,Y,'x')
```

draws a point plot using *x*-mark symbols while

```
plot(X1,Y1,':',X2,Y2,'+')
```

uses a dotted line for the first curve and the plus symbol + for the second curve. Other line and point types are:

| LINE TYPES | | POINT TYPES | |
|---|---|---|---|
| solid | – | point | . |
| dashed | – – | plus | + |
| dotted | : | star | * |
| dashdot | – . | circle | o |
| | | x-mark | x |

### 14.4.2 Color

On systems that support color, line- and mark-colors may be specified in a manner similar to line- and mark-types. For example, the statements

```
plot(X,Y,'r')
plot(X,Y,'+g')
```

use a red line on the first graph and green +-marks on the second. Other colors are:

| COLORS | |
|---|---|
| red | r |
| green | g |
| blue | b |
| white | w |
| invisible | i |

If your hard-copy device does not support color, the various colors on the interactive display are mapped to different linetypes for output.

## 14.5 Imaginary and Complex Data

When the arguments to plot are complex (have nonzero imaginary parts), the imaginary part is ignored *except* when plot is given a single complex argument. For this special case, the result is a shortcut to a plot of the real part versus the imaginary part. Thus plot(Z), when Z is a complex vector of matrix, is equivalent to plot(real(Z),imag(Z)).

To plot multiple lines in the complex plane, there is no shortcut, and the real and imaginary parts must be taken explicitly.

## 14.6 Logarithmic, Polar, and Bar Plots

The use of `loglog`, `semilogx`, `semilogy`, and `polar` is identical to the use of `plot`. These commands allow data to be plotted on different types of "graph paper," i.e., in different coordinate systems:

- `polar(theta, rho)` is a plot in polar coordinates of the angle `theta`, in radians, versus the radius `rho`. Subsequent use of the `grid` command draws polar grid lines.

- `loglog` is a plot using $\log_{10}$-$\log_{10}$ scales.

- `semilogx` is a plot using semi-log scales. The x-axis is $\log_{10}$ while the y-axis is linear.

- `semilogy` is a plot using semi-log scales. The y-axis is $\log_{10}$ while the x-axis is linear.

`bar(x)` displays a bar chart of the elements of vector `x`. `bar` does not accept multiple arguments. Similar, but missing the vertical lines, is `stairs`, which produces a stairstep plot useful for graphing sampled data systems.

## 14.7 3-D Mesh Surface and Contour Plots

The statement `mesh(Z)` creates a three dimensional perspective plot of the elements in matrix `Z`. A mesh surface is defined by the Z coordinates of points above a rectangular grid in the x-y plane. The plot is formed by joining adjacent points with straight lines.

`mesh` can be used to visualize large matrices that are otherwise too large to print out in numerical form. It can also be used to graph functions of two variables.

The first step in displaying a function $z = f(x,y)$ of two variables is to generate special X and Y matrices that consist of repeated rows and columns, respectively, over the domain of the function. The function can then be evaluated directly and graphed.

Consider the *sin(r)/r* or *sinc* function that results in the "sombrero" surface that everybody likes to show. One way to create this is:

```
x = -8: .5: 8;
y = x';
X = ones(y)*x;
Y = y*ones(x);
R = sqrt(X.^2 + Y.^2) + eps;
Z = sin(R)./R;
mesh(Z)
```

The first command defines the x-domain over which the function is to be evaluated. The third statement creates a matrix X of repeated rows. After generating a corresponding Y, a matrix R is created containing the distance from the center of the matrix, which is the origin. Forming the *sinc* function and applying mesh results in

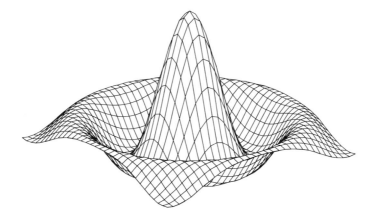

What does an identity matrix look like as a mesh surface? Try mesh(eye(14)). For an easier method of generating the special X and Y matrices required to evaluate functions of two variables, see meshdom in the *Reference* section.

A contour plot is an alternative to a mesh plot for viewing the contents of a matrix. A contour plot of the L-shaped membrane on the cover of this guide is

```
z = membrane(1,15,9,2);
contour(z)
```

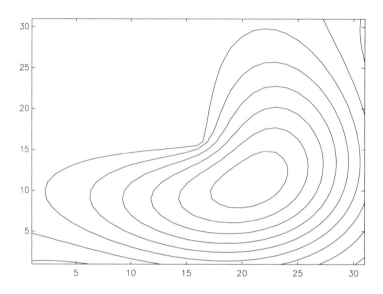

## 14.8  Screen Control

MATLAB conceptually has two displays, a *graph window* and a *command window*. Your particular hardware configuration may allow both to be seen simultaneously in different windows, or it may allow only one to be seen at a time. Several commands are available to switch back and forth between the windows, and/or erase the windows, as required:

| | |
|---|---|
| shg | show graph window |
| any key | bring back command window |
| clc | clear command window |
| clg | clear graph window |
| home | home command cursor |

For example, if during your MATLAB session only the command display is on the screen, typing `shg` will recall the last plot that was drawn on the graphing display.

By default, hardware configurations that cannot display both the command screen and the graph screen simultaneously will pause in graphics mode after a plot is drawn and wait for a key to be pressed.

It is possible to split the graph window into multiple partitions, in order to show several plots at the same time. The statement `subplot(mnp)` breaks the graph window into an *m*-by-*n* grid and uses the *p*-th box for the subsequent plot. For example,

```
subplot(211), plot(abs(y))
subplot(212), plot(angle(y))
```

breaks the screen in two, plots the magnitude of a complex vector in the top half, and plots the phase in the bottom half. The command `subplot(111)`, or just `subplot`, returns to the default single whole-screen window.

## 14.9 Manual Axis Scaling

In certain situations, it may be desirable to override the automatic axis scaling feature of the plot command and to manually select the plotting limits. Executing `axis`, by itself, freezes the current axis scaling for subsequent plots. Typing `axis` again resumes auto-scaling. `axis` returns a 4-element row vector containing the [x_min, x_max, y_min, y_max] from the last plot. `axis(V)`, where V is a 4-element vector, sets the axis scaling to the prescribed limits.

A second use of `axis` is to control the aspect ratio of the plot on the screen. `axis('square')` sets the plot region on the screen to be square. With a square aspect ratio, a line with slope 1 is at a true 45 degrees, not skewed by the irregular shape of the screen. Also, circles, like `plot(sin(t),cos(t))`, look like circles instead of ovals. `axis('normal')` sets the aspect ratio back to normal.

The `hold` command holds the current graph on the screen. Subsequent `plot` commands will add to the plot, using the already established axis limits and retaining the previously plotted curves. `hold` remains in effect until issued again.

## 14.10 Hard copy

The `prtsc` command provides printing capabilities for *The Student Edition of MATLAB*.

prtscr  prtsc initiates a graph window screen dump, like Shift-PrtSc, and allows it to be done in an M-file or in a for loop. In general, this results in a low-resolution plot, because the pixels on the screen are transferred to pixels on a printer.

The easiest way to obtain graphics hard copy is to hold the Shift key down and to press the PrtSc key. This sends a screen dump of the picture in the graph window to the printer.

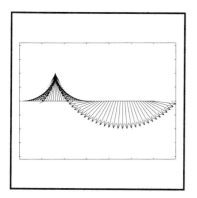

# 15
# Control Flow

MATLAB has control flow statements like those found in most computer languages. The control flow statements carry MATLAB beyond the level of a simple desk calculator, allowing it to be used as a complete high-level matrix language.

## 15.1 FOR Loops

MATLAB has its own version of the "DO" or "FOR" loop found in computer languages. It allows a statement, or group of statements, to be repeated a fixed, predetermined number of times. For example

```
for i = 1:n, x(i) = 0, end
```

assigns 0 to the first n elements of x. If n is less than 1, the construction is still legal, but the inner statement will not be executed. If x does not yet exist, or has fewer than n elements, then additional space will be allocated automatically.

The loops can be nested and are usually indented for readability.

```
for i = 1:m
    for j = 1:n
        A(i,j) = 1/(i+j-1);
    end
end
A
```

The semicolon terminating the inner statement suppresses repeated printing, while the A after the loops displays the final result.

An important point: Each for *must* be matched with an end. If you simply type

```
for i = 1:n, x(i) = 0
```

the system will patiently wait for you to enter the remaining statements in the body of the loop. Nothing will happen until you type the end.

For another example, assume

```
t =
    -1
     0
     1
     3
     5
```

and that we want to generate a Vandermonde matrix, a matrix whose columns are powers of elements of t.

```
A =
      1     -1      1     -1      1
      0      0      0      0      1
      1      1      1      1      1
     81     27      9      3      1
    625    125     25      5      1
```

Here is the most obvious double loop.

```
n = max(size(t));
for j = 1:n
    for i = 1:n
        A(i,j) = t(i)^(n-j);
    end
end
```

But the following single loop with vector operations is significantly faster and also illustrates the fact that for loops can go backwards.

```
A(:,n) = ones(n,1);
for j = n-1:-1:1
    A(:,j) = t .* A(:,j+1);
end
```

The general form of a `for` loop is

```
for v = expression
    statements
end
```

The *expression* is actually a matrix, because that's all there is in MATLAB. The columns of the matrix are assigned one by one to the variable v and then the *statements* are executed. A clearer way of accomplishing almost the same thing is

```
E = expression;
[m,n] = size(E);
for j = 1:n
    v = E(:,j);
    statements
end
```

Usually, the *expression* is something like `m:n`, or `m:i:n`, which is a matrix with only one row, and so its columns are simply scalars. In this special case, the `for` loop is like the "FOR" or "DO" loops of other languages.

## 15.2 WHILE Loops

MATLAB also has its version of the "WHILE" loop, which allows a statement, or group of statements, to be repeated an indefinite number of times, under control of a logical condition. Here is a simple problem to illustrate a `while` loop. What is the first integer $n$ for which $n!$ (that is $n$ factorial) is a 100 digit number? The following `while` loop will find it. If you don't already know the answer, you can run this yourself.

```
n = 1;
while prod(1:n) < 1.e100, n = n+1; end
n
```

A more practical computation illustrating `while` is the calculation of the exponential of a matrix, called `expm(A)` in MATLAB. One possible definition of the exponential function is the power series,

```
expm(A) = I + A + A^2/2! + A^3/3! + ...
```

It is reasonable to use this for the actual computation as long as the elements of A are not too large. The idea is to sum as many terms of this series as are needed to produce a result that would not change if more terms are added in finite precision machine arithmetic.

In the following loop, A is the given matrix, E will become the desired exponential, F is an individual term in the series, and k is the index of that term. The indented statements will be repeated until F is so small that adding it to E doesn't change E.

```
E = zeros(A);
F = eye(A);
k = 1;
while norm(E+F-E,1) > 0
    E = E + F;
    F = A*F/k;
    k = k+1;
end
```

If we want to compute the array or element-by-element exponential exp(A) instead, we just have to change the initialization of F from eye(A) to ones(A) and change the matrix multiplication A*F to array multiplication A.*F.

The general form of a while loop is

```
while expression
    statements
end
```

The *statements* are executed repeatedly as long as all of the elements in the *expression matrix* are nonzero. The expression matrix is almost always a 1-by-1 relational expression, so nonzero corresponds to TRUE. When the expression matrix is not a scalar, it can be reduced using the functions any and all.

---

## 15.3  IF and BREAK Statements

Here are a couple of examples illustrating MATLAB's if statements. The first shows how a computation might be broken down into three cases, depending upon the sign and parity of n.

```
if n < 0
    A = negative(n)
elseif rem(n,2) == 0
    A = even(n)
else
    A = odd(n)
end
```

The second example involves a fascinating problem from number theory. Take any positive integer. If it is even, divide it by 2; if it is odd, multiply it by 3 and add 1. Repeat this process until your integer becomes a one. The fascinating unsolved problem is: Is there any integer for which the process does not terminate? Our MATLAB program illustrates while and if statements. It also shows the input function, which prompts for keyboard input, and the break statement, which provides an exit jump out of loops.

```
% Classic "3n+1" problem from number theory.
while 1
    n = input('Enter n, negative quits. ');
    if n <= 0, break, end
    while n > 1
        if rem(n,2) == 0
            n = n/2
        else
            n = 3*n+1
        end;
    end
end
```

Can you make this run forever?

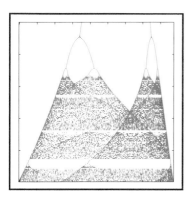

# 16
# M-files:
# Scripts and
# Functions

MATLAB is usually used in a command-driven mode; when single-line commands are entered, MATLAB processes them immediately and displays the results. MATLAB is also capable of executing sequences of commands that are stored in files. Together, these two modes form an interpretive environment.

Disk files that contain MATLAB statements are called *M-files* because they have a file type of ".m" as the last part of the filename (the ".m" is optional on the Macintosh). For example, a file named bessel.m might contain MATLAB statements that evaluate Bessel functions.

An M-file consists of a sequence of normal MATLAB statements, possibly including references to other M-files. An M-file can call itself recursively.

One use of M-files is to automate long sequences of commands. Such files are called *script files* or just *scripts*. A second type of M-file provides extensibility to MATLAB. Called *function files*, they allow new functions to be added to the existing functions. Much of the power of MATLAB derives from this ability to create new functions that solve user-specific problems.

Both types of M-files, *scripts* and *functions*, are ordinary ASCII text files, and are created using an editor or word processor of your choice.

# 16.1 Script Files

When a *script* is invoked, MATLAB simply executes the commands found in the file, instead of waiting for input from the keyboard. The statements in a *script file* operate globally on the data in the workspace. *Scripts* are useful for performing analyses, solving problems, or doing designs that require such long sequences of commands that they become cumbersome to do interactively.

As an example, suppose the MATLAB commands

```
% An M-file to calculate Fibonnaci numbers
f = [1 1];  i = 1;
while f(i) + f(i+1) < 1000
      f(i+2) = f(i) + f(i+1);
      i = i + 1;
end
plot(f)
```

are contained in a file called fibno.m. Typing the statement fibno causes MATLAB to execute the commands, calculate the first 16 Fibonnaci numbers, and create a plot. After execution of the file is complete, the variables f and i remain in the workspace.

The demos supplied with MATLAB are good examples of using *scripts* to perform more complicated tasks. The script named startup.m is executed automatically when MATLAB is invoked. Physical constants, engineering conversion factors, or anything else you would like predefined in your workspace may be put in these files. On multi-user or networked systems, a script called matlab.m is reserved for use by the system manager. It can be used to implement system-wide definitions and messages.

# 16.2 Function Files

If the first line of an M-file contains the word "function", the file is a *function file*. A *function* differs from a *script* in that arguments may be passed, and that variables defined and manipulated inside the file are local to the function and do not operate globally on the workspace. *Function files* are useful for extending MATLAB, that is, creating new MATLAB functions using the MATLAB language itself.

Here is a simple example. The file `mean.m` on your disk contains the statements:

```
function y = mean(x)
% MEAN  Average or mean value. For vectors,
%       MEAN(x) returns the mean value. For
%       matrices, MEAN(x) is a row vector
%       containing the mean value of each column.
[m,n] = size(x);
if m == 1
        m = n;            % Handle isolated row vector.
end
y = sum(x) / m;
```

The existence of this disk file defines a new function called `mean`. The new function `mean` is used just like any other MATLAB function. For example, if `Z` is a vector of the integers from 1 to 99,

```
Z = 1:99;
```

the mean value is found by typing

```
mean(Z)
```

which results in

```
ans =
    50
```

Let's examine some of the details of `mean.m`:

- The first line declares the function name, the input arguments, and the output arguments. Without this line, the file would be a *script file*, instead of a *function file*.

- The `%` symbol indicates that the rest of a line is a comment and should be ignored.

- The first few lines document the M-file and will be displayed if `help  mean` is typed.

- The variables `m`, `n`, and `y` are local to `mean` and will not exist in the workspace after `mean` has finished. (Or, if they previously existed, they will be unchanged.)

- It was not necessary to put our integers from 1 to 99 in a variable with the name `x`. In fact, we used `mean` with a variable called `Z`. The vector `Z` that contained the integers from 1 to 99 was passed or copied into `mean` where it became a local variable named `x`.

A slightly more complicated version of mean called stat calculates standard deviation too:

```
function  [mean,stdev] = stat(x)
[m,n] = size(x);
if m == 1
        m = n;             % Handle isolated row vector.
end
mean = sum(x) / m;
stdev = sqrt(sum(x.^2) / m - mean.^2);
```

stat illustrates that it is possible to return multiple output arguments.

A function that calculates the rank of a matrix uses multiple input arguments:

```
function r = rank(x,tol)
% rank of a matrix
s = svd(x);
if (nargin == 1)
        tol = max(size(x)) * s(1) * eps;
end
r = sum(s > tol);
```

This example demonstrates the use of the permanent variable nargin to find the number of input arguments. The variable nargout, although not used here, contains the number of output arguments.

*Some helpful hints*:

When a *M-function file* is invoked for the first time during a MATLAB session, it is compiled and placed into memory. It is then available for subsequent use without recompilation. It remains in memory for the duration of the session, unless you run low on free memory, in which case it may be cleared automatically.

The what command shows a directory listing of the M-files that are available in the current directory on your disk, type lists M-files, and ! is used to invoke your editor, allowing you to create or modify M-files.

In general, if you input the name of something to MATLAB, for example by typing whoopie, the MATLAB interpreter goes through the following steps:

1. Looks to see if whoopie is a variable.

2. Checks if whoopie is a built-in function.

3. Looks in the current directory for a file named whoopie.m.

4. Looks in the directories specified by the environment symbol MATLABPATH for a file named whoopie.m. (See the installation instructions to learn how to set MATLABPATH.)

Thus MATLAB first tries to use `whoopie` as a variable, if it exists, before trying to use `whoopie` as a function.

## 16.3 Echo, Input, Pause, Keyboard

Normally, while an M-file is executing, the commands in the file are not displayed on the screen. A command called `echo` causes M-files to be viewed as they execute, useful for debugging or for demonstrations. See the *Reference* section for further details.

The function `input` obtains input from the user. `n = input('How many apples')` gives the user the prompt in the text string, waits, and then returns the number or expression input from the keyboard. One use of `input` is to build menu-driven M-files. The `demo` facility is an example of this.

Similar to `input`, but more powerful, is `keyboard`. This function invokes your computer keyboard as a script. Placed in M-files, this feature is useful for debugging or for modifying variables during execution.

The `pause` command causes a procedure to stop and wait for the user to press any key before continuing. `pause(n)` pauses for n seconds before continuing.

It is also possible to define global variables, although we don't recommend it. See the *Reference* section if you insist.

## 16.4 Strings and String Macros

Text strings are entered into MATLAB surrounded by single quotes. For example,

```
s = 'Hello'
```

results in

```
s =

    Hello
```

The text is stored in a vector, one character per element. In this case,

```
size(s)

ans =
    1    5
```

indicates that `s` has five elements. The characters are stored as their ASCII values and `abs` shows these values,

```
abs(s)

ans =
    72   101   108   108   111
```

The function `setstr` sets the vector to display as text instead of showing ASCII values. Also useful are `disp`, which simply displays the text in the variable, and the functions `isstr` and `strcmp`, which detect strings and compare strings, respectively.

Text variables can be concatenated into larger strings using brackets:

```
s = [s, ' World']

s =

Hello World
```

Numeric values are converted to strings by `sprintf`, `num2str`, and `int2str`. The converted numeric values are often concatenated into larger strings to put titles on plots that include numeric values:

```
f = 70; c = (f-32)/1.8;
title(['Room temperature is ',num2str(c),'degrees C'])
```

`eval` is a function that works with text variables to implement a powerful text macro facility. `eval(t)` causes the text contained in `t` to be evaluated. If STRING is the source text for any MATLAB expression or statement, then

```
t = 'STRING';
```

encodes the text in `t`. Typing `t` prints the text and `eval(t)` causes the text to be interpreted, either as a statement or as a factor in an expression. For example

```
t = '1/(i+j-1)';
for i = 1:n
        for j = 1:n
                a(i,j) = eval(t);
        end
end
```

generates the Hilbert matrix of order n. Another example showing indexed text,

```
S = ['x = 3              '
     'y = 4              '
     'z = sqrt(x*x+y*y)'];

for k=1:3
     eval(S(k,:));
end
```

It is necessary that the strings making up the rows of the matrix S have the same lengths. Here is a final example showing how eval can use the load command to load ten sequentially numbered data files:

```
fname = 'mydata';
for i=1:10
     eval(['load ',fname,int2str(i)])
end
```

The text macro facility is particularly useful for passing function names to M-function files. For an example, see the file funm.m in the *MATLAB Toolbox.*

## 16.5 External Programs

It is possible, and often useful, to make your own external standalone programs act like new MATLAB functions. This can be done by writing M-files that

1. Save the variables on disk,

2. Run the external programs (which read the data files, process them, and write the results back out to disk), and

3. Load the processed files back into the workspace.

For example, here is a hypothetical M-function that finds the solution to Garfield's equation using an external program called GAREQN

```
function y = garfield(a,b,q,r)
save gardata a b q r
!gareqn
load gardata
```

It requires that you have written a program (in Fortran or some other language) called GAREQN that reads a file called `gardata.mat`, processes it, and puts the results back out to the same file. The utility subroutines described in the next section can be used to read and write MAT-files.

## 16.6 Speed and Memory Tips

MATLAB's built-in vector and matrix operations are more than an order of magnitude faster than its compiler/interpreter operations. This means that in order to obtain the most speed out of MATLAB, you must make every effort to vectorize the algorithms in your M-files. Wherever possible, `for` and `while` loops should be converted to vector or matrix operations. For example, one way to take the sine of 1001 numbers from 0 to 10 is:

```
i = 0;
for t = 0:.01:10
    i = i + 1;
    y(i) = sin(t);
end
```

A vectorized version of the same code is:

```
t = 0:.01:10;
y = sin(t);
```

On one machine, the first example takes 15 seconds, while the second executes in only 0.6 seconds, a speedup factor of 25. It is not always so obvious how to optimize more complex code, but the point is that when speed is important, you should always be looking for ways to vectorize your algorithms.

If you can't vectorize a piece of code, here is a tip for making your `for` loops go faster: *Preallocate any vectors in which output results are stored.* For example, inclusion of the first statement here, using `zeros`, causes the `for` loop to execute significantly faster:

```
y = zeros(1,100);
for i = 1:100
    y(i) = det(x^i);
end
```

The reason is that if you do not preallocate, the MATLAB interpreter has to resize the y vector to one element larger each time through the iteration loop. If the vector is preallocated, this step is eliminated and execution is faster.

For those of you who work with large matrices on computers with memory limitations, the preallocation scheme has a second benefit: It uses memory much more efficiently and will help if you are running out of memory. It helps because memory tends to become fragmented in the course of a MATLAB session, such that you may have plenty of free memory left, but not enough contiguous space to hold a large variable. Preallocation helps reduce fragmentation.

On the subject of memory, if the who command on your computer displays the amount of free memory remaining, then there are some caveats about this number that you ought to be aware of. If you delete a variable from the workspace, the number displayed by who usually will not get larger, *unless it is the "highest" variable in the workspace*. The number actually indicates the amount of free memory that is contiguous and has not been used. Clearing the highest variable will make it larger, but clearing a variable beneath the highest variable has no effect. What all this means, practically, is that you may have more free memory than is indicated by who.

Computers with virtual memory do not display the amount of free memory remaining because there are no MATLAB or hardware imposed limitations.

One optimization that MATLAB does for you is helpful to know about when writing M-files. The arguments that an M-file function is called with are not copied into the function's local workspace *unless* you alter the contents of the argument within the M-function. This means that there is no memory penalty for passing large variables into M-file functions.

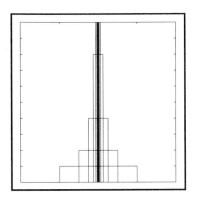

# 17
# Disk Files

load and save are the MATLAB commands to store and retrieve from disk the contents of the MATLAB workspace (see *Section 1.9* and the *Reference* entry). Other disk file related commands help manage the disk, allow external programs to be run, and provide data import/export capabilities.

## 17.1 Disk File Manipulation

The commands dir, type, delete, and chdir implement a set of generic operating system commands for manipulating files. Here is a table that indicates how these commands map to other operating systems, perhaps one you are familiar with:

| MATLAB | MS-DOS | UNIX | VAX/VMS |
|--------|--------|------|---------|
| dir | dir | ls | dir |
| type | type | cat | type |
| delete | del | rm | delete |
| chdir | chdir | cd | set default |

For most of these commands, pathnames, wildcards, and drive designators may be used in the usual way.

The `type` command differs from the usual `type` commands in an important way: If no file type is given, `.m` is used by default. This makes it convenient for the most frequent use of `type`, to list M-files on the screen.

The `diary` command creates a diary of your MATLAB session in a disk file (graphics are not saved, however). The resulting ASCII file is suitable for inclusion into reports and other documents using any word processor.

For more details on these commands, see the *Reference* section or use the online `help` facility.

## 17.2 Running External Programs

The exclamation point character ! is a *shell escape* and indicates that the rest of the input line should be issued as a command to the operating system. This is quite useful for invoking utilities or running other programs without quitting from MATLAB. For example

```
!f77 simpleprog
```

invokes a Fortran compiler called F77 and

```
!edt darwin.m
```

invokes an editor called `edt` on a file named `darwin.m`. After these programs complete, control is returned to MATLAB.

## 17.3 Importing and Exporting Data

Data from other programs and the outside world can be introduced into MATLAB by several different methods. Similarly, MATLAB data can be exported to the outside world. It is also possible to have your programs manipulate data directly in MAT-files, the file format MATLAB uses.

The best method depends upon how much data there are, whether the data are already in machine readable form, what the form is, etc. Here are some choices; select the one that looks appropriate.

1. Enter it as an explicit list of elements. If you have a small amount of data, say less than 10-15 elements, it is easy to type in the data explicitly using brackets, [ and ]. This method is awkward for larger amounts of data because you can't edit your

input if you make a mistake. See *Section 1.1*.

2. Create it in an M-file. Use your text editor to create a script M-file that enters your data as an explicit list of elements. This method is good when your data are not already in computer-readable form and you have to type them in anyway. Essentially the same as method 1, it has the advantage of allowing you to use your editor to change the data or to fix mistakes. You can then just rerun the M-file to reenter the data.

3. Load it from an ASCII flat file. If the data are stored in ASCII form, with fixed length rows terminated with newlines (carriage returns), and with spaces separating the numbers, then the file is a so-called *flat file*. (ASCII flat files can be edited using a normal text editor.) Flat files can be read directly into MATLAB using the load command. The result is put into a variable whose name is the filename.

4. Write a program in Fortran or C to translate your data into MAT-file format.

Some methods of getting MATLAB data back to the outside world are:

1. For small matrices, use the diary command to create a diary file, and then list the variables on this file. You can use your text editor to manipulate the diary file at a later time. The output of diary includes the MATLAB commands used during the session, which is useful for inclusion into documents and reports.

2. Save a variable using the save command, with the /ascii option. For example,

```
A = rand(4,3);
save temp.dat A /ascii
```

creates an ASCII file called temp.dat that contains:

```
0.2113    0.8096    0.4832
0.0824    0.8474    0.6135
0.7599    0.4524    0.2749
0.0087    0.8075    0.8807
```

3. Write a program in Fortran or C to translate the MAT-file into your own special format.

You may prefer to have your external programs read or write the data directly in the MAT-files used by the MATLAB load and save commands. The format of MAT-files is documented under load in the *Reference* section of this guide.

If you program in Fortran or C, there are some routines provided in the *MATLAB Toolbox* to help you interface your programs to MAT-files:

| | |
|---|---|
| `savemat.for` | A subroutine call that writes MAT-files. |
| `loadmat.for` | A subroutine call that reads MAT-files. |
| `testls1.for` | An example of using `savemat` and `loadmat`. |
| `testls2.for` | Another example of using `savemat` and `loadmat`. |
| `loadmat.c` | A C routine to load a matrix from a MAT-file. |
| `savemat.c` | A C routine to save a matrix to a MAT-file. |
| `testls.c` | An example of using `loadmat.c` and `savemat.c`. |

The implementation of the Fortran versions of these routines may differ from machine to machine.

# Part Three

# The Signals and Systems Toolbox

Part Three - Signals and Systems Toolbox

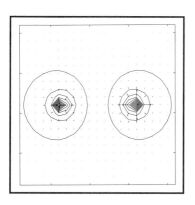

# 18
# Signals
# and Systems

The professional version of MATLAB has a number of optional toolboxes (collections of M-files) available that extends MATLAB's functionality into specific disciplines. Two of the more important ones are:

- the *Signal Processing Toolbox*, which contains commands for one-dimensional and two-dimensional signal processing (time-series analysis). It includes functions for the design and analysis of digital filters and for power spectrum estimation (FFT analysis).

- the *Control System Toolbox*, which includes commands for control engineering and systems theory.

In the directory `sigsys` on your disk there is a collection of M-files called the *Signals and Systems Toolbox*. These M-files are a selection of commands from the *Signal Processing Toolbox* and the *Control Systems Toolbox* chosen specifically for their usefulness in classroom settings. Out of the more than 150 commands available in the two professional toolboxes, 35 or so have been selected for the *Signals and Systems Toolbox*.

Chapter 19 provides a tutorial on the *Signals and Systems Toolbox* from a signal processing perspective, while Chapter 20 discusses much of the same material from a control system perspective. The math is actually the same - both are concerned with linear systems - but historically the two subjects have emphasized different approaches.

MATLAB has a rich collection of functions immediately useful for signal processing. Complex arithmetic, convolution, root finding, matrix inversion, and FFTs are just a few examples of important tools. More generally, MATLAB's linear algebra, matrix computation, and numerical analysis capabilities provide a reliable foundation for modern matrix-based signal processing.

The *Signals and Systems Toolbox* contains a collection of algorithms, expressed in M-files, that implement's a variety of modern signal processing techniques. The signal processing portion of the *Signals and Systems Toolbox* includes functions for:

- Filter analysis and implementation, including frequency response, group delay, phase delay, and filter implementation, both direct and using FFT-based frequency domain techniques.

- IIR filter design, including Butterworth, Chebyshev type I, Chebyshev type II, and elliptic.

- FIR filter design via the optimal Parks-McClellan algorithm.

- FFT processing, including the radix-2 transformation and its inverse, nonpower-of-two transform.

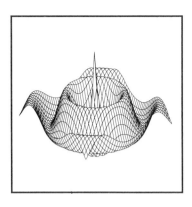

# 19
# Signal Processing

MATLAB has a rich collection of functions immediately useful for signal processing. Complex arithmetic, convolution, root finding, matrix inversion, and FFTs are just a few examples of important tools. More generally, MATLAB's linear algebra, matrix computation, and numerical analysis capabilities provide a reliable foundation for modern matrix-based signal processing.

The *Signals and Systems Toolbox* contains a collection of algorithms, expressed in M-files, that implement's a variety of modern signal processing techniques. The signal processing portion of the *Signals and Systems Toolbox* includes functions for:

- Filter analysis and implementation, including frequency response, group delay, phase delay, and filter implementation, both direct and using FFT-based frequency domain techniques.

- IIR filter design, including Butterworth, Chebyshev type I, Chebyshev type II, and elliptic.

- FIR filter design via the optimal Parks-McClellan algorithm.

- FFT processing, including the radix-2 transformation and its inverse, nonpower-of-two transform.

# 19.1 Signals as Vectors and Matrices

MATLAB is a "strongly typed" language; it works with only one kind of object, a rectangular numerical matrix with possibly complex elements. This object, a matrix, is ideal for signal processing. The basic data objects of signal processing are one-dimensional signals (sequences), multichannel signals, and two-dimensional signals. This chapter begins with a discussion of *Signal Processing Toolbox* conventions for representing these various types of signals in matrices.

Vectors, which are 1-by-*n* or *n*-by-1 matrices, are used to hold ordinary one-dimensional sampled data signals, or sequences. One way to introduce a sequence into MATLAB is to enter it as an explicit list of elements. The statement

```
x = [4 3 7 -9 1]
```

creates a simple five element real sequence in a row vector. The sequence can be turned into a column vector by transposition,

```
x = x'
```

which results in

```
x =
    4
    3
    7
   -9
    1
```

Column orientation is preferred over row orientation for single channel signals because it extends naturally to the multichannel case. For multichannel data, matrices are used to hold the different channels, each channel in a column. Each row of such a matrix then corresponds to a sample point. For example, a three channel signal that consists of $x$, $2x$, and $x/\pi$ is formed with

```
y = [x 2*x x/pi]
```

which results in

```
y =
     4.0000     8.0000     1.2732
     3.0000     6.0000     0.9549
     7.0000    14.0000     2.2282
    -9.0000   -18.0000    -2.8648
     1.0000     2.0000     0.3183
```

The data for our length five sequence were entered manually into MATLAB. More often, experimental data exists in disk files, having been generated by other programs or otherwise obtained from the outside world. There is a variety of methods whereby external data can be read into MATLAB, most centering around use of the `load` command. For example, if a disk file called `telemetry.dat` contains ASCII data, then it can be read directly into MATLAB with the line

```
load telemetry.dat
```

The data will appear in the MATLAB workspace with the name `telemetry`. See *Importing and Exporting Data* in the *Tutorial* section of the main MATLAB guide or `load` in the *Reference* section, for more information.

MATLAB has a variety of functions for synthesizing signals. Most require starting with a vector representing a time base. Consider generating data with a 1000 Hz sample frequency. The statement

```
t = 0:.001:1;
```

uses MATLAB's colon operator to create a 1001 element row vector that represents time running from zero to one second in steps of one millisecond. The semicolon ";" tells MATLAB not to display the result – we have no interest in seeing the 1001 numbers listed out.

A sample signal  y  consisting of two sinusoids, one at 50 Hz and one at 120 Hz with twice the amplitude, can be synthesized with

```
y = sin(2*pi*50*t) + 2*sin(2*pi*120*t);
```

The new variable  y, formed from vector  t, is also 1001 elements long. We can add normally distributed white noise to the signal, call it  yn, and graph the first fifty points with

```
rand('normal')
yn = y + 0.5*rand(t);
plot(t(1:50),yn(1:50))
```

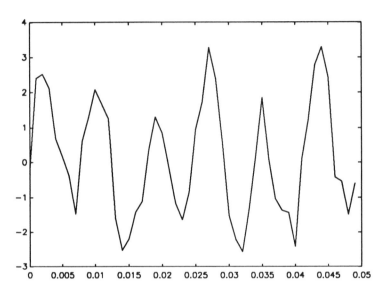

Of course, since MATLAB is a language, there is an endless variety of different signals that can be synthesized. Here are some statements that generate several commonly used sequences including unit sample, unit step, and unit ramp functions:

```
y = [1 zeros(1,99)];
y = ones(1,100);
y = t;
y = t.^2;
```

Notice that all four of these sequences are row vectors (the last two inherited their shape from  t). A multichannel signal consisting of the last two signals is

```
t = t';
z = [t  t.^2];
```

A three channel unit sample function can be generated with an outer product

```
z = [1  zeros(1,99)]'*ones(1,3)
```

which generates a 100-by-3 matrix whose first row is all ones and the rest of which is zero. If the above statement is not obvious, experiment with some smaller vectors to see how outer products can be used to replicate columns.

To give a quick preview of subjects to come in the following sections, here is how to filter the signal yn with a sixth order lowpass Butterworth filter that has a cutoff frequency of 100 Hz,

```
[b,a] = butter(6,100/500)
z = filter(b,a,yn);
```

Butterworth filter design is discussed in *Section 19.3*; spectrum estimation is covered in *Section 19.4*.

---

# 19.2 Filter Analysis and Implementation

The *Signals and Systems Toolbox* has functions to design filters, both analog and digital, and functions that apply the filters to data. It also has functions to analyze filters in terms of magnitude response, phase response, and other characterizations.

Filters are most often used to enhance signals by removing unwanted components from them. The most common filter of this type is the *frequency-selective* filter, designed from frequency response specifications, that allows only certain desired frequency bands to pass through.

Filters can also be used to represent the dynamics of a system. In this case, filter design is an inverse problem: Given input and output data, find the filter that can most nearly reproduce the measured input-output relationship. The inverse problem is usually referred to as *parametric modeling* in signal processing circles, as *system identification* in stochastic modeling and control theory circles, and as *ARMA-modeling* in econometrics and statistics.

Our discussion of filtering will start with a look at filter implementation and analysis functions and then continue into filter design methods.

## 19.2.1 Time Domain Filter Implementation

There is a function in the *Signals and Systems Toolbox* that implements time domain filtering operations:

| Time domain filtering functions |
|---|
| filter     direct filter implementation |

The function

```
y = filter(b, a, x)
```

filters the data in vector $x$ with the filter described by vectors $b$ and $a$ to create filtered data $y$. The filter structure is the general tapped delay-line filter described by the difference equation

$$y[n] = b(1)x[n] + b(2)x[n-1] + \cdots + b(nb+1)x[n-nb]$$
$$- a(2)y[n-1] - \cdots - a(na+1)y[n-na]$$

or, as we have already seen, in the frequency domain as the transfer function

$$Y(z) = \frac{b(1) + b(2)z^{-1} + \cdots + b(nb+1)z^{-nb}}{1 + a(2)z^{-1} + \cdots + a(na+1)z^{-na}} X(z)$$

For example, to find and plot the *n*-point unit impulse response of a tenth order Butterworth digital filter:

```
[b,a] = butter(10,.5);
x = [1  zeros(1,n-1)];
y = filter(b,a,x);
plot(y,'o')
```

filter is implemented as a transposed direct form II structure:

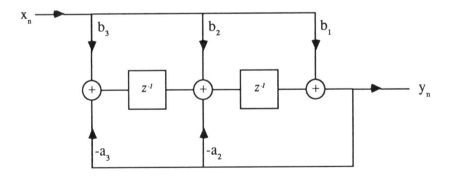

This is a canonical form; the filter implementation has the minimum number of delay elements.

This is a canonical form; the filter implementation has the minimum number of delay elements.

The `filter` function allows initial conditions to be set on its delays and it can return the final conditions after a filter run:

```
[y,zf] = filter(b,a,x,zi)
```

When filtering short data sequences, it may be important to set the initial conditions to avoid transient startup effects. With longer data lengths, it usually suffices just to disregard the first few filtered points corrupted by startup transients.

Access to initial and final conditions is also useful for filtering data in sections, especially if memory limitations are encountered. Suppose data has been collected in two chunks of 1000 points each. Perhaps the first sequence, which we'll call `yn1`, corresponds to the first ten minutes of data and the second `yn2` to an additional ten minutes. The whole sequence is `yn = [yn1 yn2]`. If there is not sufficient memory to hold the combined sequence, the subsequences `yn1` and `yn2` can be filtered one at a time. To ensure continuity of the filtered sequences, the final conditions from filtering `yn1` should be used as initial conditions to filter `yn2`:

```
[yf1,zf] = filter(b,a,yn1);
[yf2,zf2] = filter(b,a,yn2,zf);
```

## 19.2.2 Frequency Domain Filter Implementation

Duality between the time domain and the frequency domain allows anything that can be done in one domain to be done in the other. Usually one domain or the other is more convenient for a particular operation, but a given operation can always be accomplished in either domain.

General IIR filtering can be implemented in the frequency domain by multiplying the discrete Fourier transform (DFT) of the input sequence with the quotient of the DFT of the filter,

```
n = length(x);
y = ifft(fft(x).*fft(b,n)./fft(a,n));
```

which computes results that are identical to `filter`, except with different startup transients (end effects). For long sequences, this computation is very inefficient because of the large zero-padded FFT operations on the filter coefficients, and because of the dwindling efficiency of FFT algorithms with increasing $n$.

### 19.2.3 Frequency Response

Several functions in the *Signal Processing Toolbox* are available to characterize the frequency domain behavior of analog and digital filters:

| Frequency domain analysis | |
|---|---|
| abs | magnitude |
| angle | phase angle |
| freqs | Laplace transform frequency response |
| freqz | $z$-transform frequency response |
| grpdelay | group delay |
| unwrap | unwrap phase |

The statement

```
[h,w] = freqz(b,a,n)
```

returns the $n$-point complex frequency response, $H(e^{j\omega})$, of the digital filter,

$$H(z) = \frac{B(z)}{A(z)} = \frac{b(1) + b(2)z^{-1} + \cdots + b(nb+1)z^{-nb}}{a(1) + a(2)z^{-1} + \cdots + a(na+1)z^{-na}}$$

given the numerator and denominator coefficients in vectors b and a. freqz returns both h, the complex frequency response, and w, a vector containing the $n$ frequency points. The frequency response is evaluated at $n$ points equally spaced around the upper half of the unit circle, so w contains n points between 0 and $\pi$.

The magnitude and phase of the filter are extracted from the complex frequency response h and graphed, with the phase in degrees, by

```
m = abs(h);
p = angle(h);
semilogy(w,m), plot(w,p*180/pi)
```

while the statement p = unwrap(p) "unwraps" the phase to make it continuous across 180° boundaries.

The *group delay* of a filter is a measure of the average delay of the filter as a function of frequency. It is defined as the negative first derivative of a filter's phase response. If the complex frequency response of a filter is $H(e^{j\omega})$, then the group delay is

$$\tau_g(\omega) = -\frac{d\theta(\omega)}{d\omega}$$

where $\theta$ is the phase angle of $H(e^{j\omega})$. In the *Signals and Systems Toolbox*, group delay is computed with

```
[gd,w] = grpdelay(b,a,n)
```

which returns the $n$-point group delay, $\tau_g(\omega)$, of the digital filter in b and a.

The *phase delay* of a filter is the negative of phase divided by frequency

$$\tau_p(\omega) = -\frac{\theta(\omega)}{\omega}$$

Here's how to plot both the group and phase delays of a system on the same graph:

```
gd = grpdelay(b,a,128);
[h,w] = freqz(b,a,128);
pd = -unwrap(angle(h))./w;
plot(w,gd,w,pd)
```

Many FIR filters have linear phase – the phase delay and group delay are equal and constant over the frequency band. If the phase delay is an integer $n$, the filtered signal is simply delayed by $n$ time steps.

# 19.3 Filter Design

The functions in the *Signals and Systems Toolbox* for digital filter design can be grouped into four methodologies:

- IIR filter design using analog prototypes

- Direct IIR filter design

- Direct FIR filter design

- Inverse filter design

The first three of these produce frequency selective filters that are designed from magnitude response performance specifications. The last category encompasses techniques that find filter coefficients that are responsible for a given set of time-response or complex frequency-response data.

The first step in digital filter design by analog filter transformation is the design of a suitable analog filter. As a byproduct of the digital filter design tools, the *Signals and Systems Toolbox* contains functions for classical analog filter design.

### 19.3.1 Filter Performance Specification

So you need a filter for some purpose. There is more than one way in which you might specify the filter you need. A loose specification might be "For my system with a 100 Hz sample rate, I need a filter that removes the noise above 30 Hz." A more rigorous specification might call for a specific amount of passband ripple, stopband attenuation, or transition width. A very precise specification could ask to achieve the performance goals with the minimum filter order, or it could call for an arbitrary magnitude shape, or it might require an FIR filter.

The various filter design techniques differ primarily in how performance is specified. If you have only "loosely specified" requirements, as defined above, the class of Butterworth IIR filters is sufficient for most needs. For example, to design a fifth order 30 Hz lowpass Butterworth filter and to apply it to data, use

```
[b,a] = butter(5,30/50)
y = filter(b,a,x);
```

The second input argument to butter indicates the cutoff frequency, normalized to half the sample frequency (the Nyquist frequency).

More rigorous requirements may call for specific amounts of passband ripple ($Rp$), stopband attenuation ($Rs$), or transition width ($Ws-Wp$). The traditional definitions of these parameters are:

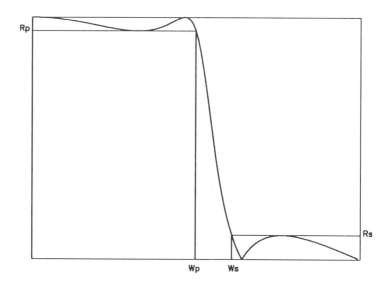

Butterworth, Chebyshev I, Chebyshev II, and elliptic filters can be used to meet this type of performance specification. Order selection functions are available to indicate the minimum filter order that meets the requirements.

To meet specifications with more rigid constraints like linear phase or arbitrary filter shape, the direct FIR and direct IIR filter design techniques should be used.

All of the filter design functions operate with normalized frequencies so that system sample rate does not have to be included as an extra input argument. We use the convention that unit frequency is the Nyquist frequency, half the sample frequency. This means that normalized frequency is always specified over the interval $0 \le \omega \le 1$. Thus for a system with a 1000 Hz sample frequency, 300 Hz is indicated as $300/500 = 0.6$. To convert normalized frequency to angular frequency around the unit circle, multiply by $\pi$. To convert normalized frequency back to Hz, multiply by half the sample frequency.

## 19.3.2 IIR Filter Design using Analog Prototypes

An important class of IIR digital filter design is based on converting classic analog Butterworth, Chebyshev I, Chebyshev II, and elliptic filters to their digital equivalents. The four functions in the *Signals and Systems Toolbox* for designing the lowpass versions of these filters are:

```
[b,a] = butter(N,Wn)
[b,a] = cheby1(N,Rp,Wn)
[b,a] = cheby2(N,Rs,Wn)
[b,a] = ellip(N,Rp,Rs,Wn)
```

These four functions design order N lowpass filters with cutoff frequency Wn, where *Wn* is a number between 0 and 1, with 1.0 corresponding to half the sample frequency (the Nyquist frequency). For cheby1 and ellip, the variable Rp indicates the decibels of ripple in the passband, and for cheby2 and ellip the stopband can be set to be Rs decibels down from the peak value in the passband.

These functions return the filter coefficients in length N+1 row vectors b and a. The filter coefficients are ordered in descending powers of $z$:

$$H(z) = \frac{B(z)}{A(z)} = \frac{b(1) + b(2)z^{-1} + \cdots + b(n+1)z^{-n}}{1 + a(2)z^{-1} + \cdots + a(n+1)z^{-n}}$$

Smaller values of passband ripple Rp and larger values of stopband attenuation Rs both lead to wider transition widths (shallower rolloff characteristics).

If Wn is a two-element vector, Wn = [w1 w2], the four functions design order 2N bandpass filters with passband w1 < $\omega$ < w2.

Highpass filters are designed by including the string `'high'` as a final argument:

```
[b,a] = ellip(N,Rp,Rs,Wn,'high')
```

Bandstop filters are designed by including the string `'stop'` as the final argument, and by specifying `Wn` as a two-element vector. For example,

```
[b,a] = butter(N,Wn,'stop')
```

is an order `2N` bandstop filter if `Wn = [w1 w2]`. The stopband is `w1 < ω < w2`.

The filter design functions can be used with different numbers of output arguments to obtain other realizations of the filter. For example, when `butter` is used with three output arguments,

```
[z,p,k] = ellip(N,Wn)
```

it returns the zeros and poles in length `N` column vectors `z` and `p`, and the gain in the scalar `k`. When used with four output arguments,

```
[A,B,C,D] = butter(N,Wn)
```

`butter` returns the filter in state-space form.

`butter`, `cheby1`, `cheby2`, and `ellip` are M-files that draw upon a collection of functions that form a small classical analog filter transformation design suite. The design procedure for each of the filters is as follows:

1. Compute analog, prewarped frequencies.

2. Convert to lowpass prototype specifications.

3. Design N-th order analog lowpass prototype filter using `buttap`, `cheb1ap`, `cheb2ap`, or `ellipap`.

4. Transform prototype to state-space using `zp2ss`.

5. Transform to lowpass, bandpass, highpass, or bandstop of desired natural `Wn` using `lp2lp`, `lp2bp`, `lp2hp`, or `lp2bs`.

6. Apply a bilinear transformation with frequency prewarping using `bilinear` to find the discrete equivalent.

7. Transform to zero-pole-gain or polynomial forms using `ss2zp` or `ss2tf`, if required.

The following sections will discuss the specific functions employed at each of these stages.

## Analog Prototypes

There are four functions for computing the classic analog filter prototypes:

```
[z,p,k] = buttap(N)
[z,p,k] = cheb1ap(N,Rp)
[z,p,k] = cheb2ap(N,Rs)
[z,p,k] = ellipap(N,Rp,Rs)
```

These functions find the zeros, poles, and gain of the order N normalized (unit cutoff frequency) analog lowpass filter prototypes. The Chebyshev and elliptic filters have additional parameters, including Rp, that specifies the decibels of ripple in the passband, and Rs, that indicates a stopband Rs decibels down from the peak value in the passband. The zeros and poles are returned in length N column vectors z and p, and the gain in scalar k. The transfer function is

$$H(s) = \frac{z(s)}{p(s)} = k\frac{(s - z(1))(s - z(2))...(s - z(n))}{(s - p(1))(s - p(2))...(s - p(n))}$$

We can compute fifth order prototypes for each of these filters

```
[zb,pb,kb] = buttap(5);
[z1,p1,k1] = cheb1ap(5,.5)
[z2,p2,k2] = cheb2ap(5,30)
[ze,pe,ke] = ellipap(5,.5,30)
```

and their frequency responses, to show the magnitude characteristics of each of these filters:

```
w = logspace(-1,1);
hb = freqs(kb*poly(zb),poly(pb),w);
h1 = freqs(k1*poly(z1),poly(p1),w);
h2 = freqs(k2*poly(z2),poly(p2),w);
he = freqs(ke*poly(ze),poly(pe),w);
loglog(w,abs(hb),w,abs(h1),w,abs(h2),w,abs(he))
```

Signals and Systems

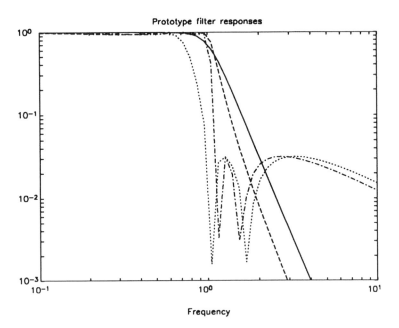

The Butterworth filter prototype has no zeros (or, equivalently, $n$ zeros at infinity) and the poles are evenly spaced on the unit circle in the left half-plane. The magnitude response (solid line) is 1 at zero frequency and $1/\sqrt{2}$ at unit frequency (3 dB down at the normalized cutoff frequency). The response is maximally flat in both the passband and the stopband.

The Chebyshev type I filter prototype (dashed line) has ripple in the passband that minimizes the maximum error over the complete passband. The stopband response is maximally flat. Again there are no zeros, and the poles, in the left half-plane, lie along an ellipse.

The Chebyshev type II filter (dotted line), sometimes referred to as an inverse Chebyshev filter, has ripple in the stopband, in contrast to the Chebyshev type I filter. The zeros are zeros of a Chebyshev polynomial that places them in complex conjugate pairs on the imaginary axis; they are independent of the stopband ripple. The poles are reciprocal values of the poles from the Chebyshev type I filter of the same order. The passband is maximally flat; the ripple serves to minimize the maximum error in the stopband. The ripple in this case determines how far down (in dB) the maximum in the stopband is from the passband.

The elliptic, or Cauer, filter (dash-dot line) is characterized by equiripple pass- and stop-bands. The two ripple parameters insure minimization of the maximum error in both the bands. The passband ripple is the peak amplitude variation, in decibels, as in the case of the Chebyshev type I filter. The stopband ripple corresponds to the stopband attenuation relative to the maximum passband response. Given the filter order and the two ripple parameters, the elliptic filter minimizes the transition width from passband to stopband.

In general, an elliptic filter will satisfy performance constraints (such as meeting a specific attenuation level at a given frequency) with a lower order filter than the other filter types. The price paid for this performance is the time to compute the actual filter. The equations governing the locations of the zeros and poles require finding zeros of a Jacobian elliptic function. The zeros lie on the imaginary axis in complex conjugate pairs. There is a detailed discussion of the relevant governing equations in [2].

## Linear System Transformations

A set of functions allows linear models to be converted between various representations:

| Linear System Transformations | |
|---|---|
| `[a,b,c,d]` `= tf2ss(num,den)` | Transfer function to state-space. |
| `[a,b,c,d]` `= zp2ss(z,p,k)` | Zero-pole to state-space. |
| `[z,p,k]` `= ss2zp(a,b,c,d,iu)` | State-space to zero-pole. |
| `[r,p,k]` `= residue(num,den)` | Transfer function to residue. |
| `[num,den]` `= residue(r,p,k)` | Residue to transfer function. |

The first three of these are used in various places within the Butterworth, Chebyshev, and elliptic digital filter design processes. In particular, `zp2ss` converts the poles and zeros from the analog prototypes into the state-space form required for the frequency transformation discussed in the next section. The function `tf2ss` is used by the frequency transformations and in the `bilinear` function. `ss2zp` converts the final digital state-space filters back into pole-zero form.

A more comprehensive collection of these model transformation routines can be found in the *Control System Toolbox*.

## Frequency Transformations

A set of functions is available to transform analog lowpass prototypes into lowpass, bandpass, highpass, and bandstop filters of the desired cutoff frequency:

| Frequency Transformations | |
|---|---|
| `lp2lp` | Lowpass to lowpass. |
| `lp2bp` | Lowpass to bandpass. |
| `lp2hp` | Lowpass to highpass. |
| `lp2bs` | Lowpass to bandstop. |

These transformations are one step in the digital filter design process of `butter`, `cheby1`, `cheby2`, and `ellip`. We will consider the `lp2bp` function in more detail.

`lp2bp` is a function to transform analog lowpass filter prototypes into bandpass filters with desired bandwidth and center frequency. The `lp2bp` function can perform the transformation on two different linear system representations: transfer function form and state-space form. In both cases the input system must be an analog filter prototype: It must be a lowpass filter with unit cutoff frequency and DC gain of 1.

*Polynomial:*

`[numt,dent]` = `lp2bp(num,den,Wo,Bw)` transforms an analog lowpass filter prototype given by polynomial coefficients into a bandpass filter with center frequency `Wo` and bandwidth `Bw`. Row vectors `num` and `den` specify the coefficients of the numerator and denominator of the prototype in descending powers of $s$,

$$\frac{num(s)}{den(s)} = \frac{num(1)s^{nn} + ... + num(nn)s + num(nn+1)}{den(1)s^{nd} + ... + den(nd)s + den(nd+1)}$$

Scalars `Wo` and `Bw` specify the center frequency and bandwidth in units of radians/s. The frequency transformed filter is returned in row vectors `numt` and `dent`.

*State-space:*

`[At,Bt,Ct,Dt]` = `lp2bp(A,B,C,D,Wo,Bw)` converts the continuous time state-space lowpass filter prototype in matrices `A,B,C,D`,

$$\dot{x} = Ax + Bu$$
$$y = Cx + Du$$

into a bandpass filter with center frequency `Wo` and bandwidth `Bw`. The bandpass filter is returned in matrices `At,Bt,Ct,Dt`.

## Bilinear Transformation

The *bilinear transformation* is a mathematical mapping of variables. In digital filtering circles, it is a standard method of mapping the $s$ or analog plane into the $z$ or digital plane. Analog filters, designed using classical filter design techniques, can be transformed into discrete equivalents.

The bilinear transformation maps the $s$-plane into the $z$-plane with

$$H(z) = H(s)\big|_{s = 2f_s \frac{(z-1)}{(z+1)}}$$

The `bilinear` function can perform this transformation on three different linear system representations: zero-pole coefficients, polynomial coefficients, and state-space form.

*Zero-pole:*

`[zd,pd,kd] = bilinear(z,p,k,fs)` converts the *s*-domain transfer function specified by zeros, poles, and gain to a discrete equivalent. Inputs `z` and `p` are column vectors containing the zeros and poles, while `k` is a scalar gain. `fs` is the sample frequency in Hz. The discrete equivalent is returned in column vectors `zd`, `pd`, and scalar `kd`.

*Polynomial:*

`[numd,dend] = bilinear(num,den,fs)` converts an *s*-domain transfer function given by polynomial coefficients to a discrete equivalent. Row vectors `num` and `den` specify the coefficients of the numerator and denominator in descending powers of *s*,

$$\frac{num(s)}{den(s)} = \frac{num(1)s^{nn} +...+ num(nn)s + num(nn+1)}{den(1)s^{nd} +...+ den(nd)s + den(nd+1)}$$

and `fs` is the sample frequency in Hz. The discrete equivalent is returned in row vectors `numd` and `dend` in descending powers of *z* (ascending powers of $z^{-1}$).

*State-space:*

`[Ad,Bd,Cd,Dd] = bilinear(A,B,C,D,fs)` converts the continuous time state-space system in matrices `A,B,C,D`,

$$\dot{x} = Ax + Bu$$
$$y = Cx + Du$$

to the discrete time system:

$$x[n+1] = A_d x[n] + B_d u[n]$$
$$y[n] = C_d x[n] + D_d u[n]$$

As before, `fs` is the sample frequency in Hz. The discrete equivalent is returned in matrices `Ad,Bd,Cd,Dd`.

All three versions of `bilinear` can accept a final scalar trailing input argument `fp` that specifies a "prewarping" frequency. Frequency prewarping forces the digital frequency response to match exactly the analog frequency response at a given frequency. The match frequency `fp` is specified in Hz.

Signals and Systems

### 19.3.3 Direct IIR Filter Design

The IIR digital filters of the last section were designed first as analog filters and then transformed into discrete equivalents. A second class of IIR filters are those that are designed directly in the discrete domain.

A function called `yulewalk` designs recursive IIR digital filters by finding the best least squares fit to a specified frequency response. Rather than being limited to the standard lowpass, bandpass, highpass, bandstop configurations, `yulewalk` can design a filter to match an arbitrarily shaped, possibly multiband, frequency response.

The function

```
[b,a] = yulewalk(n,f,m)
```

returns row vectors `b` and `a` containing the `n+1` coefficients of the order `n` IIR filter whose frequency-magnitude characteristics match those given in vectors `f` and `m`.

Vectors `f` and `m` specify the frequency-magnitude characteristics of the filter:

- `f` is a vector of frequency points, specified in the range between 0 and 1, where 1.0 corresponds to half the sample frequency (the Nyquist frequency).

- `m` is a vector containing the desired magnitude response at the points specified in `f`.

- `f` and `m` must be the same length.

- The first point of `f` must be 0 and the last point 1.

- The frequencies must be in increasing order.

- Duplicate frequency points are allowed, corresponding to steps in the frequency response.

- `plot(f,m)` can be used to display the filter shape.

For example, to design a multiband filter and plot the desired and actual frequency response:

```
m = [0 0 1 1 0 0 1 1 0 0];
f = [0 .1 .2 .3 .4 .5 .6 .7 .8 1];
[b,a] = yulewalk(10,f,m);
[h,w] = freqz(b,a,128);
plot(f,m,w/pi,abs(h))
```

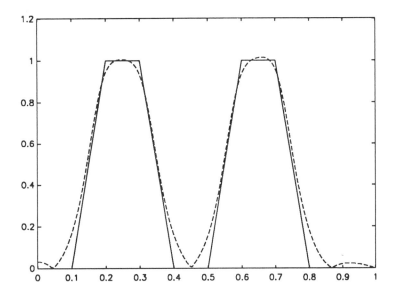

### 19.3.4 Direct FIR Filter Design

Digital filters with finite-duration impulse response (FIR filters) have both advantages and disadvantages compared to infinite-duration impulse response (IIR) filters. The primary advantages of FIR filters are:

- They can have exactly linear phase.

- They are always stable.

- The design methods are generally linear.

- They can be realized efficiently in hardware.

- The filter startup transients are finite duration.

The primary disadvantage of FIR filters is:

- They require a much higher filter order than IIR filters to achieve a given level of performance.

For most analysis done using MATLAB and the *Signals and Systems Toolbox*, IIR filters are the best choice because IIR filters give better performance with lower filter order.

Tradeoff discussions now aside, there is a method available for FIR filter design:

| FIR Filter Design | |
|---|---|
| remez | Parks-McClellan optimal FIR filter design |

The Parks-McClellan FIR filter design algorithm is perhaps the most popular and widely used FIR filter design methodology. In the *Signals and Systems Toolbox*, the function called remez designs linear phase FIR filters using the Parks-McClellan algorithm. The Parks-McClellan algorithm uses the Remez exchange algorithm and Chebyshev approximation theory to design filters with optimal fits between the desired and actual frequency responses. The filters are optimal in the sense that the maximum error between the desired frequency response and the actual frequency response is minimized. Filters designed this way exhibit an equiripple behavior in their frequency response, and hence are sometimes called *equiripple* filters.

The function

```
b = remez(n,f,m)
```

returns row vector b containing the n+1 coefficients of the order n FIR filter whose frequency-magnitude characteristics match those given by vectors f and m. Vectors f and m specify the frequency-magnitude characteristics of the filter:

- f is a vector of frequency points, specified in the range between 0 and 1, where 1.0 corresponds to half the sample frequency (the Nyquist frequency).

- m is a vector containing the desired magnitude response at the points specified in f.

- f and m must be the same length. The length must be an even number.

- The first point of f must be 0 and the last point 1.

- The frequencies must be in increasing order.

- Duplicate frequency points are allowed, but remez will separate them by 0.1 if they are exactly coincident. Note that frequency transitions much faster than 0.1 are undesirable because they can cause large amounts of ripple in the magnitude response.

- plot(f,m) can be used to display the filter shape.

Here's an example that designs a fifty-fourth order multiband filter using a weighting vector and plots its frequency response:

```
f = [0 .1 .2 .3 .36 .5 .6 .72 .82 1];
a = [0 0 1 1 0 0 1 1 0 0];
wtx = [10 1 3 1 20];
b = remez(54,f,a,wtx);
[h,w] = freqz(b,1,128);
plot(f,a,w/pi,abs(h))
```

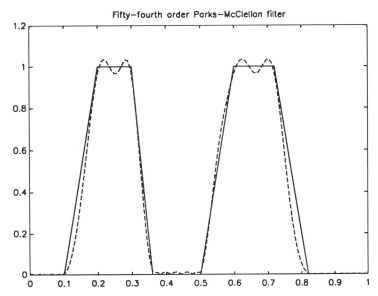

Fifty-fourth order Parks–McClellan filter

It is also possible to design Hilbert transformers and differentiators using `remez`. See the *Reference* section for more information.

# 19.4  FFT and Spectral Analysis

It is fair to say that the FFT algorithm for computing the discrete Fourier transform of a sequence is the workhorse of digital signal processing. Its uses range from filtering, convolution, computation of frequency response and group delay, to applications in power spectrum estimation.

Signals and Systems

`fft(x)` is the discrete Fourier transform of vector x, computed with a radix-2 fast Fourier transform if the length of x is a power of two, and a mixed radix algorithm if the length is not a power of two. If X is a matrix, `fft(X)` is the fast Fourier transform of each column of X.

`fft(x,n)` is the n-point FFT. If the length of x is less than n, x is padded with trailing zeros to length n. If the length of x is greater than n, the sequence x is truncated. When X is a matrix, the length of the columns is adjusted the same way.

*ifft(x)* is the inverse fast Fourier transform of vector x. `ifft(x,n)` is the n-point inverse FFT.

The two functions implement the transform - inverse transform pair given by:

$$X(k+1) = \sum_{n=0}^{N-1} x(n+1)W_N^{kn}$$

$$x(n+1) = 1/N \sum_{k=0}^{N-1} X(k+1)W_N^{-kn}$$

where $W_N = e^{-j(2\pi/N)}$ and $N = length(x)$. Note that the series is written in an unorthodox way, running over $n+1$ and $k+1$ instead of the usual $n$ and $k$ because MATLAB vectors run from 1 to $N$ instead of from 0 to $N-1$.

Suppose an even-length sequence of $N$ points is obtained at a sample frequency of $f_s$. Then, for up to the Nyquist frequency, or point $n = N/2+1$, the relationship between the bin number and the actual frequency is:

$$f = (bin\_number - 1)*f_s/N$$

The fast Fourier transform (FFT) of a column vector *x*

```
x = [4 3 7 -9 1 0 0 0]';
```

is found with

```
y = fft(x)
```

which results in

```
y =
    6.0000
   11.4853 - 2.7574i
   -2.0000 -12.0000i
   -5.4853 +11.2426i
   18.0000
   -5.4853 -11.2426i
   -2.0000 +12.0000i
   11.4853 + 2.7574i
```

Notice that although the sequence x is real, y is complex. The first component of the transformed data is the DC contribution and the fifth element corresponds to the Nyquist frequency. The last three values of y correspond to negative frequencies and, for the real sequence x, they are complex conjugates of y(4), y(3), and y(2).

### 19.4.1 Frequency Response

The function freqz, for calculating frequency response, uses an FFT-based algorithm. The frequency response is computed as the ratio of the transformed numerator and denominator coefficients, padded with zeros out to the desired length:

```
h = fft(b,n)./fft(a,n)
```

### 19.4.2 Power Spectrum Estimation

An important application of Fourier transform algorithms is the estimation of the power spectra of signals, often for the detection of narrow-band signals buried in wideband noise.

Consider the 1001 element signal yn,

```
t = 0:.001:1;
y = sin(2*pi*50*t) + 2*sin(2*pi*120*t);
rand('normal')
yn = y + 0.5*rand(t);
```

The 1024-point Fourier transform of yn

```
Yn = fft(yn,1024);
```

is the basis for a crude estimate of the power spectral density of yn:

```
n = length(Yn);
Pyy = Yn .* conj(Yn)/n;
```

In order to graph the power spectrum versus frequency in Hz, a frequency vector must be created. Because the Nyquist frequency (500 Hz) occurs at point n/2+1 of the 1024-point even length sequence, the frequency vector has 513 elements, evenly spaced between 0 and 500 Hz:

```
f = 500*(0:512)/512;
```

Using the symmetry property of real FFTs, we can remove the spectral estimates corresponding to negative frequency and compensate for them in the positive frequencies,

```
Pyy(514:1024) = [ ];
Pyy(2:512) = 2*Pyy(2:512);
```

and plot the spectrum

```
semilogy(f,Pyy)
```

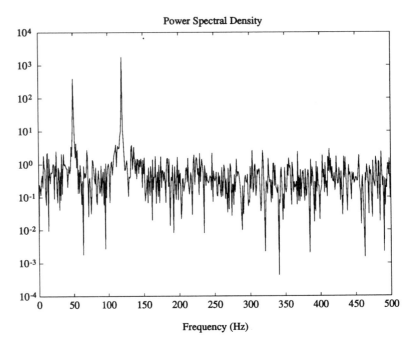

The two spectral peaks are obvious, one at 50 Hz and one at 120 Hz. The units on the y-axis are $u^2/Hz$, if the signal y has units of $u$ associated with it. The actual heights are not meaningful because they depend upon how the peaks line up with the bins. The area beneath each peak, however, is quantitatively useful and represents the energy of the signals.

Parseval's theorem states that the sum of the squared values of a sequence is equal to the sum of the squared values of the sequence's Fourier transform. This is easy to verify:

```
p = [sum(yn.^2)   sum(Pyy)]

p =   1.0e+03 *

        2.8086    2.8086
```

There are many algorithms for power spectrum estimation. In the last example we found a very crude estimate in which no smoothing was done.

## 19.5 Convolution and Deconvolution

Functions are available for convolution and deconvolution:

| Convolution and Correlation | |
|---|---|
| conv | convolution |
| deconv | deconvolution |

The statement

```
c = conv(a,b)
```

convolves vectors  a  and  b. The convolution sum is:

$$c(n+1) = \sum_{k=0}^{N-1} a(k+1)b(n-k)$$

where $N$ is the maximum sequence length. The series is written in an unorthodox way, indexed from $n+1$ and $k+1$ instead of the usual $n$ and $k$ because MATLAB vectors run from 1 to $n$ instead of from 0 to $n-1$.

Convolution is the same operation as FIR digital filtering with the input sequence padded with trailing zeros:

```
conv(b,x) = filter(b,1,[x zeros(1,length(b)-1)])
```

`[q,r] = deconv(b,a)` deconvolves vector  a  out of vector  b, using long division. The result (quotient) is returned in vector  q  and the remainder in vector  r  such that  b  = conv(q,a) + r.

If  a  and  b  are vectors of polynomial coefficients, convolving them is equivalent to multiplying the two polynomials, and deconvolution is polynomial division.

For example, to generate a list of the binomial coefficients (a portion of Pascal's triangle),

```
a = [1 1]; c = [1 1];
for i=1:5
      c(i+1,1:i+2) = conv(a,c(i,1:i+1));
end
c
```

which results in

```
c =
        1       1       0       0       0       0       0
        1       2       1       0       0       0       0
        1       3       3       1       0       0       0
        1       4       6       4       1       0       0
        1       5      10      10       5       1       0
        1       6      15      20      15       6       1
```

Deconvolution is the inverse operation of convolution. To deconvolve the polynomial

```
a = [1 1];
```

from the fifth row of c with the trailing zeros removed and the final nonzero coefficient incremented by 1:

```
p = [1 5 10 10 5 2]
```

use

```
[q,r] = deconv(p,a)
q =
        1       4       6       4       1


r =
        0       0       0       0       0       1
```

This can be verified by reconstructing p:

```
pp = conv(q,a) + r

pp =
        1       5      10      10       5       2
```

---

# 19.6  Windows

In both digital filter design and power spectrum estimation, the choice of windowing function can play an important role in determining the quality of overall results. Their major influence is to damp out the effects of the Gibbs phenomenon resulting from truncation of an infinite series.

The repertoire of available windows includes:

| Window Functions | |
| --- | --- |
| hamming | Hamming window |
| hanning | Hanning window |

Let's examine the characteristics of two windows in both the time domain and the frequency domain. First create a matrix whose columns are Hamming and Hanning windows:

```
n = 200;
x = [hamming(n) hanning(n)];
plot (x)
```

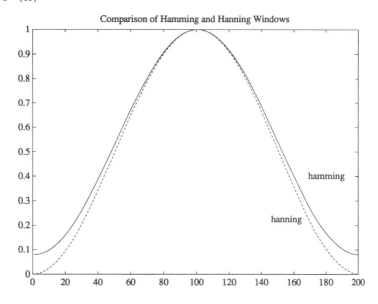

The behavior of the windows in the frequency domain can be determined by Fourier transformation of the columns of this matrix:

```
y = fft(x, 256);
[my, ny] = size(y);
```

The first fifty points, or low frequency portion, of the window spectra are graphed with

```
f = (0:25)/128;
Pyy = y(1:26,:).*conj(y(1:26,:));
semilogy(f,Pyy);
```

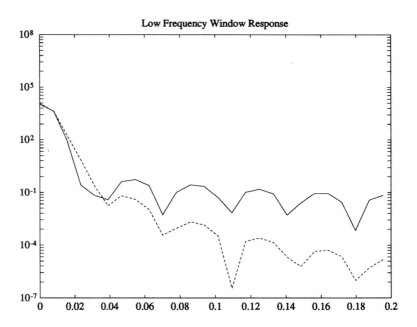

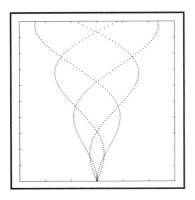

Signals and Systems

MATLAB has a rich collection of functions immediately useful for control engineering and system theory. Complex arithmetic, eigenvalues, root finding, matrix inversion, and FFTs are just a few examples of important numerical tools. More generally, MATLAB's linear algebra, matrix computation, and numerical analysis capabilities provide a reliable foundation for control design and analysis.

The *Signals and Systems Toolbox* contains a collection of algorithms, expressed in M-files, that implements a variety of modern and classical control techniques. The controls portion of the *Signals and Systems Toolbox* includes functions for:

- transformation between state-space, transfer function, and zero-pole representations
- frequency response (Bode and Nyquist plots)
- step response
- conversion from continuous-time to discrete-time
- root-locus
- design of linear quadratic regulators and estimators (LQR and Kalman filters)

# 20.1 System Models

MATLAB works with only one kind of object, a rectangular numerical matrix with possibly complex elements. The *Signals and Systems Toolbox* can be used with linear, time-invariant (LTI) models of systems. Let's begin by looking at how we use matrices to represent some different types of LTI system models:

$$\left.\begin{array}{l}\text{State-space} \\ \text{Transfer function} \\ \text{Zero-Pole-Gain} \\ \text{Partial-fraction}\end{array}\right\}\quad\begin{array}{l}\text{Continuous-time} \\ \text{Discrete-time}\end{array}$$

## 20.1.1 State-Space

A system of LTI differential equations can always be represented as a set of first order differential equations. In matrix or *state-space* form, the equations can be written as:

$$\dot{x} = Ax + Bu$$
$$y = Cx + Du$$

where $u$ is a vector of $nu$ control inputs, $x$ is an $ns$ element state vector, and $y$ is a vector of $ny$ outputs.

State-space systems are represented in MATLAB easily enough - $A$, $B$, $C$, and $D$ are matrices and are treated as individual variables. For example, suppose we have a simple second order system consisting of a pole pair with natural frequency $\omega n = 1.5$ and damping factor $\zeta = 0.2$. We enter this system in state-space form by typing:

```
Wn = 1.5;
z = 0.2;

a = [        0                1
            -Wn^2            -2*z*Wn];
b = [        0
             Wn^2];
c = [1 0];
d = 0;
```

The state-space representation is the most natural LTI model in MATLAB. As we shall see later, for multi-input-multi-output (MIMO) systems, the state-space representation is in fact the only model convenient to work with.

## 20.1.2 Transfer Function

An equivalent representation of the state-space system is the Laplace transform transfer function description:

$$Y(s) = H(s)U(s)$$

where:

$$H(s) = C(sI - A)^{-1}B + D$$

Unfortunately, $H(s)$ requires a three-dimensional matrix to be represented in the general case. The dimensions of $H(s)$ are $ny$ rows, by $nu$ columns, by $ns + 1$ layers deep, where $ns + 1$ is the number of polynomial coefficients. Because MATLAB variables are two dimensional we are limited to representing this system in a SIMO sense, from a single input of $u$:

$$H(s) = \frac{NUM(s)}{den(s)} = \frac{NUM(1)s^{nn-1} + NUM(2)s^{nn-2} + \cdots + NUM(nn)}{den(1)s^{nd-1} + den(2)^{nd-2} + \cdots + den(nd)}$$

where $nn$ and $nd$ are the number of numerator and denominator coefficients respectively. A row vector, in this case den, is used to contain the coefficients of the denominator in descending powers of $s$. A matrix NUM contains the numerator coefficients with as many rows as there are outputs in vector $y$.

Consider the SIMO system:

$$H(s) = \frac{\begin{bmatrix} 3s + 2 \\ s^3 + 2s + 5 \end{bmatrix}}{3s^3 + 5s^2 + 2s + 1}$$

This is input to MATLAB by typing:

```
num = [0 0 3 2
       1 0 2 5];
den = [3 5 2 1];
```

and illustrates that if a system is multi-output and some of the numerator polynomials are of smaller order than the others, they must be padded with leading zeros.

## 20.1.3 Zero-Pole-Gain

A transfer function can be expressed in factored or *zero-pole-gain* form, which for a single-input multiple-output (SIMO) system in MATLAB is:

$$H(s) = \frac{Z(s)}{p(s)} = k\frac{(s - Z(1))(s - Z(2)) \cdots (s - Z(n))}{(s - p(1))(s - p(2)) \cdots (s - p(n))}$$

In MATLAB we use the convention that polynomial roots are stored in column vectors, while row vectors contain polynomial coefficients. So in factored form, a column vector p contains the pole locations of the denominator of the transfer function. The numerator zeros are stored in the columns of a matrix z with as many columns as there are outputs in vector $y$. The gains for each numerator transfer function are in a column vector k. For single-input single-output (SISO) systems, k is a scalar.

We emphasize again that, by MATLAB convention, polynomial roots are stored in column vectors, while polynomial coefficients lie in row vectors. The `poly` and `roots` functions convert between the two. For example, if:

```
p = [1 3 5 2]
```

then:

```
r = roots(p)

r =
            -1.2267 + 1.4677i
            -1.2267 - 1.4677i
            -0.5466
```

and:

```
pp = poly(r)

pp =
            1.0000 3.0000 5.0000 2.0000
```

returns the original polynomial. Later we will see that, for SIMO LTI systems, `tf2zp` converts from polynomial transfer function form to the factored Zero-Pole-Gain form and `zp2tf` does the reverse.

For a SIMO example, consider the system:

$$H(s) = \frac{Z(s)}{p(s)} = \frac{\begin{bmatrix} 3(s+12) \\ 4(s+1)(s+2) \end{bmatrix}}{(s+3)(s+4)(s+5)}$$

This is entered with:

```
k = [3; 4];
z = [-12     -1
        Inf       -2];
p = [-3
      -4
      -5 ];
```

In this multi-output system, the first numerator is lower order than the second, so we use `Inf` to pad the first numerator with a zero at infinity, giving it the same order as the second numerator.

## 20.1.4 Partial-Fraction

A transfer function can also be expressed in a partial-fraction expansion or residue form, which for a SISO system is:

$$H(s) = \frac{r(1)}{s - p(1)} + \frac{r(2)}{s - p(2)} + \cdots + \frac{r(n)}{s - p(n)} + k(s)$$

A column vector $p$ is used to contain the poles, a column vector $r$ holds the residues corresponding the poles in $p$, and a row vector $k$ could contain any improper part of the original transfer function.

Transfer functions can be converted to and from partial-fraction expansion form using the residue function described in the MATLAB user's guide.

## 20.1.5 Discrete-Time

Discrete-time LTI systems are represented in MATLAB the same way as continuous-time systems: in state-space, as polynomial transfer functions, by zero-pole-gain sets, and in residue format.

*State-space systems*

A system of LTI difference equations can always be represented as a set of first order difference equations. In matrix or state-space form, the equations can be written as:

$$x[n + 1] = Ax[n] + Bu[n]$$
$$y[n] = Cx[n] + Du[n]$$

where $u$ is a vector of control inputs, $x$ is the state vector, and y is a vector of outputs.

*Transfer function systems*

An equivalent representation is the z-transform transfer function description:

$$Y(z) = H(z)U(z)$$
$$H(z) = C(zI - A)^{-1}B + D$$

or in a SIMO sense, from a single input of u:

$$H(z) = \frac{NUM(z)}{den(z)} = \frac{NUM(1)z^{nn-1} + NUM(2)z^{nn-2} + \cdots + NUM(nn)}{den(1)z^{nd-1} + den(2)z^{nd-2} + \cdots + den(nd)}$$

where *nn* and *nd* are the number of numerator and denominator coefficients. The vector `den` contains the coefficients of the denominator in decreasing powers of $z$. The matrix `NUM` contains the numerator coefficients with as many rows as there are outputs $y$. If the system is multi-output and some of the numerators are of lower order than others, then care must be taken to pad with *leading* zeros.

The same transfer function can also be represented as polynomials in ascending powers of $z^{-1}$:

$$\frac{n(z)}{d(z)} = \frac{z^{-nd+1}}{z^{-nd+1}} \cdot \frac{b_1 z^{nn-1} + \cdots + b_{nn}}{a_1 z^{nd-1} + \cdots + a_{nd}}$$

$$= \frac{b_1 z^{nn-nd} + \cdots + b_{nn} z^{-nd+1}}{a_1 + \cdots + a_{nd} z^{-nd}}$$

If the length of the numerator polynomial is the same as the length of the denominator polynomial (i.e. if *nn* = *nd*) then the two representations have have exactly the same polynomial description. However, if the numerator polynomial has a different length than the denominator polynomial, the two representations have different polynomial descriptions as the following example illustrates.

Suppose we want to represent the discrete transfer function:

$$H(z) = \frac{-3.4z + 1.5}{z^2 - 1.6z + 0.8}$$

in both the $z$ and $z^{-1}$ forms. As powers of $z$ this transfer function would be entered into MATLAB as:

```
num = [-3.4 1.5];
den = [1 -1.6 0.8];
```

and as powers of $z^{-1}$ this transfer function is:

$$H(z) = \frac{-3.4z^{-1} + 1.5z^{-2}}{1 - 1.6z^{-1} + 0.8z^{-2}}$$

and would be entered into MATLAB as:

```
num = [0 -3.4 1.5];
den = [1 -1.6 0.8];
```

Note that a leading zero was required to represent this transfer function.

The control system commands use the $z$ transfer function notation while the signal processing command `filter`, for example, uses the $z^{-1}$ notation.

Suppose the following transfer function polynomials are entered into MATLAB:

```
num = [-3.4 1.5];
den = [1 -1.6 0.8];
```

From a control perspective, we would be representing:

$$H(z) = \frac{-3.4z + 1.5}{z^2 - 1.6z - 0.8z^{-2}}$$

while from a signal processing point of view it would be:

$$H(z) = \frac{-3.4 + 1.5z^{-1}}{1 - 1.6z^{-1} + 0.8z^{-2}}$$

The two transfer functions are clearly different.

However, if instead we had entered a numerator polynomial with the same number of coefficients as the denominator polynomial:

```
num = [0 -3.4 1.5];
den = [1 -1.6 0.8];
```

then both representations are the same.

It is important to understand the distinction between these two notations since the control system functions use the $z$ transfer function notation and the signal processing functions use the $z^{-1}$ notation. To be safe, always pad the numerator polynomial so that it is the same size as the denominator polynomial. If this is done then all the functions in the *Signals and Systems Toolbox* can be used without worrying about the specific notation assumed.

*Zero-Pole-Gain systems*

The factored Zero-Pole-Gain form is:

$$H(z) = \frac{r(1)}{z} - p(1) = k\frac{(z - Z(1))(z - Z(2)) \cdots (z - Z(n))}{(z - p(1))(z - p(2)) \cdots (z - p(n))}$$

Since the z-transform representation of a system can be thought of as a digital filter, the topics discussed in the *Signals and Systems Toolbox* under filter analysis and implementation are relevant to these models. We also recommend [Fran80] as an excellent source of practical digital control methodologies.

*Partial-Fraction systems*

The partial-fraction or residue format is:

$$H(z) = \frac{r(1)}{z} - p(1) + \frac{r(2)}{z} \_ p(2) + \cdots + \frac{r(n)}{z} - p(n) + K(z)$$

## 20.1.6 Model Conversions

The *Signals and Systems Toolbox* contains a set of functions which allow LTI models to be converted between the various representations:

| Model Conversions | |
|---|---|
| residue | partial fraction expansion (see main guide) |
| ss2tf | state-space to transfer function conversion |
| ss2zp | state-space to zero-pole conversion |
| tf2ss | transfer function to state-space conversion |
| tf2zp | transfer function to zero-pole conversion |
| zp2tf | zero-pole to transfer function conversion |
| zp2ss | zero-pole to state-space conversion |

and between continuous-time and discrete-time:

| Discretization | |
|---|---|
| c2d | continuous to discrete-time conversion |

as shown in the figure below.

For more information on these functions, see the *Reference* section or use the online help facility.

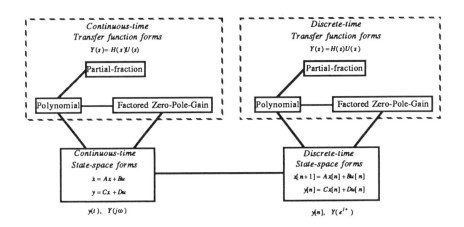

System Representations

## 20.2  Analysis Functions

The *Signals and Systems Toolbox* contains several functions for the basic linear time-domain and frequency-domain analysis tools required for control system engineering. These functions automatically generate plots or print out their results and some of the functions generate an example response if invoked with no input or output arguments.

### 20.2.1  Time Response

Time response is used to investigate the time-domain transient behavior of LTI systems to inputs and disturbances. System characteristics such as rise time, settling time, overshoot, and steady state error can be determined from the time response. The *Signals and Systems Toolbox* provides a command called `step` to compute step response.

`step` will automatically generate a plot. For instance, if `num` and `den`, or `a`, `b`, `c`, `d` are defined, the command:

```
step(num,den) or step(a,b,c,d,1)
```

generates the plot:

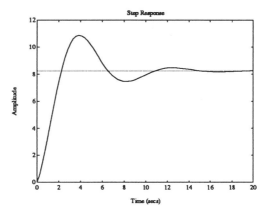

## 20.2.2 Frequency Response

Frequency response is used to investigate the frequency-domain behavior of LTI systems. System characteristics such as bandwidth, resonance, D.C. gain, gain and phase margins, and closed-loop stability can be determined from the frequency response. The *Control System Toolbox* provides functions for Bode response, Nichols response, and Nyquist response.

| Frequency Response | |
| --- | --- |
| bode | Bode plots |
| nyquist | Nyquist plots |
| freqz | z-transform frequency response (see main guide) |
| freqs | Laplace-transform frequency response (see main guide) |

The bode and nyquist functions will automatically generate a frequency response plot. For instance, if num and den, or a, b, c, d are defined, the command:

```
bode(num,den) or bode(a,b,c,d,1)
```

generates the plot:

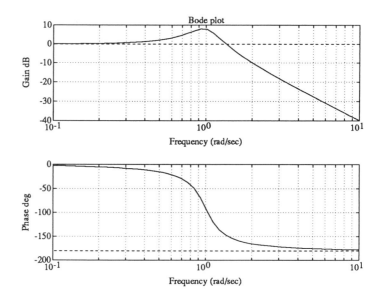

The automatic plotting algorithms are designed to work with a wide range of systems but are not perfect. In any case, it is always possible to override the automatic reduction and to manually plot the frequency response using the MATLAB plot commands.

## 20.3  Design Functions

We use the term control system *design* to refer to the process of selecting feedback gains in a closed-loop control system. Most design methods are iterative, combining parameter selection with analysis, simulation, and physical insight.

The *Signals and Systems Toolbox* has two functions for gain selection.

| Gain Selection | |
|---|---|
| lqe | linear-quadratic estimator design |
| lqr | linear-quadratic regulator design |

# Part Four

# Reference

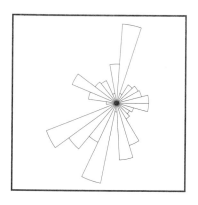

# Reference

This section contains detailed descriptions of all MATLAB functions. It begins with a list of functions grouped by subject area and continues with the reference entries in alphabetical order. Information is also available through the on-line help facility.

| General | |
|---|---|
| help | help facility |
| demo | run demonstrations |
| who | list variables in memory |
| what | list M-files on disk |
| size | row and column dimensions |
| length | vector length |
| clear | clear workspace |
| computer | type of computer |
| ^C | local abort |
| quit | terminate program |
| exit | same as quit |

| Matrix Operators | | Array Operators | |
|---|---|---|---|
| + | addition | + | addition |
| – | subtraction | – | subtraction |
| * | multiplication | .* | multiplication |
| / | right division | ./ | right division |
| \ | left division | .\ | left division |
| ^ | power | .^ | power |
| ' | conjugate transpose | .' | transpose |

| Relational and Logical Operators | | | |
|---|---|---|---|
| < | less than | & | AND |
| <= | less than or equal | \| | OR |
| > | greater than | ~ | NOT |
| >= | greater than or equal | | |
| == | equal | | |
| ~= | not equal | | |

| Special Characters | |
|---|---|
| = | assignment statement |
| [ | used to form vectors and matrices |
| ] | see [ |
| ( | arithmetic expression precedence |
| ) | see ( |
| , | separate subscripts and function arguments |
| ; | end rows, suppress printing |
| % | comments |
| : | subscripting, vector generation |
| ! | execute operating system command |

| Special Values | |
|---|---|
| ans | answer when expression is not assigned |
| eps | floating point precision |
| pi | $\pi$ |
| i,j | $\sqrt{-1}$ |
| Inf | $\infty$ |
| NaN | Not-a-Number |
| clock | wall clock |
| date | date |
| flops | floating point operation count |
| nargin | number of function input arguments |
| nargout | number of function output arguments |

| Text and Strings | |
|---|---|
| abs | convert string to ASCII values |
| eval | evaluate text macro |
| num2str | convert number to string |
| int2str | convert integer to string |
| setstr | set flag indicating matrix is a string |
| sprintf | convert number to string |
| isstr | detect string variables |
| strcmp | compare string variables |
| hex2num | convert hexadecimal string to number |

| Graph Paper | |
|---|---|
| plot | linear X-Y plot |
| loglog | loglog X-Y plot |
| semilogx | semi-log X-Y plot |
| semilogy | semi-log X-Y plot |
| polar | polar plot |
| mesh | 3-dimensional mesh surface |
| contour | contour plot |
| meshdom | domain for mesh plots |
| bar | bar charts |
| stairs | stairstep graphs |
| errorbar | add errorbars |

| Graph Annotation | |
|---|---|
| title | plot title |
| xlabel | x-axis label |
| ylabel | y-axis label |
| grid | draw grid lines |
| text | arbitrarily positioned text |
| gtext | mouse-positioned text |
| ginput | graphics input |

| Graph Window Control | |
|---|---|
| axis | manual axis scaling |
| hold | hold plot on screen |
| shg | show graph screen |
| clg | clear graph screen |
| subplot | split graph window |

| Graph Window Hardcopy | |
|---|---|
| print* | send graph to printer |
| prtsc | screen dump |
| meta* | graphics metafile |

*Not available with *The Student Edition of MATLAB*.

| Command Window | |
|---|---|
| clc | clear command screen |
| home | home cursor |
| format | set output display format |
| disp | display matrix or text |
| fprintf | print formatted number |
| echo | enable command echoing |

Reference

| Control Flow | |
|---|---|
| if | conditionally execute statements |
| elseif | used with if |
| else | used with if |
| end | terminate if, for, while |
| for | repeat statements a number of times |
| while | do while |
| break | break out of for and while loops |
| return | return from functions |
| pause | pause until key press |

| Programming and M-files | |
|---|---|
| input | get numbers from keyboard |
| keyboard | call keyboard as M-file |
| error | display error message |
| function | define function |
| eval | interpret text in variables |
| feval | evaluate function given by string |
| echo | enable command echoing |
| exist | check if variables exist |
| casesen | set case sensitivity |
| global | define global variables |
| startup | startup M-file |
| getenv | get environment string |
| menu | select item from menu |
| etime | elapsed time |

| Disk Files | |
|---|---|
| chdir | change current directory |
| delete | delete file |
| diary | diary of the session |
| dir | directory of files on disk |
| load | load variables from file |
| save | save variables on file |
| type | list function or file |
| what | show M-files on disk |
| fprintf | write to a file |
| pack | compact memory via save |

## Relational and Logical Functions

| | |
|---|---|
| any | logical conditions |
| all | logical conditions |
| find | find array indices of logical values |
| exist | check if variables exist |
| isnan | detect NaNs |
| finite | detect infinities |
| isempty | detect empty matrices |
| isstr | detect string variables |
| strcmp | compare string variables |

## Trigonometric Functions

| | |
|---|---|
| sin | sine |
| cos | cosine |
| tan | tangent |
| asin | arcsine |
| acos | arccosine |
| atan | arctangent |
| atan2 | four quadrant arctangent |
| sinh | hyperbolic sine |
| cosh | hyperbolic cosine |
| tanh | hyperbolic tangent |
| asinh | hyperbolic arcsine |
| acosh | hyperbolic arccosine |
| atanh | hyperbolic arctangent |

## Elementary Math Functions

| | |
|---|---|
| abs | absolute value or complex magnitude |
| angle | phase angle |
| sqrt | square root |
| real | real part |
| imag | imaginary part |
| conj | complex-conjugate |
| round | round to nearest integer |
| fix | round towards zero |
| floor | round towards $-\infty$ |
| ceil | round towards $\infty$ |
| sign | signum function |
| rem | remainder or modulus |
| exp | exponential base e |
| log | natural logarithm |
| log10 | log base 10 |

| Special Functions | |
|---|---|
| bessel | Bessel function |
| gamma | complete and incomplete gamma functions |
| rat | rational approximation |
| erf | error function |
| inverf | inverse error function |
| ellipk | complete elliptic integral of the first kind |
| ellipj | Jacobian elliptic functions |

| Polynomials | |
|---|---|
| poly | characteristic polynomial |
| roots | polynomial roots - companion matrix method |
| roots1 | polynomial roots - Laguerre's method |
| polyval | polynomial evaluation |
| polyvalm | matrix polynomial evaluation |
| conv | multiplication |
| deconv | division |
| residue | partial-fraction expansion |
| polyfit | polynomial curve fitting |

| Matrix Manipulation | |
|---|---|
| rot90 | rotation |
| fliplr | flip matrix left-to-right |
| flipud | flip matrix up-and-down |
| diag | extract or create diagonal |
| tril | lower triangular part |
| triu | upper triangular part |
| reshape | reshape |
| .' | transposition |
| : | general rearrangement |

| Matrix Condition | |
|---|---|
| cond | condition number in 2-norm |
| norm | 1-norm, 2-norm, F-norm, $\infty$-norm |
| rank | rank |
| rcond | condition estimate |

| Special Matrices | |
|---|---|
| compan | companion |
| diag | diagonal |
| eye | identity |
| gallery | esoteric |
| hadamard | Hadamard |
| hankel | Hankel |
| hilb | Hilbert |
| invhilb | inverse Hilbert |
| linspace | linearly spaced vectors |
| logspace | logarithmically spaced vectors |
| magic | magic square |
| meshdom | domain for mesh plots |
| ones | constant |
| rand | random elements |
| toeplitz | Toeplitz |
| vander | Vandermonde |
| zeros | zero |

| Decompositions and Factorizations | |
|---|---|
| balance | balanced form |
| backsub | backsubstitution |
| cdf2rdf | convert complex-diagonal to real-diagonal |
| chol | Cholesky factorization |
| eig | eigenvalues and eigenvectors |
| hess | Hessenberg form |
| inv | inverse |
| lu | factors from Gaussian elimination |
| nnls | nonnegative least-squares |
| null | null space |
| orth | orthogonalization |
| pinv | pseudoinverse |
| qr | orthogonal-triangular decomposition |
| qz | QZ algorithm |
| rref | reduced row echelon form |
| rsf2csf | convert real-schur to complex-schur |
| schur | Schur decomposition |
| svd | singular value decomposition |

Reference

| Elementary Matrix Functions | |
| --- | --- |
| `expm` | matrix exponential |
| `logm` | matrix logarithm |
| `sqrtm` | matrix square root |
| `funm` | arbitrary matrix functions |
| `poly` | characteristic polynomial |
| `det` | determinant |
| `trace` | trace |
| `kron` | Kronecker tensor product |

| Interpolation | |
| --- | --- |
| `spline` | cubic spline |
| `table1` | 1-D table look-up |
| `table2` | 2-D table look-up |

| Differential Equation Solution | |
| --- | --- |
| `ode23` | 2nd/3rd order Runge-Kutta method |
| `ode45` | 4th/5th order Runge-Kutta-Fehlberg method |

| Numerical Integration | |
| --- | --- |
| `quad` | numerical function integration |
| `quad8` | numerical function integration |

| Nonlinear Equations and Optimization | |
| --- | --- |
| `fmin` | minimum of a function of one variable |
| `fmins` | minimum of a multivariable function (unconstrained nonlinear optimization) |
| `fsolve` | solution to a system of nonlinear equations (zeros of a multivariable function) |
| `fzero` | zero of a function of one variable |

| Columnwise Data Analysis | |
|---|---|
| max | maximum value |
| min | minimum value |
| mean | mean value |
| median | median value |
| std | standard deviation |
| sort | sorting |
| sum | sum of elements |
| prod | product of elements |
| cumsum | cumulative sum of elements |
| cumprod | cumulative product of elements |
| diff | approximate derivatives |
| hist | histogram |
| corrcoef | correlation coefficients |
| cov | covariance matrix |
| cplxpair | reorder into complex pairs |

| Signal Processing | |
|---|---|
| abs | complex magnitude |
| angle | phase angle |
| conv | convolution |
| corrcoef | correlation coefficients |
| cov | covariance |
| deconv | deconvolution |
| fft | fast Fourier transform |
| fft2 | two-dimensional FFT |
| ifft | inverse fast Fourier transform |
| ifft2 | inverse 2-D FFT |
| fftshift | swap quadrants of matrices |

| Analog Lowpass Filter Prototypes | |
|---|---|
| buttap | Butterworth filter prototype |
| cheb1ap | Chebyshev type I filter prototype (passband ripple) |
| cheb2ap | Chebyshev type II filter prototype (stopband ripple) |
| ellipap | elliptic filter prototype |

Reference

| IIR Filter Design | |
|---|---|
| butter | Butterworth filter design |
| cheby1 | Chebyshev type I filter design |
| cheby2 | Chebyshev type II filter design |
| ellip | elliptic filter design |
| yulewalk | Yule-Walker filter design |

| FIR Filter Design | |
|---|---|
| remez | Parks-McClellan optimal FIR filter design |

| Filter Transformations | |
|---|---|
| bilinear | bilinear transformation with optional prewarping |
| lp2bp | lowpass to bandpass analog filter transformation |
| lp2bs | lowpass to bandstop analog filter transformation |
| lp2hp | lowpass to highpass analog filter transformation |
| lp2lp | lowpass to lowpass analog filter transformation |
| ss2zp | state-space to zero-pole conversion |
| tf2ss | transfer function to state-space conversion |
| zp2ss | zero-pole to state-space conversion |

| Filter Analysis/Implementation | |
|---|---|
| abs | magnitude |
| angle | phase angle |
| filter | direct filter implementation |
| freqs | Laplace transform frequency response |
| freqz | $z$-transform frequency response |
| grpdelay | group delay |
| unwrap | unwrap phase |

| Spectral Analysis | |
|---|---|
| fft | fast Fourier transform |
| ifft | inverse fast Fourier transform |

| Correlation/Convolution | |
|---|---|
| conv | convolution |

| Windows | |
|---|---|
| hamming | Hamming window |
| hanning | Hanning window |

**Purpose**

Absolute value.
Phase angle.
Phase unwrap.

**Synopsis**

```
abs(x)
angle(x)
unwrap(x)
```

**Description**

abs(Z) is the absolute value of the elements of Z. If Z is complex, abs returns the complex modulus (magnitude):

```
abs(Z) = sqrt(real(Z).^2 + imag(Z).^2)
```

angle(Z) returns the phase angles, in radians, of the elements of complex matrix Z. The angles lie between $-\pi$ and $\pi$.

For complex $z = x + iy = re^{i\theta}$, the magnitude and phase are given by

```
r = abs(z)
theta = angle(z)
```

and the statement

```
z = r.*exp(i*theta)
```

converts back to the original complex $z$.

p = unwrap(p) corrects the phase angles in vector p by adding multiples of $\pm 2\pi$, where needed, to smooth the transitions across branch cuts. When p is a matrix, the phase angles are corrected down each column. The phase must be in radians.

**Algorithm**

angle and unwrap are M-files in the *MATLAB Toolbox*. angle can be expressed as:

```
angle(x) = imag(log(x)) = atan2(imag(x),real(x))
```

## Limitations

`unwrap` does the best it can to detect branch cut crossings, but it can be fooled by sparse, rapidly changing, phase values.

## Purpose

Special values (variables and functions).

## Synopsis

*Permanent variables:*

| | |
|---|---|
| `ans` | answer when expression is not assigned |
| `eps` | machine epsilon |

*Special functions:*

| | |
|---|---|
| `i` | $\sqrt{-1}$ |
| `j` | $\sqrt{-1}$ |
| `pi` | $\pi$ |
| `Inf` | $\infty$ |
| `NaN` | Not-a-Number |
| `nargin` | number of function input arguments |
| `nargout` | number of function output arguments |

## Description

Permanent variables have special meaning in MATLAB. They cannot be cleared and are globally accessible inside M-files. Otherwise the normal rules for using variables apply.

`ans`     Variable created automatically when expressions are not assigned to anything else.

`eps`     Floating point relative accuracy. A permanent variable whose value is initially the distance from 1.0 to the next largest floating point number. It may be assigned any value, including 0. `eps` is a default tolerance for `pinv` and `rank`, as well as several other MATLAB functions. One way to calculate `eps` is:

```
eps = 1;
while (1+eps) > 1
        eps = eps/2;
end
eps = 2*eps
```

The remainder of the special values are ordinary built-in MATLAB functions that return useful scalar values:

| | |
|---|---|
| pi | $pi = 4\ atan(1) = \pi$. |
| i | $i = \sqrt{-1}$. As the basic complex unit, i is used to enter complex numbers, for example $z = 2+3*i$. Since i is a function, it can be overridden and used as a variable, if desired. Thus, you can still use i as an index in for loops, etc. |
| j | An alternative to using i, for those who prefer it. |
| Inf | The IEEE arithmetic representation for positive infinity. Infinity results from operations like division by zero, 1.0/0.0. |
| NaN | The IEEE arithmetic representation for Not-a-Number (NaN). NaNs result from undefined operations like 0.0/0.0. |
| nargin | Inside the body of a function M-file, the permanent variable nargin indicates the number of *input* arguments that the function was called with. |
| nargout | Inside the body of a function M-file, the permanent variable nargin indicates the number of *output* arguments that the function was called with. |

## See also

isnan, finite, clock

## Purpose

Test arrays for logical conditions.

## Synopsis

```
any(x)
all(x)
```

## Description

For vectors, `any(v)` returns 1 if *any* of the elements of the vector are nonzero. Otherwise it returns 0. For matrices, `any(X)` operates on the columns of X, returning a row vector of ones and zeros.

For vectors, `all(v)` returns 1 if *all* of the elements of the vector are nonzero. Otherwise it returns 0. For matrices, `all(X)` operates on the columns of X, returning a row vector of ones and zeros.

## Examples

These functions are particularly useful in `if` statements,

```
if all(A < .5)
        do something
end
```

because an `if` wants to respond to a single condition, not a vector of possibly conflicting suggestions. Applying the function twice, as in `any(any(A))`, always reduces the matrix to a scalar condition.

## See also

`&, |, ~`

Reference

## Purpose

Manual axis scaling on plots.

## Synopsis

```
axis
axis([xmin xmax ymin ymax])
axis('aspect format')
```

The *aspect format* may be `square` or `normal`.

## Description

`axis` controls manual axis scaling on plots.

`axis`, with no arguments, freezes the current axis scaling for subsequent plots. Executing `axis` again resumes auto-scaling. `axis` returns a four-element row vector that contains the values of `[xmin, xmax, ymin, ymax]` from the last plot.

`axis(V)`, where `V` is a four-element vector, sets the axis scaling to the prescribed limits.

For logarithmic plots, the elements of $V$ are $\log_{10}$ of the minimums and maximums.

`axis('square')` sets the plot region on the screen to be square. With a square aspect ratio, a line with slope 1 is at a true 45 degrees, not skewed by the irregular shape of the screen. Also, circles, like `plot(sin(t),cos(t))`, look like circles instead of ovals.

`axis('normal')` sets the aspect ratio back to normal.

## Examples

`axis([1 2 3 4]); axis;` always resets the axis scaling to automatic.

`limits = axis; axis` returns the current axis limits without freezing the scaling.

## See also

`plot, hold`

**Purpose**

    Backsubstitution to solve triangular systems of equations.

**Synopsis**

```
backsub(A,b)
```

**Description**

    `x = backsub(A,b)` uses backsubstitution to solve the equation

$$Ax = b$$

for $x$, where $A$ is upper or lower triangular. `backsub` is provided mainly for pedagogical purposes; it is usually faster to use MATLAB's built-in linear equation solver:

```
x = A \ b
```

**Examples**

    Solve the system `A*x = b` using both \ and `backsub`, for comparison.

```
A =
    0.2113    0.3710    0.9619
         0    0.4646    0.3032
         0         0    0.2774

b =
    0.1478
    0.1252
    0.4512


[ backsub(A,b)  A\b ] =

   -5.3141   -5.3141
   -0.7924   -0.7924
    1.6268    1.6268
```

Reference

## Algorithm

`backsub` is an M-file in the *MATLAB Toolbox*.

## Diagnostics

If A is singular:

```
Matrix is singular.
```

If A is not square:

```
Matrix must be square.
```

If A is not an upper or lower triangular matrix:

```
Matrix must be triangular.
```

## See also

`\, inv`

## References

C. L. Lawson and R. J. Hanson, *Solving Least Squares Problems*, Prentice Hall, 1974.

---

## Purpose

Balance a matrix to improve its conditioning.

## Synopsis

```
balance(A)
[T,Ab] = balance(A)
```

## Description

The *conditioning* of a matrix affects the accuracy of computations like matrix inverse, linear equation solution, and eigenvalues. balance is a function that attempts to find a similarity transformation that makes the row and column norms approximately equal, thereby improving the conditioning of the matrix [1]. If $T$ is a similarity transformation that balances $A$, then the balanced matrix is $T^{-1}AT$.

balance(A) returns a balanced version of matrix A whose row and column norms are approximately equal.

[T,Ab] = balance(A) returns the diagonal similarity transformation matrix T as well as the balanced matrix Ab. The relationship between A and Ab is:

```
Ab = T\A*T
```

## Examples

Row three and column four of b contain smaller elements than the other rows and columns:

```
b =
    3.1304e+00   -2.8309e+00   -9.5451e-01    4.4409e-16
   -1.9428e+00    4.0185e+00   -1.2331e+00   -2.2204e-16
   -5.5511e-17    1.1102e-16   -1.0000e+00            0
   -5.4654e-01   -5.0244e-01    1.1022e-01    1.0000e+00
```

The balanced form of b is:

```
balance(b) =
    3.1304e+00   -2.8309e+00   -7.1117e-09    1.4901e-08
   -1.9428e+00    4.0185e+00   -9.1873e-09   -7.4504e-09
   -7.4506e-09    1.4901e-08   -1.0000e+00            0
   -1.6288e-08   -1.4974e-08    2.4474e-17    1.0000e+00
```

### Algorithm

balance is built into the MATLAB interpreter. It uses the algorithm in [1] originally published in Algol, but popularized by the Fortran routines BALANC and BALBAK from EISPACK.

Successive similarity transformations via diagonal matrices are applied to A to produce Ab. The transformations are accumulated in the transformation matrix T.

The eig function automatically uses balancing to prepare its input matrix.

### Limitations

Balancing can destroy the properties of certain matrices, and should be used with some care. If a matrix contains small elements that are really due to roundoff error, balancing may scale them up to make them as significant as the other elements of the original matrix.

### Diagnostics

If A is not a square matrix:

```
Matrix must be square.
```

### See also

eig, schur, hess

### References

B.N. Parlett and C. Reinsch, "Balancing a Matrix for Calculation of Eigenvalues and Eigenvectors," *Handbook for Auto. Comp.*, Vol. II, Linear Algebra, pp. 315-326, 1971.

## Purpose

Bar graphs, stairstep graphs.

## Synopsis

```
bar(y);  bar(x,y);
[xb,yb] = bar(...)
stairs(y); stairs(x,y);
[xb,yb] = stairs(...)
```

## Description

bar(y) draws a bar graph of the elements of vector y.

bar(x,y) draws a bar graph of the elements in vector y at the locations specified in vector x. The values in x must be evenly spaced and ascending.

[xb,yb] = bar(y) and [xb,yb] = bar(x,y) do not draw graphs, but return vectors xb and yb such that plot(xb,yb) plots the bar chart. This is useful in situations where more control is needed over the appearance of a graph, for example, to combine a bar chart into a more elaborate plot statement.

stairs(y) draws a stairstep graph of the elements of vector y. A stairstep graph is similar to a bar graph, but the vertical lines dropping to the x-axis are omitted. Stairstep plots are useful for drawing time history plots of digital sampled-data systems.

stairs(x,y) draws a stairstep graph of the elements in vector y at the locations specified in vector x. The values in x must be evenly spaced in ascending order.

[xb,yb] = stairs(y) and [xb,yb] = stairs(x,y) do not draw graphs, but return vectors xb and yb such that plot(xb,yb) plots the stairstep graph.

## Examples

Create a stairstep plot of a sine wave:

```
x = 0:.25:10;
stairs(x,sin(x))
```

## Algorithm

bar and stairs are M-files in the *MATLAB Toolbox*.

Reference

---

## Purpose

Bessel functions.

## Synopsis

```
bessel(alpha,X)
besselh(alpha,X)
```

## Description

The differential equation

$$x^2 \ddot{y} + x\dot{y} + (x^2 - \alpha^2)y = 0$$

where $\alpha$ is a nonnegative constant, is called *Bessel's equation*, and its solutions are known as *Bessel functions*. `bessel` evaluates Bessel functions of the first kind.

`bessel(alpha,X)` evaluates the Bessel function of order `alpha`, $J_\alpha(x)$, at every element in array X.

`besselh(alpha,X)` returns the complex Hankel function of integer order `alpha` evaluated for the elements of X. The complex Hankel function $H_\alpha(x)$ is $J_\alpha(x) + i\, Y_\alpha(x)$.

Modified Bessel functions of integer order may be calculated using `bessel` with purely imaginary values of X. The relationship between modified Bessel functions of integer order, $I_n(x)$ and $K_n(x)$, and the usual Bessel functions, $J_n$ and $Y_n$, is:

$$I_n(x) = (-i)^n J_n(i\,x)$$
$$K_n(x) = \frac{\pi}{2}\, i^{n+1}\, [J_n(ix) + i\, Y_n(i\,x)] = \frac{\pi}{2}\, i^{n+1}\, H_n(i\,x)$$

## Examples

Plot Bessel functions of order 0 and 1,

```
x=0:.25:10;
plot(x,[bessel(0,x);bessel(1,x)])
```

---

## Algorithm

bessel consists of several M-files in the *MATLAB Toolbox*. If alpha is an integer, bessel uses besseln; otherwise it calls bessela. bessela is computed using a power series expansion [1]. besseln and besselh are computed with a backwards 3-term recurrence relationship.

## References

M. Abramowitz and I.A. Stegun, *Handbook of Mathematical Functions*, National Bureau of Standards, Applied Math. Series #55, Dover Publications, 1965, sections 9.1.1, 9.1.89, and 9.12, formulas 9.1.10 and 9.2.5.

Reference

## Purpose

Bilinear transformation.

## Synopsis

```
[zd,pd,kd]  =  bilinear(z,p,k,fs)
[zd,pd,kd]  =  bilinear(z,p,k,fs,fp)
[numd,dend]  =  bilinear(num,den,fs)
[numd,dend]  =  bilinear(num,den,fs,fp)
[ad,bd,cd,dd]  =  bilinear(a,b,c,d,fs)
[ad,bd,cd,dd]  =  bilinear(a,b,c,d,fs,fp)
```

## Description

The *bilinear transformation* is a mathematical mapping of variables. In digital filtering circles, it is a standard method of mapping the *s* or analog plane into the *z* or digital plane. It allows analog filters, designed using classical filter design techniques, to be transformed into discrete equivalents.

The bilinear transformation maps the *s*-plane into the *z*-plane with

$$H(z) = H(s)\big|_{s = 2f_s \frac{(z-1)}{(z+1)}}$$

The `bilinear` function can perform this transformation on three different linear system representations: zero-pole coefficients, polynomial coefficients, and state-space form.

*Zero-pole:*

`[zd,pd,kd] = bilinear(z,p,k,fs)` converts the *s*-domain transfer function specified by zeros, poles, and gain to a discrete equivalent. Inputs `z` and `p` are column vectors containing the zeros and poles, while `k` is a scalar gain. `fs` is the sample frequency in Hz. The discrete equivalent is returned in column vectors `zd`, `pd`, and scalar `kd`.

*Polynomial:*

`[numd,dend] = bilinear(num,den,fs)` converts an *s*-domain transfer function given by polynomial coefficients to a discrete equivalent. Row vectors `num` and `den` specify the coefficients of the numerator and denominator in descending powers of *s*,

$$\frac{num(s)}{den(s)} = \frac{num(1)s^{nn} +...+ num(nn)s + num(nn+1)}{den(1)s^{nd} +...+ den(nd)s + den(nd+1)}$$

and `fs` is the sample frequency in Hz. The discrete equivalent is returned in row vectors `numd` and `dend` in descending powers of *z* (ascending powers of $z^{-1}$).

*State-space:*

[Ad,Bd,Cd,Dd] = bilinear(A,B,C,D,fs) converts the continuous-time state-space system in matrices A,B,C,D,

$$\dot{x} = Ax + Bu$$
$$y = Cx + Du$$

to the discrete-time system:

$$x[n+1] = A_d x[n] + B_d u[n]$$
$$y[n] = C_d x[n] + D_d u[n]$$

As before, fs is the sample frequency in Hz. The discrete equivalent is returned in matrices Ad,Bd,Cd,Dd.

All three versions of bilinear can accept a final scalar trailing input argument fp that specifies a "prewarping" frequency. Frequency prewarping forces the digital frequency response and the analog frequency response to match exactly at a given frequency. The match frequency fp is specified in Hz.

## Algorithm

bilinear is an M-file in the *Signal Processing Toolbox*. When bilinear is given a system in zero-pole form, it simply applies the bilinear mapping to the zeros and poles. The polynomial form is handled by converting the transfer function into state-space form and then using the state-space algorithm. For state-space systems, bilinear uses the numerically reliable algorithm described in [1].

## References

G.F. Franklin and J.N. Little, *Digital Filter Design Formulas in State-Space*, unpublished 1988.

## Purpose

Bode frequency response plots.

## Synopsis

```
[mag,phase,w] = bode(a,b,c,d);
[mag,phase,w] = bode(a,b,c,d,iu)
[mag,phase,w] = bode(a,b,c,d,iu,w)

[mag,phase,w] = bode(num,den)
[mag,phase,w] = bode(num,den,w)
```

## Description

bode computes the magnitude and phase (Bode) frequency response of continuous-time LTI systems. Bode plots are used to analyze system properties including gain margin, phase margin, DC gain, bandwidth, disturbance rejection, and stability. When invoked without left-hand arguments, bode produces a Bode plot on the screen.

bode(A,B,C,D) produces a series of Bode plots, one for each input of the continuous state-space system:

$$\dot{x} = Ax + Bu$$
$$y = Cx + Du$$

with the frequency range automatically determined. More points are used where the response is changing rapidly.

bode(A,B,C,D,iu) produces the Bode plot from the single input iu to all the outputs of the system with the frequency range automatically determined. The scalar, iu, is an index into the inputs of the system and specifies which input to use for the Bode response.

bode(num,den) draws the Bode plot of the continuous polynomial transfer function G(s) = num(s)/den(s) where num and den contain the polynomial coefficients in descending powers of $s$.

bode(A,B,C,D,iu,w) or bode(num,den,w) uses the user-supplied frequency vector w. The vector w specifies the frequencies in radians/sec at which the Bode response will be calculated. See logspace to generate frequency vectors that are equally spaced logarithmically in frequency.

When invoked with left-hand arguments:

```
[mag,phase,w] = bode(A,B,C,D,iu)
[mag,phase,w] = bode(A,B,C,D,iu,w)
[mag,phase,w] = bode(num,den)
[mag,phase,w] = bode(num,den,w)
```

bode returns the frequency response of the system in the matrices mag, phase, and w. No plot is drawn on the screen. The matrices mag and phase contain the magnitude and phase response of the system evaluated at the frequency values w. mag and phase have as many columns as outputs and one row for each element in w:

$$G(s) = C(sI-A)^{-1} B + D$$
$$mag(\omega) = |G(j\omega)|$$
$$phase(\omega) = \angle G(j\omega)$$

The phase is returned in degrees. The magnitude can be converted to decibels with:

```
magdb = 20*log10(mag).
```

## Examples

1.  Plot the magnitude and phase responses of a second-order system with a natural frequency $\omega_{n,} = 1$ and a damping factor of $\zeta = 0.2$:

```
[a,b,c,d] = ord2(1,.2);
bode(a,b,c,d);
title('Bode plot')
```

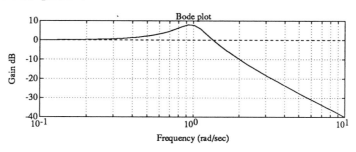

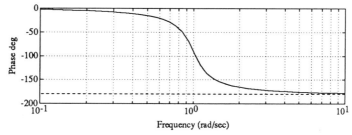

---

2.      Plot the magnitude and phase of the system in Hertz instead of radians per second:

```
[mag,phase,w]=bode(a,b,c,d);
subplot(211), semilogx(w/2*pi,20*log10(mag))
xlabel('Frequency (Hz)'), ylabel('Gain dB')
title('Bode plot')
subplot(212), semilogx(w/2*pi,phase)
xlabel('Frequency (Hz)'), ylabel('Phase deg')
```

## Algorithm

bode is an M-file in the *Signals and Systems Toolbox* and uses the Hessenberg algorithm from [1]. The A,B,C,D matrices are balanced and A is reduced to upper Hessenberg form. Next, the linear equation $C(j\omega - A)^{-1}B$ is solved directly at each frequency point, taking advantage of the Hessenberg form. The reduction to Hessenberg form provides a good compromise between efficiency and reliability. You may comment out the last line of of bode.m if you would like the magnitude returned in decibels.

The auto-selection of frequency points is performed in the M-file freqint.m which uses the poles and zeros of the system to estimate regions of rapid change.

*Warning:* Bode adds ±360 degrees to the phase, as appropriate, when the phase goes through ±180 to make the phase continuous above or below ±180, instead of "jumping" and staying within ±180. It is possible to "fool" this adjustment algorithm if you have only a few frequency points and the phase is changing rapidly. The M-file unwrap.m in the main *MATLAB Toolbox* performs this phase unwrapping. It can be commented out in bode.m if you prefer the phase to always be within ±180 degrees.

## Diagnostics

If there is a system pole on the jω axis and the w vector happens to contain this frequency point, the gain is infinite, *(jωI-A)* is singular, and bode produces the warning message:

```
Matrix is singular to working precision.
```

This message may also occasionally arise during the calculation of the frequency interval.

## See also

logspace, nyquist

**References**

Laub, A.J., *Efficient Multivariable Frequency Response Computations*, IEEE Transactions on Automatic Control, Vol. AC-26, No. 2, April 1981, pp. 407-408.

Reference

## Purpose

Break out of control structures.
Return from M-functions.
Display error messages.

## Synopsis

```
break
return
error('text')
```

## Description

break terminates the execution of for and while loops. In nested loops, break exits from the innermost loop only.

return causes a normal return to the invoking function or to the keyboard.

error('*message*') causes an error return to the keyboard and displays the text in the quoted string.

## Examples

A contrived procedure to calculate machine epsilon is really a while loop in disguise.

```
eps = 1;
for i=1:1000
        eps = eps/2; if (eps+1 <= 1), break, end
end
eps = eps*2
```

error provides an error return from M-files,

```
function foo(x,y)
if nargin ~= 2
    error('Wrong number of input arguments')
end
do_normal_things
```

## See also

while, if, for, end, disp

## Purpose

Butterworth analog lowpass filter prototype.

## Synopsis

```
[z,p,k] = buttap(n)
```

## Description

`[z,p,k] = buttap(n)` returns the zeros, poles, and gain of an order n normalized Butterworth analog lowpass filter prototype. The poles are returned in length n column vector p, the gain in scalar k, and z is an empty matrix, because there are no zeros. The transfer function is

$$H(s) = \frac{z(s)}{p(s)} = \frac{k}{(s - p(1))(s - p(2))...(s - p(n))}$$

Butterworth filters are characterized by a magnitude response that is maximally flat in the passband and monotonic overall. In the lowpass case, the first $2n - 1$ derivatives of the squared magnitude response are zero at $\omega = 0$. The squared magnitude response function is

$$|H(\omega)|^2 = \frac{1}{1 + (\omega/\omega_0)^{2n}}$$

which corresponds to a transfer function with poles equally spaced around a circle in the left half plane. The magnitude response at $\omega_0$ is always $1/\sqrt{2}$, regardless of the filter order. In the case of `buttap`, the cutoff frequency $\omega_0$ is set to 1.0 for a normalized result.

## Algorithm

`buttap` is an M-file with the three-line algorithm:

```
z = [ ];
p = exp(sqrt(-1)*(pi*(1:2:2*n-1)/(2*n) + pi/2)).';
k = real(prod(-p));
```

## See also

`butter`, `cheb1ap`, `cheb2ap`, `ellipap`

## References

T. W. Parks and C. S. Burrus, *Digital Filter Design*, chapter 7, John Wiley & Sons, 1987.

## Purpose

Butterworth filter design.

## Synopsis

```
[b,a] = butter(n,Wn)
[b,a] = butter(n,Wn,'ftype')
[z,p,k] = butter(...)
[a,b,c,d] = butter(...)
```

*ftype* can be `high` or `stop`.

## Description

`butter` designs lowpass, bandpass, highpass, and bandstop digital Butterworth filters. Butterworth filters are characterized by a magnitude response that is maximally flat in the passband and monotonic overall. In the lowpass case, the first $2n - 1$ derivatives of the squared magnitude response are zero at $\omega = 0$.

Butterworth filters sacrifice rolloff steepness for monotonicity in the pass- and stopbands. Unless the Butterworth filter's "smoothness" is needed, an elliptic or Chebyshev filter can generally provide steeper rolloff characteristics with a lower filter order.

`[b,a] = butter(n,Wn)` designs an order n lowpass digital Butterworth filter with cutoff frequency `Wn` and returns the filter coefficients in length n+1 row vectors `b` and `a`. The filter coefficients are ordered in descending powers of $z$:

$$H(z) = \frac{B(z)}{A(z)} = \frac{b(1) + b(2)z^{-1} + \cdots + b(n+1)z^{-n}}{1 + a(2)z^{-1} + \cdots + a(n+1)z^{-n}}$$

`Wn`, the cutoff frequency, must be a number between 0 and 1, where 1.0 corresponds to half the sample frequency (the Nyquist frequency).

If `Wn` is a two element vector, `Wn = [w1 w2]`, `butter` returns an order 2n bandpass filter with passband $w1 < \omega < w2$.

`[b,a] = butter(n,Wn,'high')` designs a highpass filter with cutoff frequency `Wn`.

`[b,a] = butter(n,Wn,'stop')` is an order 2n bandstop filter if `Wn` is a two element vector, `Wn = [w1 w2]`. The stopband is $w1 < \omega < w2$.

butter can be used with different numbers of output arguments to directly obtain other realizations of the filter. When used with three output arguments,

```
[z,p,k] = butter(n,wn,...)
```

butter returns the zeros and poles in length n column vectors z and p, and the gain in the scalar k. When used with four output arguments,

```
[A,B,C,D] = butter(n,wn,...)
```

butter returns the filter in state-space form, where A, B, C, and D are defined as

$$x[n+1] = Ax[n] + Bu[n]$$
$$y[n] = Cx[n] + Du[n]$$

For high order filters, the state-space form is the most numerically accurate, followed by the zero-pole-gain form. The transfer function coefficient form is the least accurate, and numerical problems can arise in filters as low as order fifteen.

## Example

Consider data sampled at 1000 Hz. Design a ninth order highpass Butterworth filter with a cutoff frequency of 300 Hz and plot its frequency response:

```
[b,a] = butter(9, 300/500, 'high')
[h,w] = freqz(b,a,128);
f = w*500/pi;
semilogy(f,abs(h)), plot(f,angle(h)*180/pi)
```

Design a tenth order bandpass Butterworth filter with a passband from 100 to 200 Hz and plot its unit sample response:

```
n = 5;
wn = [100  200]/500;
[b,a] = butter(n, wn)
y = filter(b,a,[1 zeros(1,100)]);
plot(y,'o')
```

Reference

## Algorithm

`butter` is an M-file in the *Signal Processing Toolbox.* It uses a five-step algorithm:

1.  Find lowpass analog prototype poles, zeros, and gain using the function `buttap`.

2.  Convert poles, zeros, and gain into state-space form.

3.  Transform lowpass filter to bandpass, highpass, or bandstop filter of desired cutoff frequencies. A state-space transformation is employed.

4.  Use `bilinear` to convert the analog filter into a digital filter using a bilinear transformation with frequency prewarping. Careful frequency adjustment guarantees that the analog filters and the digital filters will have the same frequency response magnitude at $\omega_n$ or $\omega_1$ and $\omega_2$.

5.  Convert the state-space filter back to transfer function, or pole-zero form, as required.

## See also

`buttord, cheby1, cheby2, ellip, cheb2ap, fir1, fir2, remez, yule-walk`

## Purpose

Conversion from continuous- to discrete-time.

## Synopsis

```
[ad,bd] = c2d(a,b,Ts)
```

## Description

c2d converts state-space models from continuous-time to discrete-time assuming a zero-order hold on the inputs.

`[Ad,Bd] = c2d(A,B,Ts)` converts the continuous-time state-space system:

$$\dot{x} = Ax + Bu$$

to the discrete time system:

$$\dot{x}[n + 1] = A_d x[n] + B_d u[n]$$

assuming the control inputs are piecewise constant over the sample time Ts.

## Algorithm

c2d is an M-file in the *Signals and Systems Toolbox*. The calculation uses a matrix exponential, which is calculated via Pade's approximation in the function expm.

## See also

expm, logm

## References

Franklin, G.F. and Powell, J.D., *Digital Control of Dynamic Systems 2/E*, Addison-Wesley, 1990.

Reference

## Purpose

Select/deselect case sensitivity.

## Synopsis

```
casesen
```

## Description

`casesen` controls the case sensitivity of MATLAB. Initially MATLAB is case sensitive; it is able to distinguish between uppercase and lowercase variable and function names.

`casesen off` makes MATLAB not case sensitive.

`casesen on` makes MATLAB case sensitive.

`casesen`, by itself, toggles the case sensitivity.

## Examples

When MATLAB is case sensitive, the variable `VAR` is different from the variable `var`. When MATLAB is not case sensitive, the two names refer to the same variable.

## Purpose

Convert a complex diagonal matrix to real diagonal form.

## Synopsis

```
[v,d] = cdf2rdf(v,d)
```

## Description

If the eigensystem `[v,d] = eig(x)` has complex eigenvalues appearing in complex-conjugate pairs, `cdf2rdf` transforms the system so it is in real diagonal form, with *2-by-2* real blocks along the diagonal replacing the complex pairs originally there. The eigenvectors are amended to correspond to the transformed eigenvalue matrix.

## Examples

Consider the system where `v = eye(3)` and

```
d =
   1.8817          0            0
        0     0+1.0000i        0
        0          0      0-1.0000i
```

The real diagonal form of this system is:

```
[v,d] = cdf2rdf(v,d)

v =
   1.0000          0          0
        0     0.5000     0-0.5000i
        0     0.5000     0+0.5000i

d =
   1.8817          0            0
        0          0       1.0000
        0    -1.0000            0
```

## Algorithm

cdf2rdf is an M-file in the *MATLAB Toolbox*. The real diagonal form for the eigenvalues is obtained from the complex form via a specially constructed similarity transformation.

## See also

eig, rsf2csf

---

## Purpose

Chebyshev type I analog lowpass filter prototype.

## Synopsis

```
[z,p,k] = cheb1ap(n,Rp)
```

## Description

`[z,p,k] = cheb1ap(n,Rp)` returns the zeros, poles, and gain of an order n normalized Chebyshev type I analog lowpass filter prototype with Rp decibels of ripple in the passband. The poles are returned in length n column vector p, the gain in scalar k, and z is an empty matrix, because there are no zeros. The transfer function is

$$H(s) = \frac{z(s)}{p(s)} = \frac{k}{(s - p(1))(s - p(2))...(s - p(n))}$$

Chebyshev type I filters are equiripple in the passband and monotonic in the stopband. The poles are evenly spaced about an ellipse in the left half plane. The Chebyshev cutoff frequency $\omega_0$ is set to 1.0 for a normalized result.

## Algorithm

`cheb1ap` is an M-file in the *Signal Processing Toolbox*.

## See also

```
cheby1, cheb2ap, buttap, ellipap
```

## References

T. W. Parks and C. S. Burrus, *Digital Filter Design*, chapter 7, John Wiley & Sons, 1987.

Reference

---

## Purpose

Chebyshev type II analog lowpass filter prototype.

## Synopsis

```
[z,p,k] = cheb2ap(n,Rs)
```

## Description

`[z,p,k] = cheb2ap(n,Rs)` returns the zeros, poles, and gain of an order $n$ normalized Chebyshev type II analog lowpass filter prototype with stopband ripple Rs decibels down from the peak value in the passband. The zeros and poles are returned in length n column vectors z and p, and the gain in scalar k. If n is odd, z is length n-1. The transfer function is

$$H(s) = \frac{z(s)}{p(s)} = k\frac{(s - z(1))(s - z(2))...(s - z(n))}{(s - p(1))(s - p(2))...(s - p(n))}$$

Chebyshev type II filters are monotonic in the passband and equiripple in the stopband. The pole locations are the inverse of the pole locations of cheb1ap, whose poles are evenly spaced about an ellipse in the left half plane. The Chebyshev cutoff frequency $\omega_0$ is set to 1.0 for a normalized result.

## Algorithm

cheb2ap is an M-file in the *Signal Proccessing Toolbox*. Chebyshev type II filters are sometimes called *inverse Chebyshev* filters because of their relationship to Chebyshev type I filters. It is easier to modify the Chebyshev type I prototype algorithm than to develop an algorithm directly. The basic idea is to replace the frequency variable $\omega$ with $1/\omega$, which turns the lowpass filter into a highpass filter while preserving the performance at $\omega = 1$, and then to subtract the filter transfer function from unity. cheb2ap is the inverse filter obtained from the equations derived from this procedure.

## See also

cheby2, cheb1ap, buttap, ellipap

## References

T. W. Parks and C. S. Burrus, *Digital Filter Design*, chapter 7, John Wiley & Sons, 1987.

---

## Purpose

Chebyshev type I filter design (passband ripple).

## Synopsis

```
[b,a] = cheby1(n,Rp,Wn)
[b,a] = cheby1(n,Rp,Wn,'ftype')
[z,p,k] = cheby1(...)
[a,b,c,d] = cheby1(...)
```

*ftype* can be `high` or `stop`.

## Description

`cheby1` designs lowpass, bandpass, highpass, and bandstop digital Chebyshev type I filters. Chebyshev type I filters are equiripple in the passband and monotonic in the stopband. Type I filters roll off faster than Chebyshev type II filters, but at the expense of passband ripple.

`[b,a] = cheby1(n,Rp,Wn)` designs an order n lowpass digital Chebyshev filter with cutoff frequency Wn and Rp decibels of ripple in the passband. It returns the filter coefficients in length n+1 row vectors b and a. The filter coefficients are ordered in descending powers of *z*:

$$H(z) = \frac{B(z)}{A(z)} = \frac{b(1) + b(2)z^{-1} + \cdots + b(n+1)z^{-n}}{1 + a(2)z^{-1} + \cdots + a(n+1)z^{-n}}$$

Wn, the cutoff frequency, must be a number between 0 and 1, where 1.0 corresponds to half the sample frequency (the Nyquist frequency).

Smaller values of passband ripple Rp lead to wider transition widths (shallower rolloff characteristics). Use `cheb1ord` to choose the filter order needed to meet a given set of performance specifications.

If Wn is a two element vector, Wn = [w1 w2], cheby1 returns an order 2n bandpass filter with passband w1 $< \omega <$ w2.

`[b,a] = cheby1(n,Rp,Wn,'high')` designs a highpass filter with cutoff frequency Wn.

`[b,a] = cheby1(n,Rp,Wn,'stop')` is an order 2n bandstop filter if Wn is a two element vector Wn = [w1 w2]. The stopband is w1 $< \omega <$ w2.

`cheby1` can be used with different numbers of output arguments to directly obtain other realizations of the filter. When used with three output arguments,

```
[z,p,k] = cheby1(n,Rp,wn,...)
```

cheby1 returns the zeros and poles in length n column vectors z and p, and the gain in the scalar k. When used with four output arguments,

```
[A,B,C,D] = cheby1(n,Rp,wn,...)
```

cheby1 returns the filter in state-space form, where A, B, C, and D are defined as

$$x[n+1] = Ax[n] + Bu[n]$$
$$y[n] = Cx[n] + Du[n]$$

For high order filters, the state-space form is the most numerically accurate, followed by the zero-pole-gain form. The transfer function coefficient form is the least accurate, and numerical problems can arise in filters as low as order fifteen.

## Examples

Consider data sampled at 1000 Hz. Design a ninth order lowpass Chebyshev filter with 0.5 dB of ripple in the passband and a cutoff frequency of 300 Hz. Plot its frequency response.

```
[b,a] = cheby1(9, 0.5, 300/500)
[h,w] = freqz(b,a,128);
f = w*500/pi;
semilogy(f,abs(h)), plot(f,angle(h)*180/pi)
```

Design a tenth order bandpass Chebyshev filter with a passband from 100 to 200Hz and plot its unit sample response:

```
n = 5; Rp = 0.5;
wn = [100 200]/500;
[b,a] = cheby1(n, Rp, wn)
y = filter(b,a,[1 zeros(1,100)]);
plot(y,'o')
```

## Algorithm

cheby1 is an M-file in the *Signal Processing Toolbox*. It uses a five-step algorithm:

1.      Find lowpass analog prototype poles, zeros, and gain using the function cheb1ap.

2.      Convert poles, zeros, and gain into state-space form.

3.    Transform lowpass filter to bandpass, highpass, or bandstop filter of desired cutoff frequencies. A state-space transformation is employed.

4.    Use `bilinear` to convert the analog filter into a digital filter using a bilinear transformation with frequency prewarping. Careful frequency adjustment guarantees that the analog filters and the digital filters will have the same frequency response magnitude at $\omega_n$ or $\omega_1$ and $\omega_2$.

5.    Convert the state-space filter back to transfer function, or pole-zero form, as required.

**See also**

cheby2, butter, ellip, buttap, remez

## Purpose

Chebyshev type II filter design (stopband ripple).

## Synopsis

```
[b,a] = cheby2(n,r,Wn)
[b,a] = cheby2(n,r,Wn,'ftype')
[z,p,k] = cheby2(...)
[a,b,c,d] = cheby2(...)
```

*ftype* can be `high` or `stop`.

## Description

`cheby2` designs lowpass, bandpass, highpass, and bandstop digital Chebyshev type II filters. Chebyshev type II filters are monotonic in the passband and equiripple in the stopband. Type II filters don't rolloff as fast as Chebyshev type I filters, and the stopband does not head toward zero like type I filters, but type II filters are free of passband ripple.

`[b,a] = cheby2(n,r,Wn)` designs an order n lowpass digital Chebyshev filter with cutoff frequency `Wn` and stopband ripple  r decibels down from the peak value in the passband. It returns the filter coefficients in length n+1 row vectors b and a. The filter coefficients are ordered in descending powers of $z$:

$$H(z) = \frac{B(z)}{A(z)} = \frac{b(1) + b(2)z^{-1} + \cdots + b(n+1)z^{-n}}{1 + a(2)z^{-1} + \cdots + a(n+1)z^{-n}}$$

`Wn`, the cutoff frequency, must be a number between 0 and 1, where 1.0 corresponds to half the sample frequency (the Nyquist frequency).

Larger values of stopband attenuation $r$ lead to wider transition widths (shallower rolloff characteristics).

If `Wn` is a two element vector, `Wn = [w1 w2]`, `cheby2` returns an order 2n bandpass filter with passband `w1` < $\omega$ < `w2`.

`[b,a] = cheby2(n,r,Wn,'high')` designs a highpass filter with cutoff frequency  `Wn`.

`[b,a] = cheby2(n,r,Wn,'stop')` is an order 2n bandstop filter if `Wn` is a two element row vector `Wn = [w1 w2]`. The stopband is `w1` < $\omega$ < `w2`.

`cheby2` can be used with different numbers of output arguments directly to obtain other realizations of the filter. When used with three output arguments,

```
[z,p,k] = cheby2(n,r,wn,...)
```

cheby2 returns the zeros and poles in length n column vectors z and p, and the gain in the scalar k. When used with four output arguments,

```
[A,B,C,D] = cheby2(n,r,wn,...)
```

cheby2 returns the filter in state-space form, where A, B, C, and D are defined as,

$$x[n+1] = Ax[n] + Bu[n]$$
$$y[n] = Cx[n] + Du[n]$$

For high order filters, the state-space form is the most numerically accurate, followed by the zero-pole-gain form. The transfer function coefficient form is the least accurate, and numerical problems can arise in filters as low as order fifteen.

## Examples

Consider data sampled at 1000 Hz. Design a ninth order lowpass Chebyshev filter with stopband 20 dB down from the passband and a cutoff frequency of 300 Hz. Plot its frequency response.

```
[b,a] = cheby2(9, 20, 300/500)
[h,w] = freqz(b,a,128);
f = w*500/pi;
semilogy(f,abs(h)), plot(f,angle(h)*180/pi)
```

Design a twentieth order bandpass Chebyshev filter with a passband from 100 to 200Hz and plot its unit sample response:

```
n = 10; r = 20;
wn = [100 200]/500;
[b,a] = cheby2(n, r, wn)
y = filter(b,a,[1 zeros(1,100)]);
plot(y,'o')
```

## Algorithm

cheby2 is an M-file in the *Signal Processing Toolbox*. It uses a five-step algorithm:

1.  Find lowpass analog prototype poles, zeros, and gain using the function cheb2ap.

2.  Convert poles, zeros, and gain into state-space form.

Reference

3.     Transform lowpass filter to bandpass, highpass, or bandstop filter of desired cutoff frequencies. A state-space transformation is employed.

4.     Use `bilinear` to convert the analog filter into a digital filter using a bilinear transformation with frequency prewarping. Careful frequency adjustment guarantees that the analog filters and the digital filters will have the same frequency response magnitude at $\omega_n$ or $\omega_1$ and $\omega_2$.

5.     Convert the state-space filter back to transfer function, or pole-zero form, as required.

**See also**

    `cheby1, butter, ellip, buttap, remez`

## Purpose

Cholesky factorization.

## Synopsis

```
chol(X)
```

## Description

`chol` computes the Cholesky factorization of a matrix. If X is positive definite, then

```
R = chol(X)
```

produces an upper triangular R so that `R'*R = X`. `chol` uses only the diagonal and upper triangle of X; the lower triangular is assumed to be the (complex-conjugate) transpose of the upper.

## Algorithm

`chol` uses the algorithm from the LINPACK subroutine ZPOFA. For a detailed write-up on the use of the Cholesky decomposition, see chapter 8 of the *LINPACK User's Guide*.

## Diagnostics

If X is not positive definite,

```
Matrix must be positive definite.
```

## References

J.J. Dongarra, J.R. Bunch, C.B. Moler, and G.W. Stewart, *LINPACK User's Guide*, SIAM, Philadelphia, 1979.

Reference

## Purpose

Command window control.
Graph window control.

## Synopsis

```
clc
clg
shg
home
```

## Description

Conceptually, MATLAB has two displays, a *graph window* and a *command window*. Your particular hardware configuration may allow both to be seen simultaneously in different windows, or it may allow only one to be seen at a time. Several commands are available to switch back and forth between the windows, and/or erase the windows, as required:

| Screen Control | |
|---|---|
| shg | show graph window |
| any key | bring back command window |
| clc | clear command window |
| clg | clear graph window |
| home | home command cursor |

By default, hardware configurations that cannot display both the command screen and the graph screen simultaneously will pause in graph mode after a plot is drawn and wait for any key to be pressed.

## Examples

Show a "movie" of a random matrix:

```
clc, for i=1:25, home, a = rand(5), end
```

## See also

```
plot, hold, subplot
```

## Purpose

Remove items from memory.

## Synopsis

```
clear
clear name
clear name1  name2 name3 ...
clear functions
clear variables
```

The *name* can be either a variable name or a function name.

## Description

Executing `clear`, by itself, clears all variables and compiled functions from the workspace. It leaves the workspace empty, as if MATLAB were just invoked.

`clear` X removes just variable or function X from the workspace.

`clear` X Y Z removes X, Y, and Z from the workspace.

Assigning a variable to null does NOT clear it. For example, X=[ ] frees the space occupied by the data, but leaves behind a matrix of dimension zero named X.

`clear functions` clears all the currently compiled M-functions from memory.

`clear variables` clears the variables, leaving the compiled M-functions behind.

## See also

```
pack
```

## Purpose

Wall clock, elapsed time, and date.

## Synopsis

```
clock
etime(t2,t1)
date
```

## Description

`clock` returns a six-element row vector containing the current time and date in decimal form:

```
clock = [year month day hour minute seconds]
```

The first five elements are integers. The *seconds* element is accurate to several digits beyond the decimal point.

`etime` calculates the elapsed time between `clock` output vectors. `etime(t2,t1)` returns the time in seconds between `t1` and `t2`.

`s = date` returns a string containing the date in *dd-mmm-yy* format.

## Examples

Rounding to the nearest second results in an integer display:

```
fix(clock)

ans =
    1985    10    28    13     5    52
```

Calculate how long a 2048-point real FFT takes:

```
x = rand(2048,1);
t = clock; fft(x); etime(clock,t)
```

Calculate the smallest time interval `clock` and `etime` are capable of resolving:

```
t1 = clock; etime(clock,t1)
```

Display the date as a string:

```
date

ans =
   16-Jan-89
```

**Algorithm**

clock is built into the interpreter; etime and date are M-files in the *MATLAB Toolbox.*

**Limitations**

etime will fail across month and year boundaries. It could be fixed with some effort; see the etime M-file.

## Purpose

Companion matrix.

## Synopsis

```
compan(p)
```

## Description

If p is a vector of polynomial coefficients, `compan(p)` is the corresponding companion matrix whose first row is p(2:n)/p(1).

The eigenvalues of `compan(p)` are the roots of p.

## Examples

The polynomial $(x-1)(x-2)(x+3) = x^3 - 7x + 6$ has a companion matrix of:

```
p = [1 0 -7 6]
a = compan(p)

a =
        0       7      -6
        1       0       0
        0       1       0
```

The eigenvalues are the polynomial roots:

```
eig(compan(p)) =

    -3.0000
     2.0000
     1.0000
```

## Algorithm

`compan` is an M-file in the *MATLAB Toolbox*.

## See also

```
roots, hankel, toeplitz
```

**Purpose**

    Computer description.

**Synopsis**

    `[c,maxsize] = computer`

**Description**

    `computer`, by itself, returns a string containing the type of computer on which MATLAB is running. Possibilities include

| String | Computer |
|--------|----------|
| VAX | VAX |
| SUN | Sun workstation |
| APOLLO | Apollo workstation |
| PC | Personal Computer |
| 386 | 386-MATLAB |
| MAC | Macintosh Plus or SE |
| MAC2 | Macintosh II |

    `[c,maxsize] = computer` returns the computer type in `c` and integer `maxsize`, which contains the maximum number of elements allowed in a matrix for the specific MATLAB implementation.

    For PC and MAC computers, $maxsize = 2^{16}/8 - 4 = 8,188$.

    For the other machines, $maxsize = 2^{32}/8 = 536,870,912$, unless the operating system imposes other constraints.

Reference

## Purpose

Condition number of a matrix.

## Synopsis

```
cond(X)
rcond(X)
```

## Description

The *condition number* of a matrix measures the sensitivity of the solution of a system of linear equations to errors in the data. It gives an indication of the accuracy of the results from matrix inversion and linear equation solution.

`cond(X)` returns the 2-norm condition number, the ratio of the largest singular value of X to the smallest.

The usual rule of thumb is that the exponent on the condition number, `log10(cond(X))`, indicates the number of decimal places that the computer can lose to roundoff errors from Gaussian elimination.

`rcond` is a more efficient, but less reliable, method of estimating the condition of a matrix. `rcond(X)` is an estimate for the reciprocal of the condition of X in 1-norm using the LINPACK condition estimator. If X is well conditioned, `rcond(X)` is near 1.0. If X is badly conditioned, `rcond(X)` is near 0.0.

## Algorithm

`cond` uses the singular value decomposition (`svd`) and is implemented in an M-file in the *MATLAB Toolbox*.

`rcond` uses the condition estimator from the LINPACK routine ZGECO.

## See also

```
norm, svd, rank
```

## References

J.J. Dongarra, J.R. Bunch, C.B. Moler, and G.W. Stewart, *LINPACK User's Guide*, SIAM, Philadelphia, 1979.

## Purpose

Contour plot of a matrix.

## Synopsis

```
contour(z)
contour(z,n)
contour(z,v)
contour(z,n,x,y)
contour(z,v,x,y)
```

## Description

contour(z) draws a contour plot of matrix z. The contours are level lines in the units of array z. The upper left corner of the plot corresponds to z(1,1). The number of contour lines and their values are chosen automatically by contour.

contour(z,n) produces a contour plot of matrix z with n contour levels. When n is not specified, the default value is 10.

contour(z,v) draws a contour plot of z with contour levels at the values specified in vector v.

contour(z,n,x,y) and contour(z,v,x,y) produce contour plots of z and use the data in vectors x and y to control the axis scaling on the x- and y-axes.

## Examples

To view a contour plot of the function

$$z = x \, e^{(-x^2 - y^2)}$$

over the range

$$-2 \le x \le 2, \quad -2 \le y \le 3$$

use the statements

```
[x,y] = meshdom(-2:.2:2, -2:.2:3);
z = x .* exp(-x.^2 - y.^2);
contour(z,10,-2:.2:2, -2:.2:3)
```

### Diagnostics

If the smallest dimension of $z$ is less than 3:

```
Minimum dimension for CONTOUR is 3.
```

### See also

```
plot, mesh, meshdom
```

## Purpose

Convolution and deconvolution.
Polynomial multiplication and division.

## Synopsis

```
c = conv(a,b)
[q,r] = deconv(b,a)
```

## Description

conv(a,b) convolves vectors a and b. The convolution sum is:

$$c(n+1) = \sum_{k=0}^{N-1} a(k+1)b(n-k)$$

where $N$ is the maximum sequence length. The series is written in an unorthodox way, indexed from $n+1$ and $k+1$ instead of the usual $n$ and $k$, because MATLAB vectors run from 1 to $n$ instead of from 0 to $n-1$.

[q,r] = deconv(b,a) deconvolves vector a out of vector b, using long division. The quotient is returned in vector q and the remainder in vector r such that b = conv(q,a) + r.

If a and b are vectors of polynomial coefficients, convolving them is equivalent to multiplying the two polynomials, and deconvolution is polynomial division. The result of dividing b by a is quotient q and remainder r.

## Examples

If a = [1 2 3], b = [4 5 6], the convolution is

```
c = conv(a,b)

c =
        4     13     28     27     18
```

Use deconvolution to divide a back out,

```
[q,r] = deconv(c,a)

q =
      4     5     6
r =
      0     0     0     0     0
```

## Algorithm

These functions are all M-files in the *MATLAB Toolbox* that use the `filter` primitive. Convolution is the same as FIR filtering with an appropriate number of zeros appended to the input. Deconvolution is the impulse response of an IIR filter.

## See also

```
residue
convmtx,  filter,  conv2 later in the Signal Processing Functions section of this guide.
```

## Purpose

Covariance and correlation matrices.

## Synopsis

```
cov(X), cov(x,y)
corrcoef(X), corrcoef(x,y)
```

## Description

cov computes the covariance matrix. For a single vector, cov(x) returns a scalar containing the variance. For matrices, where each row is an observation, and each column a variable, cov(X) is the covariance matrix. diag(cov(X)) is a vector of variances for each column, and sqrt(diag(cov(X))) is a vector of standard deviations.

cov(X) is the zero-th lag of the covariance function, i.e., the zero-th lag of xcov(x)/(n-1) packed into a square array.

cov(x,y), where x and y are column vectors of equal length, is equivalent to cov([x y]).

corrcoef(X) returns a matrix of correlation coefficients calculated from an input matrix whose rows are observations and whose columns are variables. If C = cov(X) then corrcoef(X) is the matrix whose element $(i,j)$ is

$$corrcoef(i,j) = \frac{C(i,j)}{\sqrt{C(i,i)\,C(j,j)}}$$

corrcoef(X) is the zero-th lag of the covariance function, i.e., the zero-th lag of xcov(x,'coeff') packed into a square array.

Both cov and corrcoef remove the mean from each column before calculating their results.

## Algorithm

Both functions are M-files; the basic algorithm for cov is

```
[n,p] = size(x);
x = x - ones(n,1)*(sum(x)/n);
y = x'*x/(n-1);
```

## See also

```
mean, std
xcov, xcorr (See also Signals and Systems section of this guide).
```

## Purpose

Group complex numbers into complex-conjugate pairs.

## Synopsis

```
x = cplxpair(x)
x = cplxpair(x,tol)
```

## Description

cplxpair(x) returns x with complex-conjugate pairs grouped together. The conjugate pairs are ordered by increasing real part. Within a pair, the element with negative imaginary part comes first. The purely real values are returned following all the complex pairs.

The complex-conjugate pairs are forced to be exact complex conjugates. A default tolerance of 100*eps relative to abs(x(i)) determines which numbers are real and which elements are paired complex conjugates. The default tolerance may be overridden with cplxpair(x,tol).

## Examples

Order into complex pairs five poles evenly spaced around the unit circle,

```
cplxpair(exp(2*pi*sqrt(-1)*(0:4)/5)')

ans =
  -0.8090 - 0.5878i
  -0.8090 + 0.5878i
   0.3090 - 0.9511i
   0.3090 + 0.9511i
   1.0000
```

## Diagnostics

If there is an odd number of complex numbers, or if the complex numbers cannot be grouped into complex-conjugate pairs within the tolerance, cplxpair generates the error message:

```
Complex numbers can't be paired.
```

## Purpose

Diagonal matrices.

Upper and lower triangular parts.

## Synopsis

```
diag(X), diag(X,k)
triu(X), triu(X,k)
tril(X), tril(X,k)
```

The optional argument k indicates the *k*-th diagonal. k = 0 is the main diagonal, k > 0 is above the main diagonal, and k < 0 is below the main diagonal.

## Description

If V is a vector with *n* components, diag(V,k) is a square matrix of order *n+abs(k)* with the elements of V on the *k*-th diagonal. k = 0 is the main diagonal, k > 0 is above the main diagonal, and k < 0 is below the main diagonal. diag(V) simply puts V on the main diagonal.

If X is a matrix, diag(X,k) is a column vector formed from the elements of the *k*-th diagonal of X. diag(X) is the main diagonal of X.

triu(X) are the upper triangular part of X. triu(X,k) are the elements on and above the *k*-th diagonal of X, with k defined as before.

tril(X) is the lower triangular part of X. tril(X,k) are the elements on and below the *k*-th diagonal of X.

## Examples

diag(diag(X)) is a diagonal matrix.

sum(diag(X)) is the trace of X.

The statement

```
diag(-m:m) + diag(ones(2*m,1),1) + diag(ones(2*m,1),-1)
```

produces a tridiagonal matrix of order *2m+1*.

## Algorithm

triu and tril are M-files in the *MATLAB Toolbox*; diag is built into the interpreter.

## Purpose

Save the session in a disk file, possibly for later printing.

## Synopsis

```
diary file
diary
diary on
diary off
```

## Description

The command `diary` *file*, where *file* is a filename, causes a copy of all subsequent keyboard input and most of the resulting output (but not graphs) to be written on the named file. If the file already exists, the output is appended to the end of the file.

`diary off` suspends the diary.

`diary on` turns it back on again, using the current filename, or the default filename `diary` if none had yet been specified.

`diary`, by itself, toggles `diary` on and off.

The output of `diary` is an ASCII file, suitable for printing or for inclusion in reports and other documents.

## Limitations

No, you can't put a diary into the files named `off` and `on`.

## Purpose

Difference functions, approximate derivatives.

## Synopsis

```
diff(x)
diff(x,n)
```

The optional argument n indicates the *n*-th difference function.

## Description

`diff` calculates differences. If X is a row or column vector

$$X = [x(1) \quad x(2) \quad \ldots \quad x(n)]$$

then `diff(X)` returns a vector of differences between adjacent elements

$$[x(2)-x(1) \quad x(3)-x(2) \quad \ldots \quad x(n)-x(n-1)]$$

The output vector will be one element shorter than the input vector.

If X is a matrix, the differences are calculated down each column:

$$\text{diff}(X) = X(2:m,:) - X(1:m-1,:)$$

`diff(X,n)` is the *n*-th difference function.

## Examples

`diff(y)./diff(x)` is an approximate derivative.

## Algorithm

`diff` is an M-file in the *MATLAB Toolbox*.

## See also

```
sum, prod
```

## Purpose

File manipulation.

## Synopsis

```
dir
type file
delete file
chdir dir
```

## Description

`dir`, `type`, `delete`, and `chdir` implement a set of generic operating system commands for manipulating files. Here is a table that indicates how these commands map to other operating systems, perhaps one you are familiar with:

| MATLAB | MS-DOS | UNIX | VAX/VMS |
|--------|--------|------|---------|
| dir    | dir    | ls   | dir     |
| type   | type   | cat  | type    |
| delete | del    | rm   | delete  |
| chdir  | chdir  | cd   | set default |

Pathnames, wildcards, and drive designators may be used in the usual way for your operating system.

The `type` command differs from the usual `type` commands in an important way; if no filename extension is given, `.m` is added by default. This makes it convenient for the most frequent use of `type`: to list M-files on the screen.

Other operating system commands can be issued using the exclamation point character `!`.

## Examples

`type foo.bar` lists the ASCII file `foo.bar`.
`type foo` lists the ASCII file `foo.m`.

## See also

`who, what, !`

## References

The manual for your operating system.

## Purpose

Display text or matrix.

## Synopsis

```
disp(X)
```

## Description

`disp(X)` displays a matrix, without printing the matrix name. If X contains a text string, the string is displayed.

Another way to display a matrix on the screen is to type its name, but this prints a leading "A = ", which is not always desirable.

## Examples

One use of `disp` is to display a matrix with column labels,

```
disp('      Corn        oats        hay')
disp(rand(5,3))
```

which results in

```
        Corn    oats    hay
       0.2113  0.8474  0.2749
       0.0824  0.4524  0.8807
       0.7599  0.8075  0.6538
       0.0087  0.4832  0.4899
       0.8096  0.6135  0.7741
```

It shows the use of `disp` on both data and text strings.

## See also

```
setstr, num2str, sprintf
```

Reference

## Purpose

Echo M-files during execution.

## Synopsis

```
echo on,  echo off
echo fun
echo on all,  echo off all
```

## Description

echo controls the echoing of M-files during execution. The commands in M-files are normally not displayed on the screen during execution. Command echoing can be enabled for debugging, or for demonstrations, allowing the commands to be viewed as they execute.

echo behaves slightly differently, depending upon which of the two types of M-files, *script files* or *function files*, is being considered. For *script files*, the use of echo is simple; echoing can be either on or off, in which case any *script* used is affected: echo on turns on the echoing of commands, in all *script files*. echo off turns off the echoing of all *script files*. echo, by itself, toggles the echo state.

This use of echo does not affect *function files*.

With *function files*, the use of echo is more complicated. If echo is enabled on a *function file*, the file is interpreted, rather than compiled, so that each input line can be viewed as it is executed. Since this results in inefficient execution and should only be used for debugging, provision is made to use echo on just a single *function file*, instead of operating globally on all files: echo *file* on, where *file* is a function name, causes the named *function file* to be echoed when it is used. echo *file* off turns off the echoing of the named *function file*. echo *file* toggles the echo state of the named file. echo on all and echo off all set echoing for all *function files*.

## See also

M-files

## Purpose

Eigenvalues and eigenvectors.

## Synopsis

```
eig(X)
[V,D] = eig(X)
[V,D] = eig(X,'nobalance')
eig(A,B)
[V,D] = eig(A,B)
```

## Description

The eigenvalue problem is to determine the nontrivial solutions of the equation

$$Ax = \lambda x$$

where $A$ is an $n$-by-$n$ matrix, $x$ is a length $n$ column vector, and $\lambda$ is a scalar. The $n$ values of $\lambda$ that satisfy the equation are the *eigenvalues* and the corresponding values of $x$ are the *right eigenvectors*.

In MATLAB the function `eig` solves for the eigenvalues $\lambda$ and optionally the eigenvectors $x$: `eig(A)` is a vector containing the eigenvalues of matrix A. `[X,D] = eig(A)` produces a diagonal matrix D of eigenvalues and a full matrix X whose columns are the corresponding eigenvectors so that `A*X = X*D`.

The eigenvectors are scaled so that the norm of each is 1.0.

`[V,D] = eig(A,'nobalance')` finds eigenvalues and eigenvectors without a preliminary balancing step. Ordinarily, balancing improves the conditioning of the input matrix, enabling more accurate computation of the eigenvectors and eigenvalues. However, if a matrix contains small elements that are really due to roundoff error, balancing may scale them up to make them as significant as the other elements of the original matrix, leading to incorrect eigenvectors. The `nobalance` option should be used in this event.

When a matrix has no repeated eigenvalues - the $\lambda_i$ are distinct - then the eigenvectors are always independent and the eigenvector matrix V will "diagonalize" the original matrix A if applied as a similarity transformation. However, if a matrix has repeated eigenvalues, it is not diagonalizable unless it has a full (independent) set of eigenvectors. If the eigenvectors are not independent then the original matrix is said to be *defective*. Even if a matrix is defective, the solution from `eig` satisfies `A*X = X*D`.

Reference

The *generalized* eigenvalue problem is to determine the nontrivial solutions of the equation

$$Ax = \lambda Bx$$

where both $A$ and $B$ are *n*-by-*n* matrices and $\lambda$ is a scalar. The values of $\lambda$ that satisfy the equation are the *generalized eigenvalues* and the corresponding values of $x$ are the *generalized right eigenvectors*.

If $B$ is nonsingular, the problem could be solved by reducing it to a standard eigenvalue problem,

$$B^{-1}Ax = \lambda x$$

with $A$ replaced by $B^{-1}A$. Because B could be singular, an alternative algorithm, called the QZ method, is necessary.

In MATLAB the function eig solves for the generalized eigenvalues and eigenvectors when used with two input arguments: eig(A,B), if A and B are square matrices, returns a vector containing the generalized eigenvalues. [X,D] = eig(A,B) produces a diagonal matrix D of generalized eigenvalues and a full matrix X whose columns are the corresponding eigenvectors so that A*X = B*X*D.

The eigenvectors are scaled so that the norm of each is 1.0.

## Examples
The matrix

```
b = [ 3 -2 -.9 2*eps
     -2 4 -1 -eps
     -eps/4 eps/2 -1 0
     -.5 -.5 .1 1 ];
```

has elements on the order of roundoff error. It is an example for which the  nobalance option is necessary to compute the eigenvectors correctly. Try the statements:

```
[vb, db] = eig(b)
b*vb-vb*db
[vn, dn] = eig(b, 'nobalance')
b*vn - vn*dn
```

## Algorithm

For real matrices, `eig(X)` uses the EISPACK routines BALANC, BALBAK, ORTRAN, ORTHES, and HQR2. BALANC and BALBAK balance the input matrix. ORTHES converts a real general matrix to Hessenberg form using orthogonal similarity transformations. ORTRAN accumulates the transformations used by ORTHES. HQR2 finds the eigenvalues and eigenvectors of a real upper Hessenberg matrix by the QR method. The EISPACK subroutine HQR2 is modified to make the computation of eigenvectors optional.

When `eig` is used with two arguments, the EISPACK routines QZHES, QZIT, QZVAL, and QZVEC solve for the generalized eigenvalues via the QZ algorithm. They have been modified for the complex case.

When `eig` is used with one complex argument, the solution is computed using the QZ algorithm as `eig(X,eye(X))`. Modifications to the QZ routines handle the special case $B = I$.

For detailed write-ups on these algorithms, see the *EISPACK User's Guide*.

## Diagnostics

If the limit of *30n* iterations is exhausted while seeking an eigenvalue:

```
Solution will not converge.
```

## See also

`qz,hess,schur,balance`

## References

1.  B. T. Smith, J. M. Boyle, J. J. Dongarra, B. S. Garbow, Y. Ikebe, V. C. Klema, C. B. Moler, *Matrix Eigensystem Routines -- EISPACK Guide*, Lecture Notes in Computer Science, volume 6, second edition, Springer-Verlag, 1976.

2.  B. S. Garbow, J. M. Boyle, J. J. Dongarra, C. B. Moler, *Matrix Eigensystem Routines -- EISPACK Guide Extension*, Lecture Notes in Computer Science, volume 51, Springer-Verlag, 1977.

3.  C.B Moler and G.W. Stewart, *An Algorithm for Generalized Matrix Eigenvalue Problems*, SIAM J. Numer. Anal., Vol. 10, No. 2, April 1973.

Reference

# ellip                                                            ellip

**Purpose**

Elliptic or Cauer filter design.

**Synopsis**

```
[b,a] = ellip(n,Rp,Rs,Wn)
[b,a] = ellip(n,Rp,Rs,Wn,'ftype')
[z,p,k] = ellip(...)
[a,b,c,d] = ellip(...)
```

*ftype* can be `high` or `stop`.

**Description**

`ellip` designs lowpass, bandpass, highpass, and bandstop digital elliptic filters. Elliptic filters are equiripple in both the pass- and stopbands. They offer steeper rolloff characteristics than Butterworth and Chebyshev filters, but at the expense of pass- and stopband ripple. In general, elliptic filters, although the most expensive to compute, will meet a given set of filter performance specifications with the lowest filter order.

`[b,a] = ellip(n,Rp,Rs,Wn)` designs an order n lowpass digital elliptic filter with cutoff frequency Wn, Rp decibels of ripple in the passband, and a stopband Rs decibels down from the peak value in the passband. It returns the filter coefficients in length n+1 row vectors b and a. The filter coefficients are ordered in descending powers of $z$:

$$H(z) = \frac{B(z)}{A(z)} = \frac{b(1) + b(2)z^{-1} + \cdots + b(n+1)z^{-n}}{1 + a(2)z^{-1} + \cdots + a(n+1)z^{-n}}$$

Wn, the cutoff frequency, must be a number between 0 and 1, where 1.0 corresponds to half the sample frequency (the Nyquist frequency).

Smaller values of passband ripple Rp and larger values of stopband attenuation Rs both lead to wider transition widths (shallower rolloff characteristics).

If Wn is a two element vector, Wn = [w1 w2], `ellip` returns an order 2n bandpass filter with passband $w1 < \omega < w2$.

`[b,a] = ellip(n,Rp,Rs,Wn,'high')` designs a highpass filter with cutoff frequency Wn.

`[b,a] = ellip(n,Rp,Rs,Wn,'stop')` is an order 2n bandstop filter if Wn is a two element vector Wn = [w1 w2]. The stopband is $w1 < \omega < w2$.

ellip can be used with different numbers of output arguments directly to obtain other realizations of the filter. When used with three output arguments,

```
[z,p,k] = ellip(n,Rp,...)
```

ellip returns the zeros and poles in length n column vectors z and p, and the gain in the scalar k. When used with four output arguments,

```
[A,B,C,D] = ellip(n,Rp,...)
```

ellip returns the filter in state-space form, where A, B, C, and D are defined as,

$$x[n+1] = Ax[n] + Bu[n]$$
$$y[n] = Cx[n] + Du[n]$$

For high order filters, the state-space form is the most numerically accurate, followed by the zero-pole-gain form. The transfer function coefficient form is the least accurate, and numerical problems can arise in filters as low as order fifteen.

## Examples

Consider data sampled at 1000 Hz. Design a ninth order lowpass elliptic filter with 0.5 dB of ripple in the passband and a stopband 20 dB down at 300 Hz. Plot its frequency response:

```
[b,a] = ellip(9, 0.5, 20, 300/500);
[h,w] = freqz(b,a,128);
f = w*500/pi;
semilogy(f,abs(h)), plot(f,angle(h)*180/pi)
```

Design a tenth order bandpass elliptic filter with a passband from 100 to 200Hz and plot its unit sample response:

```
n = 5; Rp = 0.5; Rs = 20;
Wn = [100 200]/500;
[b,a] = ellip(n, Rp, Rs, Wn)
y = filter(b,a,[1 zeros(1,100)]);
plot(y,'o')
```

## Algorithm

ellip is an M-file in the *Signal Processing Toolbox*.  It uses a five-step algorithm:

1.  Find lowpass analog prototype poles, zeros, and gain using the function ellipap.

2.  Convert poles, zeros, and gain into state-space form.

3.  Transform lowpass filter to bandpass, highpass, or bandstop filter of desired cutoff frequencies.  A state-space transformation is employed.

4.  Use bilinear to convert the analog filter into a digital filter using a bilinear transformation with frequency prewarping.  Careful frequency adjustment guarantees that the analog filters and the digital filters will have the same frequency response magnitude at $\omega_n$ or $\omega_1$ and $\omega_2$.

5.  Convert the state-space filter back to transfer function, or pole-zero form, as required.

## See also

cheby2, butter, ellip, buttap, remez

## Purpose

Elliptic analog lowpass filter prototype.

## Synopsis

```
[z,p,k] = ellipap(n,Rp,Rs)
```

## Description

`[z,p,k] = ellipap(n,Rp,Rs)` returns the zeros, poles, and gain of an order n normalized elliptic analog lowpass filter prototype, with Rp decibels of ripple in the passband, and a stopband Rs decibels down from the peak value in the passband. The zeros and poles are returned in length n column vectors z and p, and the gain in scalar k. If n is odd, z is length n-1. The transfer function is

$$H(s) = \frac{z(s)}{p(s)} = k\frac{(s - z(1))(s - z(2))...(s - z(n))}{(s - p(1))(s - p(2))...(s - p(n))}$$

Elliptic filters are equiripple in both pass- and stopbands. They offer steeper rolloff characteristics than Butterworth and Chebyshev filters, but at the expense of pass- and stopband ripple. Of the four classical filter types, elliptic filters usually meet a given set of filter performance specifications with the lowest filter order.

The cutoff frequency $\omega_0$ of the elliptic filter is set to 1.0 for a normalized result.

## Algorithm

`ellipap` is an M-file in the *Signal Processing Toolbox* that uses the algorithm outlined in [1]. It employs the M-file `ellipk` to calculate the complete elliptic integral of the first kind and the M-file `ellipj` to calculate Jacobi elliptic functions.

## See also

`ellip`, `buttap`, `cheb1ap`, `cheb2ap`

## References

T. W. Parks and C. S. Burrus, *Digital Filter Design*, chapter 7, John Wiley & Sons, 1987.

Reference

## Purpose

Jacobian elliptic functions.

## Synopsis

```
[sn,cn,dn] = ellipj(u,m)
```

## Description

`[sn,cn,dn] = ellipj(u,m)` returns the Jacobian elliptic functions *sn*, *cn* and *dn* for the values in u evaluated at the corresponding parameters in m. Inputs u and m may contain scalars or matrices, but if they are both matrices, they must be the same size.

The Jacobian elliptic functions are defined in terms of the integral

$$u = \int_0^\phi \frac{d\theta}{(1 - m\sin^2\theta)^{1/2}}$$

Then

$$sn(u) = \sin(\phi), \quad cn(u) = \cos(\phi), \quad dn(u) = (1 - m\sin^2(\phi))^{1/2}$$

The angle $\phi$ is also called the amplitude, or $am(u)$.

Sometimes the elliptic functions are defined differently, which can lead to some confusion. The alternate definitions are usually in terms of the modulus *k*, which is related to *m* by

$$k^2 = m = \sin^2(\alpha)$$

The Jacobian elliptic functions obey many mathematical identities; for a good sample, see [1].

The accuracy of the result is eps; the value of eps can be changed for a less accurate, but more quickly computed answer.

## Algorithm

The Jacobian elliptic functions are computed using the method of the arithmetic-geometric mean [1]. Start with the triplet of numbers,

$$a_0 = 1, \; b_0 = \sqrt{1-m}, \; c_0 = \sqrt{m}$$

Compute successive iterations of $a_i$, $b_i$, and $c_i$ with:

$$a_i = \frac{1}{2}(a_{i-1} + b_{i-1})$$
$$b_i = (a_{i-1}b_{i-1})^{1/2}$$
$$c_i = \frac{1}{2}(a_{i-1} - b_{i-1})$$

stopping at iteration $n$ when $c_n \approx 0$, within the tolerance specified by eps.

Next, calculate $\phi_n = 2^n a_n u$ in radians and calculate $\phi_{n-1}, ..., \phi_1, \phi_0$ using

$$\sin(2\phi_{n-1} - \phi_n) = \frac{c_n}{a_n}\sin(\phi_n)$$

being careful to unwrap the phases $\phi_i$ correctly. The Jacobian elliptic functions are then simply

$$sn(u|m) = \sin\phi_0$$
$$cn(u|m) = \cos\phi_0$$
$$dn(u|m) = (1 - m\ sn(u|m)^2)^{1/2}$$

## Limitations

ellipj is limited to the input domain $0 \leq m \leq 1$. Other values of $m$ may be mapped into this range using the transformations described in [1], equations 16.10 and 16.11.

## See also

ellipk

## References

M. Abramowitz and I.A. Stegun, *Handbook of Mathematical Functions*, Dover Publications, 1965, 17.6.

---

**Purpose**

Complete elliptic integral of the first kind.

**Synopsis**

    ellipk(1,m)

**Description**

ellipk(1,m) returns the complete elliptic integral of the first kind for the elements of m. The complete elliptic integral of the first kind is:

$$F(\phi|m) = \int_0^\phi (1 - \sin^2\alpha\sin^2\theta)^{-\frac{1}{2}} d\theta$$
$$= \int_0^{\sin\phi} \frac{dt}{\sqrt{((1 - t^2)(1 - mt^2))}}$$

where $\sin\phi = sn(u,m)$ and $\phi = 2\pi$. Some definitions of $F$ use the modulus $k = \sin\alpha$ instead of the parameter $m$. The relationships are:

$$F(\phi\backslash\alpha) = F(\phi|m) = K(\alpha)$$
$$k^2 = m$$

The accuracy of the result is eps; the value of eps can be changed for a less accurate, but more quickly computed answer.

**Algorithm**

The elliptic integral is computed using the method of the arithmetic-geometric mean described in [1], section 17.6. Start with the triplet of numbers,

$$a_0 = 1, \; b_0 = \sqrt{1-m}, \; c_0 = \sqrt{m}$$

Compute successive iterations of $a_i$, $b_i$ and $c_i$ with:

$$a_i = \frac{1}{2}(a_{i-1} + b_{i-1})$$
$$b_i = (a_{i-1}b_{i-1})^{1/2}$$
$$c_i = \frac{1}{2}(a_{i-1} - b_{i-1})$$

stopping at iteration $n$ when $c_n \approx 0$, within the tolerance specified by `eps`. The complete elliptic integral of the first kind is then:

$$K(\alpha) = \frac{\pi}{2a_n}$$

## Limitations

`ellipk` is limited to the input domain $0 \le m \le 1$.

## See also

`ellipj`

## References

M. Abramowitz and I.A. Stegun, *Handbook of Mathematical Functions*, Dover Publications, 1965, 17.6.

Reference

## Purpose

Terminate `for`, `while`, and `if` statements.

## Synopsis

```
while s
  statements end
```

## Description

`end` terminates the scope of `for`, `while`, and `if` statements. Without an `end`, `for`, `while`, and `if` wait for further input. Each `end` is paired with the closest previous unpaired `for`, `while`, or `if` and serves to delimit its scope.

## Examples

This example shows `end` used with `for` and `if`.

```
for i=1:n
      for j=1:n
            if i == j
                  a(i,j) = 2;
            elseif abs(i-j) == 1
                  a(i,j) = -1;
            else
                  a(i,j) = 0;
            end
      end
end
```

The indentation is important only to human readers.

## See also

```
while, if, for, break, return
```

## Purpose

Error function and inverse error function.

## Synopsis

```
erf(x), erf(x,'high')
erf(x,y), erf(x,y,'high')
inverf(x)
```

## Description

The error function $erf(x)$ is the integral of the Gaussian distribution function from 0 to $x$:

$$erf(x) = \frac{2}{\sqrt{\pi}} \int_0^x e^{-t^2} \, dt$$

The error function is related to the integral of the normal probability distribution function by

$$\frac{1}{\sqrt{2\pi}} \int_0^x e^{-\frac{1}{2}t^2} \, dt = \frac{1}{2} erf(\frac{x}{\sqrt{2}})$$

`erf(x)` returns the value of the error function for each value of `x`, accurate to about 1e-5.

`erf(x,y)` returns the value of the generalized error function. That is,

$$erf(x,y) = \frac{2}{\sqrt{\pi}} \int_x^y e^{-t^2} \, dt = erf(y) - erf(x)$$

If `x` is a scalar, `erf(x,y)` is calculated for each element of `y` with constant `x`. The same is true for scalar `y` and matrix `x`.

`erf(x,'high')` and `erf(x,y,'high')` return very accurate, but slowly computed, values of the error function.

`erf(x,Inf)` is the complementary error function.

`erf(-Inf,y)` integrates from minus infinity.

`inverf(x)` returns the value of the inverse error function for each value of `x`, accurate to about 1e-5.

## Algorithm

`erf` and `inverf` are M-files in the *MATLAB Toolbox*.

**Purpose**

Add errorbars to a plot.

**Synopsis**

```
errorbar(x,y,e)
```

**Description**

`errorbar(x,y,e)` adds errorbars to a preexisting plot of vector x versus vector y. e must be a vector the same size as x and y containing the lengths of the errorbars to be drawn above and below each (x,y) pair. Error bars are therefore 2*e in height.

**Examples**

Draw errorbars with unit standard deviation on a sine curve:

```
x = 1:10;
y = sin(x);
plot(x,y)
e = ones(y);
errorbar(x,y,e)
```

**Algorithm**

`errorbar` is an M-file in the *MATLAB Toolbox*.

**See also**

```
plot, std
```

## Purpose

Text macro facility.

## Synopsis

```
eval(t)
```

## Description

`eval(t)` executes the text contained in `t`. If `STRING` is the source text for any MATLAB expression or statement, then

```
t = 'STRING';
```

encodes the text in `t`. Typing `t` prints the text and

```
eval(t)
```

causes the text to be interpreted, either as a statement or as a factor in an expression. If the text is an expression, `eval` returns the result, which can be assigned to a variable. For example, these statements assign $\pi$ to `p`:

```
t = '4*atan(1)';
p = eval(t);
```

The text macro facility is particularly useful as a mechanism for passing function names to *M-function files*. For example, see the file `funm.m` in the *MATLAB Toolbox*.

## Examples

Generate the Hilbert matrix of order *n*:

```
t = '1/(i+j-1)';
for i = 1:n
    for j = 1:n
        a(i,j) = eval(t);
    end
end
```

Reference

Here is an example showing indexed text:

```
S = ['x = 3              '
     'y = 4              '
     'z = sqrt(x*x+y*y)'];
for k=1:3
    eval(S(k,:))
end
```

It is necessary that the strings making up the "rows" of the "matrix" S have the same lengths.

eval returns multiple output arguments if it is used on a function that does so as well:

```
s = 'eig(a)';
[v,d] = eval(s)
```

**See also**

```
M-files, setstr
```

## Purpose

Exponential, logarithmic, and square root functions.

## Synopsis

```
exp(x)
log(x)
log10(x)
sqrt(x)
```

## Description

`exp`, `log`, and `log10` are elementary functions that operate elementwise on matrices. Their domain includes complex numbers that can lead to unexpected results if used unintentionally.

`exp(X)` returns $e^x$ for each of the elements of `X`. For complex $z = x + iy$, the complex exponential is returned:

$$e^z = e^x(cos(y) + i\ sin(y))$$

`log(X)` is the natural logarithm of the elements of `X`. For complex or negative `z`, the complex logarithm is returned:

$$log(z) = log(abs(z)) + i\ atan2(y,x)$$

`log10(X)` is $log_{10}$ of the elements of `X`.

`sqrt(X)` is the square root of the elements of `X`. Complex results are produced for the elements of `X` that are negative or complex.

## Examples

The statement `log(-1)` is a clever way to generate $\pi$:

```
ans   =
     0.0000 + 3.1416i
```

## See also

```
trig, expm, logm, sqrtm, funm, abs, angle
```

## Purpose

Matrix exponential and other matrix functions.

## Synopsis

```
expm(X)
logm(X)
sqrtm(X)
funm(X,'function')
```

For `funm`, the *function* can be `log`, `sqrt`, `sin`, `cos`, or any other elementary function.

## Description

`expm(X)` is the matrix exponential of X. Complex results are produced if X has nonpositive eigenvalues. `expm` uses a Pade expansion after scaling X for more reliable computation. `funm` can also be used, but `expm` gives a much faster and sometimes more accurate result.

`funm` can evaluate more general matrix functions. For matrix arguments X, `funm(X,'fun')` evaluates the matrix function specified by *fun* using Parlett's method [1]. For example, `funm(X,'exp')` calculates the matrix exponential, `funm(X,'log')` the matrix logarithm, and `funm(X,'sqrt')` the matrix square root.

`sqrtm(X)` and `logm(X)` are equivalent to `funm(X,'sqrt')` and `funm(X,'log')`.

## Algorithm

`expm` is a built-in function, but it uses the Pade approximation algorithm expressed in the file `expm1.m` in the *MATLAB Toolbox*.

A second method of calculating the matrix exponential is via a Taylor series approximation. This method can be found in the file `expm2.m`.

A third way of calculating the matrix exponential, found in the file `expm3.m`, is to diagonalize the matrix, apply the function to the individual eigenvalues, and then transform back.

Many algorithms for computing `expm(x)` are described and compared in references [1] and [2]. Our built-in method, `expm1`, is essentially method 3 of [2].

`funm` evaluates other matrix functions using Parlett's method [1], and is an M-file in the *MATLAB Toolbox*.

**References**

1.      G. H. Golub and C. F. Van Loan, *Matrix Computation*, Johns Hopkins University Press, 1983, p. 384.

2.      C. B. Moler and C. F. Van Loan, "Nineteen Dubious Ways to Compute the Exponential of a Matrix", *SIAM Review 20*, pp. 801-836, 1979.

Reference

## Purpose

Function evaluation.

## Synopsis

```
feval('function',x1,...,xn)
[y1,y2,...] = feval('function',x1,...,xn)
```

## Description

`feval('fun',x1,...,xn)` evaluates `fun(x1,...,xn)`.

`[y1,y2...] = feval('function',x1,...)` returns multiple output arguments.

## Examples

The statements

```
[V,D] = feval('eig',a)
[V,D] = eig(a)
```

are equivalent. Usually `feval` finds application in functions that accept string arguments specifying function names. For example, the function

```
function plotf(fun,x)
y = feval(fun,x);
plot(x,y)
```

can be used to graph arbitrary elementary functions:

```
x = 0:.1:10;
plotf('sin',x), plotf('cos',x), plotf('exp',x)
```

See `funm`, `ode23`, and `fmin` for other examples.

## Algorithm

`feval` is built into the MATLAB interpreter.

## See also

```
eval
```

## Purpose

1-D and 2-D fast Fourier transforms and inverses.

## Synopsis

```
fft(x),  fft(x,n)
ifft(x),  ifft(x,n)
fft2(X),  ifft2(X)
fftshift(X)
```

## Description

fft(x) is the discrete Fourier transform of vector x, computed with a fast Fourier transform algorithm (FFT). If X is a matrix, fft(X) is the FFT of each column of the matrix.

fft(x,n) is the n-point FFT. If the length of x is less than n, x is padded with trailing zeros to length n. If the length of x is greater than n, the sequence x is truncated. When X is a matrix, the length of the columns are adjusted in the same manner.

The fft function employs a radix-2 fast Fourier transform algorithm if the length of the sequence is a power of two, and a slower mixed-radix algorithm if it is not.

ifft(x) is the inverse fast Fourier transform of vector x.  ifft(x,n) is the n-point inverse FFT.

The two functions implement the transform - inverse transform pair given by:

$$X(k+1) = \sum_{n=0}^{N-1} x(n+1) W_N^{kn}$$
$$x(n+1) = 1/N \sum_{k=0}^{N-1} X(k+1) W_N^{-kn}$$

where $W_N = e^{-j(2\pi/N)}$ and $N = length(x)$. Note that the series is written in an unorthodox way, running over $n+1$ and $k+1$ instead of the usual $n$ and $k$ because MATLAB vectors run from 1 to $N$ instead of from 0 to $N-1$.

Suppose a sequence of $N$ points is obtained at a sample frequency of $f_s$. Then, for up to the Nyquist frequency, or point $n = N/2+1$, the relationship between the bin number and the actual frequency is:

$$f = (bin\_number - 1)*f_s/N$$

fft2 and ifft2 perform the two-dimensional FFT and inverse.

Reference

fftshift(x) rearranges the outputs of fft and fft2 by moving the zero frequency component to the center of the spectrum, which is sometimes a more convenient form. For vectors, fftshift(x) returns a vector with the left and right halves swapped. For matrices, fftshift(X) swaps quadrants one and three with quadrants two and four.

## Examples

A common use of Fourier transforms is to find the frequency components of a signal buried in a noisy time domain signal. Consider data sampled at 1000 Hz. Form a signal containing 50 Hz and 120 Hz and corrupt it with some zero-mean random noise,

```
t = 0:0.001:0.6;
x = sin(2*pi*50*t) + sin(2*pi*120*t);
rand('normal')
y = x + 2*rand(t);
plot(y(1:50))
```

It is difficult to identify the frequency components from looking at the original signal. Converting to the frequency domain, the discrete Fourier transform of the noisy signal y is found by taking the 512-point fast Fourier transform (FFT):

```
Y = fft(y,512);
```

The power spectral density, a measurement of the energy at various frequencies, is:

```
Pyy = Y .* conj(Y) / 512;
```

The first 256 points (the other 256 points are symmetric) can be graphed on a meaningful frequency axis with:

```
f = 1000*(0:255)/512;
plot(f,Pyy(1:256))
```

## Algorithm

ifft, fft2, ifft2, and fftshift are M-files while fft is built into the interpreter. When the sequence length is a power of two, a high-speed radix-2 fast Fourier transform algorithm is employed. The radix-2 FFT routine is optimized to perform a real FFT if the input sequence is purely real, otherwise it computes the complex FFT. This causes a real power-of-two FFT to be about 40% faster than a complex FFT of the same length.

When the sequence length is not an exact power of two, a non-power-of-two algorithm finds the prime factors of the sequence length and computes the mixed-radix discrete Fourier transforms of the shorter sequences.

The time it takes to compute an FFT varies greatly depending upon the sequence length. The FFT of sequences whose lengths have many prime factors is computed quickly; the FFT of those that have few is not. Sequences whose lengths are prime numbers are reduced to the raw (and slow) DFT algorithm. For this reason it is generally better to stay with power-of-two FFTs unless other circumstances dictate that this cannot be done. For example, on one machine a 4096-point real FFT takes 2.1 seconds and a complex FFT of the same length takes 3.7 seconds. The FFTs of neighboring sequences of length 4095 and 4097, however, take 7 seconds and 58 seconds, respectively.

**See also**

spectrum, specplot, filter, freqz, dftmtx (in the *Signals and Systems Toolbox*).

## Purpose

Filter data.

## Synopsis

```
y = filter(b, a, x)
[y, zf] = filter(b, a, x, zi)
```

## Description

filter filters data using a digital filter. The filter realization is the *transposed direct form II* structure [1], which can handle both FIR and IIR filters. Access to initial and final conditions is available.

y = filter(b, a, x) filters the data in vector x with the filter described by coefficient vectors a and b to create filtered data vector y. The operation performed by filter is described in the *time domain* by the difference equation:

$$y(n) = b(1)x(n) + b(2)x(n-1) + \ldots + b(nb+1)x(n-nb)$$
$$- a(2)y(n-1) - \ldots - a(na+1)y(n-na)$$

An equivalent representation is the $z$-transform or *frequency-domain* description:

$$Y(z) = \frac{b(1) + b(2)z^{-1} + \cdots + b(nb+1)z^{-nb}}{1 + a(2)z^{-1} + \cdots + a(na+1)z^{-na}}X(z)$$

If $a(1) \neq 1$, the filter coefficients are normalized by $a(1)$.

The block diagram for the transposed direct form II realization of filter is:

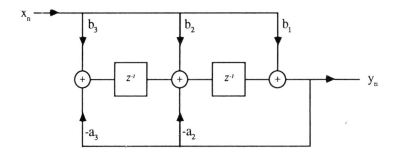

When used with two left hand arguments, `filter` returns the final values of the delays (states):

```
[y,zf] = filter(b, a, x)
```

When used with an extra right hand argument, initial conditions on the delays are specified:

```
y = filter(b, a, x, zi)
```

The size of the initial/final condition vector is *max(na,nb)*.

## Examples

Find and graph the *n*-point unit impulse response of a digital filter:

```
x = [1 zeros(1,n-1)];
y = filter(b,a,x);
plot(y,'o')
```

Filter two sequences, the second of which starts with initial conditions left over from the first:

```
[y1,z] = filter(b,a,x1);
y2 = filter(b,a,x2,z);
```

Filter a sequence with initial conditions that reduce the startup transient by matching the DC offset of the first element of the signal:

```
z = fliplr(cumsum(fliplr(b-a)))*x(1); z(1) = [ ];
y = filter(b,a,x,z);
```

Eliminate all phase changes by refiltering the data, in reverse:

```
y = filter(b,a,x);
y = filter(b,a,y(n:-1:1));
```

## Algorithm

`filter` is a built-in function.

**Diagnostics**

If $a(1) = 0$, `filter` produces the error message:

```
First denominator coefficient must be nonzero.
```

If the initial condition vector is not length $max(na, nb)$:

```
Initial condition vector has incorrect dimensions.
```

**References**

A.V. Oppenheim and R.W. Schafer, *Digital Signal Processing*, Prentice Hall, 1975, page 155.

## Purpose

Find indices of the nonzero elements in a vector.

## Synopsis

```
find(A)
```

## Description

`find(A)` returns a vector containing the indices of the nonzero elements of vector A. If none are found, `find` returns an empty matrix (a matrix of size 0-by-0).

If A is a matrix, `find` regards A as `A(:)`, which is the long column vector formed from the columns of A.

## Examples

The statement

```
i = find(x>100)
```

returns the indices of x where the elements of x are greater than 100.

The statements

```
i = find(isnan(x));
x(i) = zeros(i);
```

replace all occurrences of NaN in x with zero. It will work even if x is a matrix, because a matrix can be referenced as a long column vector with a single subscript.

## See also

```
<, <=, >, >=, ==, ~=, isnan, finite, isempty
```

Reference

**Purpose**

    Flip matrices left-right and up-down.

**Synopsis**

```
fliplr(x)
flipud(x)
```

**Description**

    `fliplr(X)` returns X with columns flipped in the left/right direction.

```
a =
    1 2 3
    4 5 6

fliplr(a) =

    3 2 1
    6 5 4
```

    `flipud(X)` returns X with rows flipped in the up/down direction.

```
a =
    1 4
    2 5
    3 6

flipud(a) =
    3 6
    2 5
    1 4
```

**Algorithm**

    `fliplr` and `flipud` are simple M-files in the *MATLAB Toolbox*.

**See also**

```
reshape, rot90, :,   '
```

## Purpose

Count of floating point operations.

## Synopsis

```
flops
flops(0)
```

## Description

`flops` returns the cumulative number of floating point operations.

`flops(0)` resets the count to zero.

It is not feasible to count absolutely all floating point operations, but most of the important ones are counted. Additions and subtractions are each one flop if real and two if complex. Multiplications and divisions count one flop each if the result is real and six flops if it is complex. Elementary functions count one if real and more if complex.

## Examples

If A and B are real $n$-by-$n$ matrices, some typical flop counts for different operations are:

| Operations | Flop Count |
|------------|------------|
| A + B      | $n^2$      |
| A * B      | $2n^3$     |
| A ^ 100    | $99*2n^3$  |
| lu(A)      | $(2/3)n^3$ |

## Purpose

Minimum of a function of one variable.

## Synopsis

```
fmin('function', x1, x2)
fmin('function', x1, x2, tol)
fmin('function', x1, x2, tol, trace)
```

## Description

fmin finds the minimum of a function of one variable within a fixed interval.

x = fmin('fun', x1, x2) returns the value of x that minimizes fun(x) on the interval x1 $<x<$ x2. The solution is accurate to within a relative error of 1e-3 or better.

fmin('fun', x1, x2, tol) returns an answer accurate to within a relative error of tol.

If the final argument trace is nonzero, fmin displays the algorithm steps.

## Examples

A minimum of $sin(x)$ occurs at:

```
x = fmin('sin',0,2*pi)
x =
      4.7118
```

The value of the function at the minimum is:

```
y = sin(x)
y =
      -1.0000
```

To find the minimum of the function

$$f(x) = (x-3)^2 - 1$$

on the interval (0,5), write an M-file called f.m

```
function y = f(x)
y = (x-3).^2 - 1;
```

and invoke `fmin`

```
x = fmin('f', 0, 5)
x =
      3
```

The value of the function at the minimum is:

```
y = f(x)

y =
      -1
```

## Algorithm

`fmin` is an M-file in the *MATLAB Toolbox* that uses the algorithm of the same name from [1].

## See also

`fmins, \, nnls, fsolve, fzero`

## References

G.E. Forsythe, M.A. Malcolm, and C.B. Moler, *Computer Methods for Mathematical Computations*, Prentice Hall, 1976.

## Purpose

Minimum of a multivariable function.

## Synopsis

```
fmins('function', x0)
fmins('function', x0, tol)
fmins('function', x0, tol, trace)
[x, count] = fmins(...)
```

## Description

fmins finds the minimum of a function of several variables, starting from an initial estimate. In some circles this is referred to as "unconstrained nonlinear optimization."

x = fmins('fun', x0) returns vector x that minimizes function fun(x), starting from the guess in vector x0. fun(x) is a scalar output cost function with a vector input. The solution is accurate to within a relative error of 1e-3 or better.

fmins('fun', x0, tol) returns an answer accurate to within a relative error of tol.

If the final argument trace is nonzero, the algorithm steps are displayed.

## Examples

Generate exponentially decaying 5 Hz sinusoid data, $e^{-4t}\sin(10\pi t)$:

```
T = 0:.01:1;
p = [4; 5];
Data = exp(-p(1)*T).*sin(2*pi*p(2)*T);
```

To do a nonlinear least squares curve fit to $e^{-at}\sin(2\pi bt)$, write an M-file that returns the sum of the squared residuals between a model with parameters in vector p and the data.

```
function q = decay(p)
a = p(1); b = p(2);
q = exp(-a*T).*sin(2*pi*b*T) - Data;
q = sum(q.^2);
```

Define variables T and Data as global, and invoke fmins:

```
global T Data
est = fmins('decay', [3 6]')

est =
      3.9998
      5.0001
```

## Algorithm

fmins, an M-file in the *MATLAB Toolbox*, is an implementation of the Nelder-Meade simplex algorithm, described in detail in [1]. It is a direct search method for finding a function's minimum. Suppose $f(x_1, x_2, ...x_n)$ is the function to be minimized. Then, at each iteration, evaluate $f$ at $n+1$ specially selected points $\mathbf{y}_1$, $\mathbf{y}_2$, ..., $\mathbf{y}_{n+1}$ to choose the direction in which to step. These points can be thought of as vertices of an $n$-dimensional simplex. A trial point is accepted or rejected based on $f$ at that point relative to $f(\mathbf{y}_1)$, $f(\mathbf{y}_n)$, and $f(\mathbf{y}_{n+1})$. Iteration continues until the diameter of the simplex is less than tol.

## Limitations

For functions with multiple local minima, it is important to choose the starting guess x0 carefully or fmins may find a minimum different from the one you are seeking. fmins is best for finding the minimum of functions with five or fewer unknown parameters.

## See also

\, nnls, fmin, fsolve

## References

J. E. Dennis, Jr. and D. J. Woods, *New Computing Environments: Microcomputers in Large-Scale Computing*, edited by A. Wouk, SIAM, 1987, pp. 116-122.

## Purpose

Repeat statements a specific number of times.

## Synopsis

```
for  v = e
   statements
end
```

## Description

for allows statements to be repeated a specific number of times. The general format is:

```
for  variable = expression
      statement

             . . .
      statement
end
```

The *columns* of the *expression* are stored one at a time in the variable while the following statements, up to the end, are executed.

In practice, the *expression* is almost always of the form x:y, in which case its columns are simply scalars.

## Examples

Assume n has already been assigned a value:

1. The Hilbert matrix:

```
for  i=1:n,
        for  j=1:n,
                a(i,j)  =  1/(i+j-1);
        end
end
```

2. Step s with increments of –0.1:

```
for  s  =  1.0:  -0.1:  0.0,...  end
```

3. Successively set e to the unit n-vectors:

```
for e = eye(n), ... end
```

4. The line:

```
for V = A, ... end
```

has the same effect as

```
for j = 1:n, V = A(:,j); ... end
```

except j is also set here.

## See also

```
while, if, end, break, return
```

Reference

**Purpose**

Output display format.

**Description**

format controls the output format. By default, MATLAB displays numbers in a "short" format with 5 decimal digits. format switches between different display formats:

| COMMAND | RESULT | EXAMPLE |
|---|---|---|
| format short | 5 digit scaled fixed point | 1.3333 |
| format long | 15 digit scaled fixed point | 1.33333333333333 |
| format short e | 5 digit floating point | 1.3333E+000 |
| format long e | 15 digit floating point | 1.33333333333333E+000 |
| format hex | Hexadecimal | 3FF5555555555555 |
| format + | +,– format | + |
| format bank | Fixed dollars and cents | 1.33 |

format compact suppresses excess line-feeds and results in a slightly more compact display. format loose reverts to the more airy display. These two commands do not affect the numeric format.

format, by itself, returns to the default formats.

**Examples**

The + format displays +, –, and blank symbols for positive, negative, and zero real elements. It is especially useful for displaying large matrices. Here is a simple example on a small matrix:

```
format +
E = ones(5);   P = triu(E) - tril(E)
P =
    ++++
  - +++
  -- ++
  --- +
  ----
```

**See also**

num2str, sprintf, fprintf

## Purpose

Frequency response of analog filters.

## Synopsis

```
h = freqs(b,a,w)
```

## Description

H = freqs(b,a,w) returns the complex frequency response, $H(j\omega)$, of the analog filter (Laplace transform),

$$H(s) = \frac{B(s)}{A(s)} = \frac{b(1)s^{nb} + b(2)s^{(nb-1)} + \cdots + b(nb+1)}{a(1)s^{na} + a(2)s^{(na-1)} + \cdots + a(na+1)}$$

given the numerator and denominator coefficients in vectors b and a. The frequency response is evaluated along the imaginary axis in the complex plane at the frequencies specified in real vector w.

## Examples

Given a transfer function

$$H(s) = \frac{.2s^2 + .3s + 1}{s^2 + .4s + 1}$$

find and graph its frequency response:

```
a = [1 0.4 1];  b = [0.2 0.3 1];
w = logspace(-1,1);
h = freqs(b,a,w);
mag = abs(h);  phase = angle(h);
loglog(f,mag), semilogx(f,phase)
```

To convert to Hz, degrees, and decibels,

```
f = w/(2*pi);
phase = phase*180/pi;
mag = 20*log10(mag);
```

Reference

---

### Algorithm

`freqs` is an M-file in the *Signal Processing Toolbox*. It evaluates the polynomials at each frequency point, and then divides the numerator response by the denominator response. The complete algorithm is:

```
s = sqrt(-1)*w;
h = polyval(b,s) ./ polyval(a,s);
```

### See also

`freqz, logspace, abs, angle`

## Purpose

Frequency response of digital filters.

## Synopsis

```
[h,w] = freqz(b,a,n)
[h,w] = freqz(b,a,n,'whole')
h = freqz(b,a,w)
```

## Description

`[h,w] = freqz(b,a,n)` returns the *n*-point complex frequency response, $H(e^{j\omega})$, of the digital filter,

$$H(z) = \frac{B(z)}{A(z)} = \frac{b(1) + b(2)z^{-1} + \cdots + b(nb+1)z^{-nb}}{a(1) + a(2)z^{-1} + \cdots + a(na+1)z^{-na}}$$

given the numerator and denominator coefficients in vectors b and a. `freqz` returns both h, the complex frequency response, and w, a vector containing the n frequency points. The frequency response is evaluated at *n* points equally spaced around the upper half of the unit circle, so w contains n points between 0 and $\pi$.

It is best, although not necessary, to choose a value for n that is an exact power of two, because this allows fast computation using an FFT algorithm.

`freqz(b,a,n,'whole')` uses *n*-points around the *whole* unit circle (from 0 to $2\pi$).

`freqz(b,a,w)` returns the frequency response at the arbitrary frequencies designated in vector w (they should still be between 0 and $2\pi$, however).

## Examples

The output of `freqz` is a complex vector. The magnitude and phase, in this example from a Butterworth filter, can be graphed on a frequency axis from 0 to $\pi$ with:

```
[b,a] = butter(5,.2);
[h,w] = freqz(b,a,128);
mag = abs(h); phase = angle(h);
semilogy(w,mag), plot(w,phase)
```

Reference

To graph on a frequency axis running from 0 to 1, where 1 corresponds to the Nyquist frequency, form a normalized frequency vector. This can be done by dividing the w output of `freqz` by $\pi$,

```
w = w/pi;
semilogy(w,mag), plot(w,phase)
```

or by creating the vector from scratch:

```
n = 128; w = (0:n-1)/n;
semilogy(w,mag), plot(w,phase)
```

To graph with a frequency axis in units of Hz, multiply the normalized w by half the sample frequency.

## Algorithm

`freqz` is an M-file that uses an FFT algorithm when invoked with argument n. The frequency response is computed as the ratio of the transformed numerator and denominator coefficients, padded with zeros out to the desired length:

```
h = fft(b,n)./fft(a,n)
```

If $n$ is not a power of two, the FFT algorithm is not as efficient and may cause long computation times.

When `freqz` is invoked with frequency vector w, `freqz` evaluates the polynomials at each frequency point, using Horner's method of polynomial evaluation, and then divides the numerator response by the denominator response.

## See also

```
filter, fft, freqs logspace, angle, abs
```

## Purpose

Extensibility, programming, functions, and procedures.

## Description

### Script files:

A *script file* is an external file that contains a sequence of MATLAB statements. By typing the filename, subsequent MATLAB input is obtained from the file. *Script files* must have a filename extension of .m (except on the Macintosh, where the extension is optional). To make a *script file* into a function, see below.

### Function files:

New functions may be added to MATLAB's vocabulary if they are expressed in terms of other existing functions. The commands and functions that comprise the new function are put in a file whose name defines the name of the new function, with a filename extension of .m appended. A line is put at the top of the file that contains the syntax definition for the new function. For example, the existence of a file on disk called stat.m with:

```
function  [mean,stdev] = stat(x)
n = length(x);
mean = sum(x) ./ n;
stdev = sqrt(sum(x^2) / n - mean^2);
```

defines a new function called stat that calculates the mean and standard deviation of a vector. The variables within the body of the function are all local variables.

When a function is used that MATLAB does not recognize, it will search for a file by the same name on disk. If it is found, the function is compiled into memory for subsequent use.

If echo is enabled, the file will be interpreted instead of compiled so that each input line can be viewed as it is executed. clear can be used to remove the function from memory.

In general, if you input the name of something to MATLAB, for example by typing foo, the MATLAB interpreter:

1.    Looks to see if foo is a variable.

2.    Checks if foo is a built-in function.

3.  Looks in the current directory for a file named `foo.m`.

4.  Looks in the directories specified by the environment symbol MATLABPATH for a file named `foo.m`.

## Examples

A function called `pinv` that finds the pseudoinverse of a matrix is:

```
function X = pinv(A,tol)
% Pseudoinverse,
% Ignore singular values <= tol.
% Default tol = max(size(A)) * s(1) * eps.
[U,S,V] = svd(A);
S = diag(S);
if (nargin == 1)
   tol = max(size(A)) * S(1) * eps;
end
r = sum(S > tol);
if (r == 0)
   X = zeros(A');
else
   S = diag(ones(r,1)./S(1:r));
   X = V(:,1:r)*S*U(:,1:r)';
end
```

## See also

type, echo, nargin, nargout, what, MATLABPATH

## Purpose

Zero of a function of one variable.

## Synopsis

```
fzero('function', x0)
fzero('function', x0, tol)
fzero('function', x0, tol, trace)
```

## Description

fzero('fun', x0) finds a zero of the function fun(x) that is near x0.

fzero('fun', x0, tol) returns an answer accurate to within a relative error of tol. The default value for tol is eps.

Information at each iteration is displayed if the optional fourth argument, trace, is nonzero.

## Examples

Calculate $\pi$ by finding the zero of the sine function near 3:

```
x = fzero('sin', 3)
x =

    3.1416
```

To find a zero of the function $f(x) = (x-3)^2 - 1$, write an M-file called f.m:

```
function y = f(x)
y = (x-3).^2 -1;
```

and use fzero to find the zero near 1:

```
z = fzero('f',1)

z =
    2
```

The function has a second zero, which can be found by starting from a different point:

```
z2 = fzero('f',5)

z2 =
     4
```

## Algorithm

`fzero` is an M-file in the *MATLAB Toolbox*. The original algorithm was originated by T. Dekker. An Algol 60 version, with some improvements, is given in [1]. A Fortran version, upon which the `fzero` M-file is based, is in [2].

## See also

`zerodemo` M-file in the *MATLAB Toolbox*.
`roots, fsolve, fmin`

## References

1.      R. Brent, *Algorithms for Minimization Without Derivatives*, Prentice Hall, 1973.

2.      G. E. Forsythe, M. A. Malcolm and C. B. Moler, *Computer Methods for Mathematical Computations*, Prentice Hall, 1976.

---

## Purpose

A "gallery" of interesting matrices.

## Synopsis

```
gallery(n)
```

## Description

`gallery` is a function that returns some famous, and not so famous, test matrices.

`gallery(n)` returns an *n*-by-*n* matrix with some special property. Only $n$ = 3, 5, 8, and 21 are available at this time.

`gallery(3)` is a matrix that is poorly conditioned with respect to inversion.

`gallery(5)` is an interesting eigenvalue problem.

`gallery(8)` is the Rosser matrix, a classic symmetric eigenvalue problem.

`gallery(21)` is Wilkinson's W21+ example, another difficult eigenvalue problem.

## Algorithm

`gallery` is an M-file in the *MATLAB Toolbox*.

## See also

```
magic, hilb, invhilb, hadamard
```

Reference

## Purpose

Gamma function.

## Synopsis

```
gamma(a)
gamma(a,x)
```

## Description

`gamma(a)` returns the gamma function evaluated at the elements of `a`. The gamma function is defined by the integral

$$\Gamma(a) = \int_0^\infty e^{-t} t^{a-1} dt, \ \ a > 0$$

`gamma(a,x)` returns the incomplete gamma function of `a`, integrated from `x` to infinity. Either `a`, `x`, or both may be matrices, in which case the function is evaluated at all the elements. The incomplete gamma function is defined by

$$P(a,x) = \frac{1}{\Gamma(a)} \int_0^x e^{-t} t^{a-1} dt, \ \ a > 0$$

With this definition, `gamma(p,Inf)` is equal to one.

## Algorithm

`gamma` is an M-file in the *MATLAB Toolbox* that calls `gammac` to compute the complete gamma function and `gammai` for the incomplete gamma function. The computation of `gammac`, based on the algorithm outlined in [1], uses two different minimax rational approximations depending upon the value of `p`. Computation of the incomplete gamma function is based on the algorithm in [2].

## See also

`bessel`

## References

W. J. Cody, *An Overview of Software Development for Special Functions*, Lecture Notes in Mathematics, 506, Numerical Analysis Dundee, 1975, G. A. Watson (ed.), Springer-Verlag, Berlin, 1976.

**Purpose**

Get environment variable.

**Synopsis**

`getenv('`*string*`')`

**Description**

`getenv('`*string*`')` returns the text associated with the environment variable specified by *string*.

**Examples**

To fetch `MATLABPATH` on a Unix system:

```
s = getenv('MATLABPATH')

s =
        /matlab:/matlab/signal
```

**See also**

`MATLABPATH`

**References**

See `getenv` in any C library or Unix reference.

Reference

**Purpose**

Graphical input function.

**Synopsis**

```
[x,y] = ginput
[x,y] = ginput(n)
[x,y] = ginput(n, 'sc')
[x,y,button] = ginput(...)
```

**Description**

ginput provides a means of picking off (selecting) points from the graph window using a mouse or arrow keys.

[x,y] = ginput(n) displays the graph window, puts up a crosshair, and gets n points in data coordinates from the graph window, returning them in column vectors x and y. The crosshair can be positioned with the mouse (or by the arrow keys on some terminals). Data points are entered by pressing a mouse button or any key on the keyboard.

[x,y] = ginput gathers an unlimited number of points. Pressing the return key terminates the input.

[x,y,button] = ginput returns a third argument that contains a vector of integers corresponding to the ASCII equivalent of the keys pressed. The mouse buttons return 1,2,... from left to right.

[x,y] = ginput(...,'sc') returns the position of the crosshair in screen coordinates, where (0,0) is the lower left corner and (1,1) is the upper right.

**See also**

plot, gtext

# global                                                                    global

## Purpose

Define global variables.

## Synopsis

```
global  variable-name
global  name-1  name-2  ...
```

## Description

The `global` declaration makes variables global in scope, allowing them to be referenced inside function M-files without passing them through the argument list. The statement

```
global x y z
```

makes variables x, y, and z global, immediately making them available inside the bodies of functions. The variable names are separated by spaces, and need not have previously existed in the workspace.

The `global` statement *cannot* be issued in the body of a function, nor inside a `for` or `while` loop. It must be issued interactively or in a script M-file, and is normally used at the beginning of the session. Variables remain global unless the entire workspace is `cleared`.

## Limitations

Variable name clash can occur between local function variable names and global variable names. If you make common variable names like X or A global, you are virtually guaranteed to get unpredictable effects when using functions out of the *MATLAB Toolbox*. We recommend that you maximize the chance of getting unique names by using long names or by using an underscore "_" in the variable name.

When clash occurs, the global variable name wins, unless the local variable name is defined in the function argument list or the variable was defined as global *after* the function was compiled into memory.

Global variables are, in general, bad programming practice. We hope you seldom have to use this facility, and, as a matter of principle, we discourage its use.

Reference

## Purpose

Group delay.

## Synopsis

```
[gd,w] = grpdelay(num,den,n)
[gd,w] = grpdelay(num,den,n,'whole')
```

## Description

The *group delay* of a filter is a measure of the average delay of the filter as a function of frequency. It is defined as the negative first derivative of a filter's phase response. If the complex frequency response of a filter is $H(e^{j\omega})$, then the group delay is

$$\tau_g(\omega) = -\frac{d\theta(\omega)}{d\omega}$$

where $\omega$ is frequency and $\theta$ is the phase angle of $H(e^{j\omega})$.

`[gd,w] = grpdelay(b,a,n)` returns the *n*-point group delay, $\tau_g(\omega)$, of the digital filter,

$$H(z) = \frac{B(z)}{A(z)} = \frac{b(1) + b(2)z^{-1} + \cdots + b(nb+1)z^{-nb}}{a(1) + a(2)z^{-1} + \cdots + a(na+1)z^{-na}}$$

given the numerator and denominator coefficients in vectors b and a. `grpdelay` returns both gd, the group delay, and w, a vector containing the n frequency points. The group delay is evaluated at *n* points equally spaced around the upper half of the unit circle, so w contains n points between 0 and $\pi$.

It is best, although not necessary, to choose a value for n that is an exact power of two, because this allows fast computation using an FFT algorithm.

`grpdelay(b,a,n,'whole')` uses *n*-points around the *whole* unit circle (from 0 to $2\pi$).

## Examples

*Phase delay*, not to be confused with group delay, is the negative of phase divided by frequency

$$\tau_p(\omega) = -\frac{\theta(\omega)}{\omega}$$

Plot both the group and phase delays of a system on the same graph:

```
gd = grpdelay(b,a,128);
[h,w] = freqz(b,a,128);
pd = -unwrap(angle(h))./w;
plot(w,gd,w,pd)
```

## Algorithm

grpdelay is an M-file in the *Signal Processing Toolbox* that, using the algorithm of [1], multiplies the filter coefficients by a unit ramp, which, after Fourier transformation, corresponds to differentiation.

## See also

freqz, fft

## References

J. O. Smith, *Note on Calculation of Group Delay*, unpublished.

Reference

## Purpose

Place text on a graph using a mouse.

## Synopsis

```
gtext('string')
```

## Description

`gtext('string')` displays the graph window, puts up a crosshair, and waits for a mouse button or keyboard key to be pressed. The crosshair can be positioned with the mouse (or with the arrow keys on some computers). Pressing a mouse button or any key writes the text string onto the graph at the selected location.

## Examples

Label an interesting portion of the current plot with:

```
gtext('Note this peak!')
```

## Algorithm

`gtext` is an M-file in the *MATLAB Toolbox* that uses the functions `ginput` and `text`.

## Diagnostics

If `string` is not a text variable:

```
Argument must be a string.
```

## See also

```
ginput, text
```

## Purpose

Hadamard matrix.

## Synopsis

```
hadamard(k)
```

## Description

`hadamard(k)` returns the Hadamard matrix of order $n = 2^k$.

The accumulation of roundoff error during the solution of linear equations using Gaussian elimination tends to be more pronounced as the order of a matrix increases. The error is proportional to the largest element of the transformed matrix. The Hadamard matrix has the maximum possible roundoff error for matrices of a given size when Gaussian elimination is performed with complete pivoting (see [1]). The Hadamard matrix also arises in 2-D signal processing [2].

## Examples

`contour(hadamard(5))` is an interesting plot.

## Algorithm

`hadamard` is an M-file in the *MATLAB Toolbox*. The Hadamard matrix is computed recursively with:

```
if k < 1
    H = 1;
else
    T = hadamard(k-1);
    H = [T T; T -T];
end
```

## See also

```
magic, gallery
```

## References

1.      H. J. Ryser, *Combinatorial Mathematics*, John Wiley and Sons, 1963.

2.      W. K. Pratt, *Digital Signal Processing*, John Wiley and Sons, 1978.

**Purpose**

      Hamming and Hanning windows.

**Synopsis**

      `hamming(N)`
      `hanning(N)`

**Description**

      `hamming(N)` returns an N-point Hamming window in a column vector. The coefficients of a Hamming window are given by

$$w[n] = 0.54 - 0.46\ cos(2\pi\frac{n-1}{N-1})\ ,\quad n = 1,\ \cdots\ N$$

      `hanning(N)` returns an N-point Hanning window in a column vector. The coefficients of a Hanning window are given by

$$w[n] = 0.5\ (1 - cos(2\pi\frac{n}{N+1}))\ ,\quad n = 1,\ \cdots\ N$$

**Examples**

      Graph length 55 Hamming and Hanning windows:

      `plot([hamming(55) hanning(55)])`

---

**Purpose**

Hankel matrix.

**Synopsis**

```
hankel(c)
hankel(c,r)
```

**Description**

A Hankel matrix is a matrix that is symmetric, constant across the antidiagonals, and has elements $h(i,j)=r(i+j-1)$, where vector $r$ completely determines the Hankel matrix.

`hankel(c)` is the square Hankel matrix whose first column is $c$ and whose elements are zero below the first antidiagonal.

`hankel(c,r)` is a Hankel matrix whose first column is $c$ and whose last row is $r$. If the last element of $c$ differs from the first element of $r$, the last element of $c$ wins the disagreement.

**Examples**

A Hankel matrix with antidiagonal disagreement is

```
c = 1:3;  r = 7:10;
h = hankel(c,r)
h =
        1       2       3       8
        2       3       8       9
        3       8       9      10
```

**Algorithm**

`hankel` is an M-file in the *MATLAB Toolbox*.

**Diagnostics**

If the last element of $c$ differs from the first element of $r$:

```
Column wins antidiagonal conflict.
```

**See also**

```
toeplitz, vander
```

Reference

**Purpose**

Help facility.
Demonstrations.

**Description**

demo brings up a menu of the available demonstrations.

Executing help gives a list of HELP topics, including the M-files in the various libraries on disk.

help *topic* gives help on the specified *topic*. If the topic is not found in the help file, the help facility looks on the disk for an M-file with the filename *topic.m*. If it finds it, the first comment lines in the file are displayed. This allows you to use HELP on your own M-files.

**See also**

who, what, MATLABPATH

## Purpose

Hessenberg form.
Schur decomposition.

## Synopsis

```
H = hess(X)
[P,H] = hess(X)
T = schur(X)
[U,T] = schur(X)
[U,T] = rsf2csf(U,T)
```

## Description

`hess` finds the Hessenberg form of a matrix. A Hessenberg matrix is all zero below the first sub-diagonal. If the matrix is symmetric or Hermitian, the form is tridiagonal.

`[P,H] = hess(A)` produces a Hessenberg matrix `H` and a unitary matrix `P` so that `A = P*H*P'` and `P'*P = eye(A)`. By itself, `hess(A)` returns `H`.

`schur` computes the Schur form of a matrix. The *complex Schur form* of a matrix is upper triangular with the eigenvalues of the matrix on the diagonal. The *real Schur form* has the real eigenvalues on the diagonal and the complex eigenvalues in 2-by-2 blocks on the diagonal.

`[U,T] = schur(A)` produces a Schur matrix `T`, and a unitary matrix `U` so that `A = U*T*U'` and `U'*U = eye(A)`. By itself, `schur(A)` returns just `T`.

If the matrix `A` is real, `schur` returns the *real Schur form*. If `imag(A)` is nonzero, `schur` returns the *complex Schur form*. The function `rsf2csf` converts the real form to the complex form.

## Algorithm

For real matrices, `hess` and `schur` use the EISPACK routines ORTRAN, ORTHES, and HQR2. ORTHES converts a real general matrix to Hessenberg form using orthogonal similarity transformations. ORTRAN accumulates the transformations used by ORTHES. HQR2 finds the eigenvalues of a real upper Hessenberg matrix by the QR method.

The EISPACK subroutine HQR2 is modified to allow access to the Schur form, ordinarily just an intermediate result, and to make the computation of eigenvectors optional.

Reference

When `hess` and `schur` are used with a complex argument, the solution is computed using the QZ algorithm by the EISPACK routines QZHES, QZIT, QZVAL, and QZVEC. They have been modified for complex problems and to handle the special case $B = I$.

For detailed write-ups on these algorithms, see the EISPACK User's Guide.

**Diagnostics**

From `schur`, if the limit of *30n* iterations is exhausted while seeking an eigenvalue:

```
Solution will not converge.
```

**See also**

`eig, qz, rsf2csf`

**References**

1.     B. T. Smith, J. M. Boyle, J. J. Dongarra, B. S. Garbow, Y. Ikebe, V. C. Klema, and C. B. Moler, *Matrix Eigensystem Routines -- EISPACK Guide*, Lecture Notes in Computer Science, volume 6, second edition, Springer-Verlag, 1976.

2.     B. S. Garbow, J. M. Boyle, J. J. Dongarra, and C. B. Moler, *Matrix Eigensystem Routines -- EISPACK Guide Extension*, Lecture Notes in Computer Science, volume 51, Springer-Verlag, 1977.

3.     C.B. Moler and G.W. Stewart, "An Algorithm for Generalized Matrix Eigenvalue Problems," *SIAM J. Numer. Anal.*, Vol. 10, No. 2, April 1973.

---

### Purpose

Hexadecimal to double precision number conversion.

### Synopsis

```
hex2num(s)
```

### Description

`hex2num(s)` converts the hex value in string `s` to the IEEE double precision floating point number it represents. `NaN`, `Inf`, and denormalized numbers are all handled correctly.

### Examples

```
f = hex2num('400921fb54442d18')

f =
   3.14159265358979
```

### Algorithm

`hex2num` is an M-file in the *MATLAB Toolbox.*

### Limitations

`hex2num` only works for IEEE numbers; it will not work for the floating point representation of the VAX or other non-IEEE computers.

### See also

```
format
```

## Purpose

Hilbert and inverse Hilbert matrices.

## Synopsis

```
hilb(n)
invhilb(n)
```

## Description

`hilb(n)` is the Hilbert matrix of order n. Hilbert matrices consist of elements:

$$hilb(i,j) = \frac{1}{i+j-1}$$

The Hilbert matrix is a notable example of a poorly conditioned matrix [1].

`invhilb(n)` gives the exact inverse of `hilb(n)` for $n \leq 12$. Compare with the result from `inv(hilb(n))`.

## Examples

Even third order Hilbert matrices show signs of poor conditioning.

```
cond(hilb(3)) =

    524.0568
```

## Algorithm

`hilb` and `invhilb` are M-files in the *MATLAB Toolbox*. The algorithm for `hilb` is:

```
x = ones(n);
for i=1:n
        for j=1:n
                x(i,j) = (1)./(i+j-1);
        end
end
```

## References

G. E. Forsythe and C. B. Moler, *Computer Solution of Linear Algebraic Systems*, Prentice Hall, 1967, chapter 19.

## Purpose

Histograms.

## Synopsis

```
hist(y), hist(y,nb), hist(y,x)
[n,x] = hist(y)
[n,x] = hist(y,nb)
[n,x] = hist(y,x)
```

## Description

hist calculates or plots histograms.

hist(y) draws a 10-bin histogram for the data in vector y. The bins are equally spaced between the minimum and maximum values in y.

hist(y,nb) draws a histogram with nb bins.

hist(y,x), if x is a vector, draws a histogram using the bins specified in x.

[n,x] = hist(y), [n,x] = hist(y,nb), and [n,x] = hist(y,x) do not draw graphs, but return vectors n and x containing the frequency counts and the bin locations such that bar(x,n) plots the histogram. This is useful in situations where more control is needed over the appearance of a graph, for example, to combine a histogram into a more elaborate plot statement.

## Examples

Generate bell-curve histograms from Gaussian data:

```
rand('normal')
y = rand(1500,1);
hist(y);  % This is in bar chart form.
[n,x] = hist(y,30);
plot(x,n,'x')   % This uses x-marks.
```

## Algorithm

hist is an M-file in the *MATLAB Toolbox*.

## Purpose

Hold plot on screen.

## Synopsis

```
hold
hold on
hold off
```

## Description

`hold` holds the current graph on the screen. Subsequent `plot` commands will add to the plot, using the already established axis limits and retaining the previously plotted curves.

If `hold` is not in effect, each `plot` command starts by clearing the screen and finding fresh auto-ranging limits.

`hold on` sets holding on.

`hold off` turns holding off.

`hold`, by itself, toggles the hold state.

## See also

```
axis
```

## Purpose

Conditional control flow statements.

## Synopsis

```
if expression
    statements
elseif expression
    statements
else
    statements
end
```

## Description

`if` conditionally executes statements. The simple form is:

```
if expression
    statements
end
```

The statements execute if the *expression* has all nonzero elements. The expression is usually the result of

```
expression rop expression
```

where *rop* is `==`, `<`, `>`, `<=`, `>=`, or `~=`.

More complicated forms use `else` or `elseif` in the normal way. (Be careful not to put a space between the `else` and the `if` when you really mean `elseif`.)

Reference

## Examples

Here is an example showing `if`, `else`, and `elseif`.

```
for i=1:n,
        for j=1:n,
                if i == j,
                        a(i,j) = 2;
                elseif abs(i-j) == 1,
                        a(i,j) = -1;
                else
                        a(i,j) = 0;
                end
        end
end
```

## See also

```
while, for, end, break, return
```

## Purpose

Manipulation of complex numbers.

## Synopsis

```
imag(X)
real(X)
conj(X)
```

## Description

The functions `real`, `imag`, and `conj` operate on the individual elements of matrices:

- `real(X)` is the real part of X.

- `imag(X)` is the imaginary part of X.

- `conj(X)` is the complex-conjugate of X.

Imaginary numbers can be entered into MATLAB using the functions `i` and `j`. For example, $3+2i$ can be entered as

```
3+2*j
```

or you might prefer

```
3+2*i
```

This won't work, however, if you've redefined `i` or `j` to be another variable. In this case, you might use `3+2*sqrt(-1)`.

## Examples

If X is a complex vector or matrix:

```
conj(X) = real(X) - i*imag(X)
```

Reference

## Purpose

User input.

## Synopsis

```
x = input('prompt')
x = input('prompt','s')
```

## Description

n = input('How many apples') displays the text string as a prompt on the screen, waits for input from the keyboard, and returns the value entered by the user.

It is legal to feed an *expression* like [1 2 3] or rand(3,3) to the prompt. input can also be used with multiple output arguments if the expression entered by the user returns more than one output.

t = input('What''s your name','s') returns the *string* typed by the user as a text variable.

If the user strikes the return key without entering input, input returns an empty matrix.

## Examples

Allow the user to strike the return key to select a default value by detecting an empty matrix:

```
i = input('Do you want more? Y/N [Y]: ','s');
if isempty(i)
    i = 'Y';
end
```

## See also

keyboard

## Purpose

Matrix inverse.
Determinant.
LU decomposition.

## Synopsis

```
inv(X)
det(X)
[L,U] = lu(X)
[L,U,P] = lu(x)
```

## Description

inv(X) is the inverse of the square matrix X. A warning message is printed if X is badly scaled or nearly singular.

In practice, it is seldom necessary to form the explicit inverse of a matrix. A frequent misuse of inv arises when solving the system of linear equations $Ax = b$. One way to solve this is with x = inv(A)*b. A better way, from a numerical accuracy standpoint, is to use the "matrix division" operator, x = A\b. This produces the solution using Gaussian elimination, without forming the inverse. See \ and / for further information.

det(X) is the determinant of the square matrix X. If X contains only integers, the result will be an integer.

The most basic factorization expresses any square matrix as the product of two essentially triangular matrices, one of them a permutation of a lower triangular matrix and the other an upper triangular matrix. The factorization is often called the "LU," or sometimes the "LR," factorization. Most of the algorithms for computing it are variants of Gaussian elimination.

The factors themselves are available from the lu function. The factorization is a key step in obtaining the inverse with inv and the determinant with det. It is also the basis for the linear equation solution or "matrix division" obtained with \ and /.

[L,U] = lu(X) stores an upper triangular matrix in U and a "psychologically lower triangular matrix," i.e., a product of lower triangular and permutation matrices, in L, so that X = L*U.

Reference

[L,U,P] = lu(X) stores an upper triangular matrix in U, a lower triangular matrix in L, and a permutation matrix in P, so that L*U = P*X.

By itself, lu(X) returns the output from the LINPACK routine ZGEFA.

## Examples

Start with

```
A =
        1       2       3
        4       5       6
        7       8       0
```

To see the LU factorization, use MATLAB's double assignment statement:

```
[L,U]  = lu(A)

L =
    0.1429      1.0000      0
    0.5714      0.5000      1.0000
    1.0000      0           0


U =
    7.0000      8.0000      0.0000
    0           0.8571      3.0000
    0           0           4.5000
```

Notice that L is a permutation of a lower triangular matrix that has ones on the permuted diagonal, and that U is upper triangular. To check that the factorization does its job, we can compute the product

```
L*U
```

which gives us back the original A. If we use three arguments on the left-hand side to get the permutation matrix as well

```
[L,U,P]  = lu(A)
```

U is the same as before but L is reordered

```
L =
     1.0000            0            0
     0.1429       1.0000            0
     0.5714       0.5000       1.0000

U =
     7.0000       8.0000            0
          0       0.8571       3.0000
          0            0       4.5000

P =
        0        0        1
        1        0        0
        0        1        0
```

To verify that L*U is a permuted version of A, compute L*U and subtract it from P*A:

```
L*U - P*A
```

The inverse of the example matrix, X = inv(A), is actually computed from the inverses of the triangular factors

```
X = inv(U)*inv(L)
```

The determinant of the example matrix is:

```
d = det(A)
```

which gives

```
d =
    27
```

It is computed from the determinants of the triangular factors

```
d = det(L)*det(U)
```

Reference

The solution to $Ax = b$ is obtained with "matrix division":

```
x = A\b
```

The solution is actually computed by solving two triangular systems,

```
y = L\b, x = U\y
```

Triangular factorization is also used by a specialized function, `rcond`. This quantity is produced by several of the LINPACK subroutines as an estimate of the reciprocal condition number of the input matrix.

## Algorithm

`inv`, `lu`, and `det` use the subroutines ZGEDI and ZGEFA from LINPACK. For more information, see the *LINPACK User's Guide*.

## Diagnostics

From `inv`, if the matrix is singular:

```
Matrix is singular to working precision.
```

On machines with IEEE arithmetic, this is only a warning message. `inv` then returns a matrix with each element set to `Inf`. On machines without IEEE arithmetic, like the VAX, this is treated as an error.

If the inverse was found, but is not reliable:

```
Warning: Matrix is close to singular or badly scaled.
         Results may be inaccurate. RCOND = xxx
```

## See also

`rcond, rref, \, /`

## References

J.J. Dongarra, J.R. Bunch, C.B. Moler, and G.W. Stewart, *LINPACK User's Guide*, SIAM, Philadelphia, 1979.

## Purpose

Detect NaNs, infinities, and empty matrices.

## Synopsis

```
isnan(x)
finite(x)
isempty(x)
```

## Description

`isnan(X)` returns ones where the elements of X are NaNs and zeros where they are not.

`finite(X)` returns ones where the elements of X are finite and zeros where they are infinite or NaN.

`isempty(X)` returns 1 if X is an empty matrix and 0 otherwise. An empty matrix has size 0-by-0.

## Examples

You might think that the statement

```
K = (A == NaN)
```

would return a matrix with ones where there are NaNs, and zeros elsewhere, but it does not - it returns NaNs everywhere because any operation with a NaN results in another NaN. The correct way to detect NaNs is with `isnan`:

```
K = isnan(A)
```

## Algorithm

`isempty` is an M-file; `isnan` and `finite` are built into the interpreter.

## See also

```
find, any, all, <, <=, >, >=, ==, ~=
```

## Purpose

Invoke keyboard as an M-file.

## Synopsis

```
keyboard
```

## Description

keyboard invokes the keyboard as if it were a script M-file. When placed in an M-file, key-board stops execution of the file and gives control to the user's keyboard. The special status is indicated by a K appearing before the prompt. Variables may be examined or changed; all MATLAB commands are valid. The keyboard mode is terminated by excuting the command "return" (i.e., typing out the six letters "r-e-t-u-r-n" and pressing the return key). Control returns to the invoking M-file.

keyboard is useful as a tool for debugging M-files. To examine variables in a buggy M-file, insert it into the M-file before the line the error occurs on.

## See also

```
input, quit
```

---

**Purpose**

Kronecker product.

**Synopsis**

```
kron(X,Y)
```

**Description**

`kron(X,Y)` is the Kronecker tensor product of X and Y. The result is a large matrix formed by taking all possible products between the elements of X and those of Y. For example, if X is 2-by-3, then `kron(X,Y)` is

```
[ X(1,1)*Y   X(1,2)*Y   X(1,3)*Y
  X(2,1)*Y   X(2,2)*Y   X(2,3)*Y ]
```

**Algorithm**

`kron` is an M-function in the *MATLAB Toolbox*.

**Purpose**

Saving and loading variables on disk.

**Synopsis**

```
load file
save file
save file A B C
save file variable /ascii
save file variable /ascii /double
save file variable -ascii -double
```

**Description**

save and load are the MATLAB commands to store and retrieve variables on disk. They can also import and export ASCII data files.

**MAT-files**

MAT-files are full-precision binary MATLAB format files created by the save command and readable by the load command.

save temp stores all variables in a MAT-file named temp.mat.

save temp X saves only variable X.

save temp X Y Z saves X, Y, and Z.

save, by itself, saves everything in a file named matlab.mat.

The load command is the inverse of save.

load temp retrieves all variables from the MAT-file named temp.mat.

load, by itself, loads the variables from the file matlab.mat.

Double-precision MAT-files can be transferred between PC, VAX, Sun, Macintosh, and other implementations of MATLAB. MAT-files contain a signature that indicates the machine that wrote the file. The load command checks the signature and performs conversion, if necessary. Full numeric precision is retained when moving between IEEE arithmetic machines, such as the PC, Sun, and Macintosh. Precision is lost when files are exchanged with the VAX, however.

### ASCII file import/export

`save temp.dat X /ascii` or `save temp.dat X -ascii` exports variable `X` in 8-digit ASCII format to the file named `temp.dat`.
`save temp.dat X /ascii /double` exports variable `X` in 16-digit ASCII form.

`load temp.dat` imports the ASCII flat file `temp.dat`, putting the result into a variable named `temp`. If the data are stored in ASCII form, with fixed-length rows terminated with new-lines (carriage returns), and with spaces separating the numbers, then the file is called a *flat file*. (ASCII flat files can be edited using a normal text editor.) The `load` command directly imports flat files, putting the result into a variable with the same name as the file, with the extension stripped.

## Algorithm

The `save` command saves MATLAB variables on disk in a specially structured file we call a MAT-file, so called because the filename ends with ".mat". It is possible to read and write MAT-files from your own programs, provided you use the special file structure.

A MAT-file may contain one or more variables. The variables are written sequentially on disk, with the bytes conceptually forming a continuous stream. Each variable starts with a fixed-length 20-byte header that contains information describing certain attributes of the variable. The 20-byte header consists of 5 four-byte long integers (words):

`type`   Type flag. Word 1 contains an integer whose decimal digits encode the variable type. If the integer is represented as *MOPT* where *M* is the thousands digit, *O* is the hundreds digit, *P* is the tens digit, and *T* is the ones digit, then:

*M* indicates the numeric format of binary numbers on the machine that wrote the file. Use this table to determine the number to use for your machine:

| Machine ID | |
|---|---|
| PC | 0 |
| Other Intel | 0 |
| Sun | 1 |
| Apollo | 1 |
| Macintosh | 1 |
| Other Motorola | 1 |
| VAX D-float | 2 |
| VAX G-float | 3 |

$O$ is normally 0, which means the data are stored in a *column-wise* orientation (varies fastest down a column). If $O = 1$, the data are transposed and stored in a *row-wise* orientation (varies fastest across a row).

$P$ is normally 0, which means the data are stored on disk in double-precision (8 bytes/element). If $P = 1$, the data are stored in single precision (4 bytes/element). $P = 2$ is signed 32-bit integer data, $P = 3$ is 16-bit signed integers, and $P = 4$ is unsigned 16-bit integers.

$T$ is normally 0, indicating that the data that follow describe a matrix. If $T = 1$, the variable is a text variable. This means that the numbers in the variable are floating point numbers between 0 and 255 representing the ASCII code of characters.

For PCs, type is usually 0000, or 0, which indicates PC double precision matrix data stored by columns. Note that $P \neq 0$ and $O = 1$ are not produced by the save command, but they could be generated outside of MATLAB (to save file space) and accepted by load.

| | |
|---|---|
| mrows | Row dimension. Word 2 contains an integer with the row dimension of the variable. |
| ncols | Column dimension. Word 3 contains an integer with the column dimension of the variable. |
| imagf | Imaginary flag. Word 4 is an integer that is either 0 or 1. If 1, then the variable has an imaginary part. If 0, there is only real data. |
| namlen | Name length. Word 5 contains an integer with the length of the variable name plus 1. |

Immediately following the fixed length header are data that have a length dependent on the variables in the fixed length header:

name    Variable name. The name consists of `namlen` ASCII bytes, the last one of which must be a NUL character (encoded as 0).

real    Real part of the matrix. The `real` data consists of `mrow` * `ncol` double precision (8-byte) floating point numbers. Matrices are stored column-wise, first the first column, then the second column, etc., unless otherwise specified by `type` in the fixed header.

imag    Imaginary part of the matrix, if any. If the imaginary flag `imagf` is nonzero, the imaginary part of a matrix is here. It is stored in the same way as real data.

The structure is repeated for each variable stored in the file.

Here is some C language code that writes a single matrix on disk:

```
typedef struct {
     long type;    /* type */
     long mrows;   /* row dimension */
     long ncols;   /* column dimension */
     long imagf;   /* flag indicating imag part */
     long namlen;  /* name length (including NULL) */
} Fmatrix;

char *pname;       /* pointer to matrix name */
double *pr;        /* pointer to real data */
double *pi;        /* pointer to imag data */
FILE *fp;
Fmatrix x;
int mn;

fwrite(&x, sizeof(Fmatrix), 1, fp);
fwrite(pname, sizeof(char), x.namlen, fp);
mn = x.mrows * x.ncols;
fwrite(pr, sizeof(double), mn, fp);
if (x.imagf)
     fwrite(pi, sizeof(double), mn, fp);
```

Reference

The Fortran and C equivalents of this code are available in the *MATLAB Toolbox*. Perhaps you'll find code for other languages there too.

## Limitations

There are some rules that MATLAB uses when it looks for data files. If the filename does not contain an extension beginning with period ".", MATLAB appends the extension .mat before opening the file. If the filename contains an extension, i.e., it has a period in it, MATLAB will open the file with the complete name. This means that files without an extension cannot be saved or loaded, because MATLAB will append the .mat before trying to open them.

On VAX/VMS and MS-DOS computers, you can load extensionless files by putting a period at the end of the filename, for example, "load temp.". This does not work on Unix systems because Unix does not require filename extensions.

## Purpose

Generate logarithmically and linearly spaced vectors.

## Synopsis

```
y = logspace(d1,d2)
y = logspace(d1,d2,n)
y = logspace(d1,pi)
y = linspace(x1,x2)
y = linspace(x1,x2,n)
```

## Description

`logspace` generates logarithmically spaced vectors. Especially useful for creating frequency vectors, it is a logarithmic equivalent of `linspace` and the `":"` or colon operator.

`logspace(d1,d2)` generates a vector of 50 points logarithmically equally spaced between decades $10^{d1}$ and $10^{d2}$.

`logspace(d1,d2,n)` generates n points.

If `d2` is `pi`, the points are between $10^{d1}$ and $\pi$, which is useful for digital signal processing where frequencies go over this interval around the unit circle.

`linspace` generates linearly spaced vectors. It is similar to the `":"` or colon operator, but gives direct control over the number of points.

`linspace(x1,x2)` generates a vector of 100 points linearly equally spaced between `x1` and `x2`.

`linspace(x1,x2,n)` generates n points.

## Examples

Generate 50 points between .01 and 10,

```
w = logspace(-2,1);
```

## Algorithm

`logspace` and `linspace` are M-files in the *MATLAB Toolbox*.

## See also

## Purpose

Lowpass to bandpass analog filter transformation.

## Synopsis

```
[numt,dent] = lp2bp(num,den,Wo,Bw)
[at,bt,ct,dt] = lp2bp(a,b,c,d,Wo,Bw)
```

## Description

lp2bp is a function to transform analog lowpass filter prototypes into bandpass filters with desired bandwidth and center frequency. The transformation is one step in the digital filter design process of butter, cheby1, cheby2, and ellip.

The lp2bp function can perform the transformation on two different linear system representations: transfer function form and state-space form. In both cases, the input system must be an analog filter prototype: It must be a lowpass filter with a cutoff frequency of one radian/s and a DC gain of one.

*Polynomial:*

[numt,dent] = lp2bp(num,den,Wo,Bw) transforms an analog lowpass filter prototype given by polynomial coefficients into a bandpass filter with center frequency Wo and bandwidth Bw. Row vectors num and den specify the coefficients of the numerator and denominator of the prototype in descending powers of $s$,

$$\frac{num(s)}{den(s)} = \frac{num(1)\,s^{nn} + ... + num(nn)\,s + num(nn+1)}{den(1)\,s^{nd} + ... + den(nd)\,s + den(nd+1)}$$

Scalars Wo and Bw specify the center frequency and bandwidth in units of radians/s. The frequency transformed filter is returned in row vectors numt and dent.

*State-space:*

[At,Bt,Ct,Dt] = lp2bp(A,B,C,D,Wo,Bw) converts the continuous-time state-space lowpass filter prototype in matrices A,B,C,D

$$\dot{x} = Ax + Bu$$
$$y = Cx + Du$$

into a bandpass filter with center frequency Wo and bandwidth Bw. The bandpass filter is returned in matrices At,Bt,Ct,Dt.

## Algorithm

lp2bp is an M-file with a highly accurate state-space formulation of the classic analog filter frequency transformation. Consider the state-space system

$$\dot{x} = Ax + Bu$$
$$y = Cx + Du$$

The Laplace transform of the first equation is:

$$sx = Ax + Bu$$

Now if a bandpass filter is to have center frequency $\omega_o$ and bandwidth $B_w$, the standard $s$-domain transformation is:

$$s = Q(p^2 + 1) / p$$

where $Q = \omega_o/B_w$ and $p = s/\omega_o$. If we substitute this equation for $s$ in the Laplace transformed state-space equation, and consider the operator $p$ as $d/dt$, the equation becomes

$$Q\,\ddot{x} + Q\,x = A\,\dot{x} + B\,\dot{u}$$

or

$$Q\,\ddot{x} - A\dot{x} - B\,\dot{u} = -Q\,x$$

Now define

$$Q\,\dot{\omega} = -Q\,x$$

which when substituted, leads to

$$Q\,\dot{x} = A\,x + Q\,\omega + B\,u$$

The equations of state are given by these last two equations. If we write these in the standard form and multiply the differential equations by $\omega_o$ to recover the time/frequency scaling represented by $p$, state matrices for the bandpass filter are readily obtained:

```
Q  = Wo/Bw;
At = Wo*[A/Q eye(A); -eye(A) zeros(A)];
Bt = Wo*[B/Q; zeros(ma,nb)];
Ct = [C zeros(mc,ma)];
Dt = d;
```

If lp2bp is given a system in transfer function form, it first transforms it into state-space form before applying this algorithm.

**See also**

lp2lp, lp2hp, lp2bs, bilinear

## Purpose

Lowpass to bandstop analog filter transformation.

## Synopsis

```
[numt,dent] = lp2bs(num,den,Wo,Bw)
[at,bt,ct,dt] = lp2bs(a,b,c,d,Wo,Bw)
```

## Description

lp2bs is a function to transform analog lowpass filter prototypes into bandstop filters with desired bandwidth and center frequency. The transformation is one step in the digital filter design process of butter, cheby1, cheby2, and ellip.

The lp2bs function can perform the transformation on two different linear system representations: transfer function form and state-space form. In both cases, the input system must be an analog filter prototype: It must be a lowpass filter with a cutoff frequency of one radian/s and a DC gain of one.

*Polynomial:*

[numt,dent] = lp2bs(num,den,Wo,Bw) transforms an analog lowpass filter prototype given by polynomial coefficients into a bandstop filter with center frequency Wo and bandwidth Bw. Row vectors num and den specify the coefficients of the numerator and denominator of the prototype in descending powers of *s*,

$$\frac{num(s)}{den(s)} = \frac{num(1)\,s^{nn} + ... + num(nn)\,s + num(nn+1)}{den(1)\,s^{nd} + ... + den(nd)\,s + den(nd+1)}$$

Scalars Wo and Bw specify the center frequency and bandwidth in units of radians/s. The frequency transformed filter is returned in row vectors numt and dent.

*State-space:*

[At,Bt,Ct,Dt] = lp2bs(A,B,C,D,Wo,Bw) converts the continuous-time state-space lowpass filter prototype in matrices A,B,C,D,

$$\dot{x} = Ax + Bu$$
$$y = Cx + Du$$

into a bandstop filter with center frequency Wo and bandwidth Bw. The bandstop filter is returned in matrices At,Bt,Ct,Dt.

## Algorithm

lp2bs is an M-file with a highly accurate state-space formulation of the classic analog filter frequency transformation. If a bandstop filter is to have center frequency $\omega_o$ and bandwidth $B_w$, the standard $s$-domain transformation is:

$$s = \frac{p}{Q(p^2 + 1)}$$

where $Q = \omega_o/B_w$ and $p = s/\omega_o$. The state-space version of this transformation is:

```
Q = Wo/Bw;
At =   [Wo/Q*inv(A)  Wo*eye(ma);  -Wo*eye(ma) zeros(ma)];
Bt = -[Wo/Q*(A\B); zeros(ma,nb)];
Ct = [C/A zeros(mc,ma)];
Dt = D - C/A*B;
```

See lp2bp for a derivation of the bandpass version of this transformation.

## See also

lp2lp, lp2hp, lp2bp, bilinear

## Purpose

Lowpass to highpass analog filter transformation.

## Synopsis

```
[numt,dent] = lp2hp(num,den,Wo)
[at,bt,ct,dt] = lp2hp(a,b,c,d,Wo)
```

## Description

lp2hp is a function to transform analog lowpass filter prototypes into highpass filters with desired cutoff frequency. The transformation is one step in the digital filter design process of butter, cheby1, cheby2, and ellip.

The lp2hp function can perform the transformation on two different linear system representations: transfer function form and state-space form. In both cases, the input system must be an analog filter prototype: It must be a lowpass filter with a cutoff frequency of one radian/s and a DC gain of one.

*Polynomial:*

[numt,dent] = lp2hp(num,den,Wo,Bw) transforms an analog lowpass filter prototype given by polynomial coefficients into a highpass filter with cutoff frequency Wo. Row vectors num and den specify the coefficients of the numerator and denominator of the prototype in descending powers of *s*,

$$\frac{num(s)}{den(s)} = \frac{num(1)s^{nn} + ... + num(nn)s + num(nn+1)}{den(1)s^{nd} + ... + den(nd)s + den(nd+1)}$$

Scalar Wo specifies the cutoff frequency in units of radians/s. The frequency transformed filter is returned in row vectors numt and dent.

*State-space:*

[At,Bt,Ct,Dt] = lp2hp(A,B,C,D,Wo,Bw) converts the continuous-time state-space lowpass filter prototype in matrices A,B,C,D,

$$\dot{x} = Ax + Bu$$
$$y = Cx + Du$$

into a highpass filter with cutoff frequency Wo. The highpass filter is returned in matrices At,Bt,Ct,Dt.

Reference

## Algorithm

lp2hp is an M-file with a highly accurate state-space formulation of the classic analog filter frequency transformation. If a highpass filter is to have cutoff frequency $\omega_o$, the standard $s$-domain transformation is:

$$s = \frac{\omega_o}{p}$$

The state-space version of this transformation is:

```
At  =  Wo*inv(A);
Bt  =  -Wo*(A\B);
Ct  =  C/A;
Dt  =  D - C/A*B;
```

See lp2bp for a derivation of the bandpass version of this transformation.

## See also

lp2lp, lp2bs, lp2bp, bilinear

## Purpose

Lowpass to lowpass analog filter transformation.

## Synopsis

```
[numt,dent] = lp2lp(num,den,Wo)
[at,bt,ct,dt] = lp2lp(a,b,c,d,Wo)
```

## Description

lp2lp is a function to transform analog lowpass filter prototypes into lowpass filters with desired cutoff frequency. The transformation is one step in the digital filter design process of butter, cheby1, cheby2, and ellip.

The lp2lp function can perform the transformation on two different linear system representations: transfer function form and state-space form. In both cases, the input system must be an analog filter prototype: It must be a lowpass filter with a cutoff frequency of one radian/s and a DC gain of one.

*Polynomial:*

[numt,dent] = lp2lp(num,den,Wo,Bw) transforms an analog lowpass filter prototype given by polynomial coefficients into a lowpass filter with cutoff frequency Wo. Row vectors num and den specify the coefficients of the numerator and denominator of the prototype in descending powers of *s*,

$$\frac{num(s)}{den(s)} = \frac{num(1)s^{nn} +...+ num(nn)s + num(nn+1)}{den(1)s^{nd} +...+ den(nd)s + den(nd+1)}$$

Scalar Wo specifies the cutoff frequency in units of radians/s. The frequency transformed filter is returned in row vectors numt and dent.

*State-space:*

[At,Bt,Ct,Dt] = lp2lp(A,B,C,D,Wo,Bw) converts the continuous-time state-space lowpass filter prototype in matrices A,B,C,D,

$$\dot{x} = Ax + Bu$$
$$y = Cx + Du$$

into a lowpass filter with cutoff frequency Wo. The lowpass filter is returned in matrices At,Bt,Ct,Dt.

## Algorithm

lp21p is an M-file with a highly accurate state-space formulation of the classic analog filter frequency transformation. If a lowpass filter is to have cutoff frequency $\omega_o$, the standard s-domain transformation is:

$$s = \omega_o\ p$$

The state-space version of this transformation is:

```
At = Wo*A;
Bt = Wo*B;
Ct = C;
Dt = D;
```

See lp2bp for a derivation of the bandpass version of this transformation.

## See also

lp2hp, lp2bs, lp2bp, bilinear

---

## Purpose

Linear-quadratic estimator design.

## Synopsis

```
[l,p,e] = lqe(a,g,c,q,r)
[l,p,e,] = lqe(a,g,c,q,r,n)
```

## Description

`lqe` solves the continuous-time linear-quadratic estimator problem and the associated Riccati equation.

For the continuous-time system with state and measurement equations:

$$\dot{x} = Ax + Bu + Gw$$
$$y = Cx + Du + v$$

and process and measurement noise covariances:

$$E[w] = E[v] = 0, \; E[ww'] = Q, \; E[vv'] = R, \; E[wv'] = 0$$

`L = lqe(A,G,C,Q,R)` returns the gain matrix `L` such that the continuous, stationary Kalman filter:

$$\dot{x} = Ax + Bu + L(y - Cx - Du)$$

produces an LQG optimal estimate of $x$.

`[L,P,E] = lqe(A,G,C,Q,R)` also returns the Riccati equation solution `P` which is the estimation error covariance and the closed loop eigenvalues of the estimator `E = eig(A-L*C)`.

`[L,P,E] = lqe(A,G,C,Q,R,N)` calculates the Kalman gain matrix when the process and sensor noise are correlated:

$$E[w] = E[v] = 0, \; E[ww'] = Q, \; E[vv'] = R, \; E[wv'] = N$$

## Limitations

Certain assumptions must be met in order for a unique positive definite solution to the LQE problem to exist:

1.     Matrix Q must be symmetric and positive semidefinite.

2.     Matrix R must be symmetric and positive definite.

3.     The (A, C) pair must be observable.

## Algorithm

lqe is an M-file in the *Signals and Systems Toolbox*. lqe uses lqr to calculate the estimator gains using duality.

## See also

lqr

## Purpose

Linear-quadratic regulator design.

## Synopsis

```
[k,s,e] = lqr(a,b,q,r)
[k,s,e] = lqr(a,b,q,r,n)
```

## Description

`lqr` solves the continuous-time linear-quadratic regulator problem and the associated Riccati equation.

`K = lqr(A,B,Q,R)` calculates the optimal feedback gain matrix `K` such that the feedback law:

$$u = -Kx$$

minimizes the cost function:

$$J = \int (x'Qx + u'Ru)\,dt$$

subject to the constraint equation:

$$\dot{x} = Ax + Bu$$

`[K,S,E] = lqr(A,B,Q,R)` also returns `S`, the unique positive definite solution to the associated matrix Riccati equation:

$$0 = SA + A'S - SBR^{-1}B'S + Q$$

and `E`, the closed loop eigenvalues, `E=eig(A-B*K)`:

`[K,S,E] = lqr(A,B,Q,R,N)` calculates the optimal feedback gain matrix that minimizes the cost function with the cross weighting matrix, `N`:

$$J = \int (x'Qx + 2u'Nx + u'Ru)\,dt$$

**Limitations**

Certain assumptions must be met in order for a unique positive definite solution to the LQR problem to exist:

1.  Matrix Q must be symmetric and positive semidefinite.

2.  Matrix R must be symmetric and positive definite.

3.  The (A, B) pair must be controllable.

**Algorithm**

lqr is an M-file in the *Signals and Systems Toolbox*. lqr uses eigenvector decomposition of an associated Hamiltonian matrix.

**See also**

lqe

## Purpose
Magic square.

## Synopsis
```
magic(n)
```

## Description
`magic(n)`, for $n \geq 3$, is an $n$-by-$n$ matrix constructed from the integers 1 through $n^2$ with equal row and column sums. A magic square, scaled by its magic sum, is *doubly stochastic*.

## Examples
Try this:

```
for n = 3:20
    A = magic(n);
    plot(A,'-')
    r(n) = rank(A);
end
r
```

## Algorithm
`magic` is built into the MATLAB interpreter.

## See also
```
rand, ones
```

Reference

## Purpose

MATLAB search path.

## Description

MATLAB has a *search path*. If you input the name of something to MATLAB, for example by typing FOX, the MATLAB interpreter:

1.      Looks to see if FOX is a variable.

2.      Checks if FOX is a built-in function.

3.      Looks in the current directory for a file named FOX.M.

4.      Searches the directories specified by the environment symbol MATLABPATH for FOX.M.

MATLABPATH is an operating system environmental variable that has been predefined for you, but it may be changed if you wish to add your own directories to the search path. Consult the machine-specific first section for more information.

## Examples

Here is how to set MATLABPATH on some different operating systems:

MS-DOS:

```
set MATLABPATH=c:\matlab;c:\matlab\signal
```

Unix C-shell:

```
setenv MATLABPATH "/usr/matlab:/usr/matlab/signal"
```

VAX/VMS:

```
MATLABPATH :== [matlab],[matlab.signal]
```

Macintosh:

Automatically uses all folders in the MATLAB folder.

---

## Purpose

Maximum and minimum.

## Synopsis

```
max(X)
[Y,I] = max(X)
max(A,B)
```

## Description

For vectors, `max(X)` is the largest element in X. For matrices, `max(X)` is a row vector containing the maximum element from each column.

`[Y,I] = max(X)` stores the indices of the maximum values in vector I. If there are several identical maximum values, the index of the first one found is returned.

`max(A,B)` returns a matrix the same size as A and B with the largest elements taken from A or B.

When complex, the magnitude `max(abs(x))` is used.

`min` works the same as `max`, with the obvious difference.

## See also

`sort`

**Purpose**

Basic statistical functions.

**Synopsis**

```
mean(X)
median(X)
std(X)
```

**Description**

mean calculates the average or *mean* value. For vectors, mean(X) is the mean value of the elements in vector X. For matrices, mean(X) is a row vector containing the mean value of each column.

median calculates the *median* value. For vectors, median(X) is the median value of the elements in vector X. For matrices, median(X) is a row vector containing the median value of each column. Since median is implemented using sort, it can be costly for large variables.

std calculates *standard deviation*. For vectors, std(X) is the standard deviation of the elements in vector X. For matrices, std(X) is a row vector containing the standard deviation of each column.

**Algorithm**

All three functions are M-files in the *MATLAB Toolbox*.

**See also**

```
cov, corrcoef
```

## Purpose

Generate a menu of choices for user input.

## Synopsis

```
menu(mtitle, opt1, opt2, ..., optn)
```

## Description

`menu(mtitle, opt1, opt2, ..., optn)` displays the menu whose title is in the string variable `mtitle` and whose choices are string variables `opt1`, `opt2`, etc. `menu` returns the value the user enters.

## Examples

`k = menu('Choose a color','Red','Green','Blue')` displays:

```
----- Choose a color -----

        1) Red
        2) Green
        3) Blue

    Select a menu number:
```

After the user inputs a number, use `k` to control the color of a graph:

```
if k == 1
        plot(t,s,'r')
elseif k == 2
        plot(t,s,'g')
elseif k == 3
        plot(t,s,'b')
end
```

## Algorithm

`menu` is an M-file in the *MATLAB Toolbox*.

## See also

```
input, demo
```

Reference

## Purpose

Three-dimensional mesh surface.
Evaluate functions of two variables.

## Synopsis

```
mesh(Z)
mesh(Z,M)
mesh(Z,S)
mesh(Z,M,S)
[X,Y] = meshdom(x,y)
```

## Description

mesh creates mesh surfaces like the one on the cover of this guide. mesh(Z) produces a 3-dimensional perspective plot of the values in matrix Z as heights above a plane. For example, mesh(eye(14)) shows an identity matrix.

mesh(Z,M) produces a mesh surface of Z with the viewpoint specified by M where M = [az el]. The azimuth az (horizontal rotation) and vertical elevation el are specified in degrees. A positive value for az indicates counterclockwise rotation of the viewpoint about the vertical or $z$-axis, corresponding to a clockwise rotation of the object. Positive values of elevation el view the object from above, negative from below. Some examples:

> el = 90 is directly overhead.
> M = [0 0] looks directly up the first column of Z, from the
> Z(m,1) element.
> az = 180 is behind the matrix.
> M = [-37.5 30] is the default.

mesh(Z,S) and mesh(Z,M,S) control the scale factors that set the $x$, $y$, and $z$ axes. S is a three-element vector [sx sy sz] where the size of the mesh is based on the relative values of S.

meshdom generates X and Y arrays for use with mesh.

[XX,YY] = meshdom(x,y) transforms the domains specified by vectors x and y into arrays XX and YY for evaluating functions of two variables with 3-D mesh plots.

**Examples**

To evaluate the function

$$z = x \ e^{(-x^2 - y^2)}$$

over the range

$$-2 \le x \le 2, \quad -2 \le y \le 3$$

use the statements

```
[x,y] = meshdom(-2:.2:2, -2:.2:3);
z = x .* exp(-x.^2 - y.^2);
mesh(z)
```

**Algorithm**

`meshdom` is an M-file in the *MATLAB Toolbox.*

**See also**

`contour, plot, title, format +`

Reference

---

## Purpose

Nonnegative least squares.

## Synopsis

```
nnls(A,b)
nnls(A,b,tol)
[x,w] = nnls(A,b)
[x,w] = nnls(A,b,tol)
```

## Description

`x = nnls(A,b)` solves the system of equations

$$Ax = b$$

in a least squares sense, subject to the constraint that the solution vector $x$ have nonnegative elements:

$$x_j \geq 0, \; j=1,2,...n$$

`[x,w] = nnls(A,b)` returns also the "dual vector" w. The elements of x and w are related by:

$$w_i < 0, \; (i \mid x_i = 0)$$
$$w_i = 0, \; (i \mid x_i > 0)$$

## Examples

Compare the unconstrained least squares solution to the `nnls` solution for a 4-by-2 problem

```
a =
    0.0372    0.2869
    0.6861    0.7071
    0.6233    0.6245
    0.6344    0.6170
```

```
b =
   0.8587
   0.1781
   0.0747
   0.8405


[a\b nnls(a,b)] =

   -2.5625          0
    3.1106     0.6929

[norm(a*(a\b)-b)  norm(a*nnls(a,b)-b)] =

     0.6677     0.9119
```

The solution from nnls does not fit as well, but has no negative components.

## Algorithm

nnls is an M-file in the *MATLAB Toolbox* that uses the algorithm described in [1], chapter 23. The algorithm starts with a set of possible basis vectors, computes the associated dual vector w, and selects the basis vector corresponding to the maximum value in w to swap out of the basis in exchange for another possible candidate, until w <= 0.

## See also

\

## References

C. L. Lawson and R. J. Hanson, *Solving Least Squares Problems*, Prentice Hall, 1974, chapter 23, p. 161.

Reference

**Purpose**

    Matrix norms.

**Synopsis**

```
norm(X)
norm(X,p)
norm(X,'fro')
```

**Description**

    The *norm* of a matrix is a scalar that gives some measure of the "bigness" of the matrix. Several different types of norms can be calculated:

    When the argument X is a matrix:

        `norm(X)` is the largest singular value of X.
        `norm(X,1)` is the 1-norm, or largest column sum of X,
            `max(sum(abs(real(X))+abs(imag(X))))`.
        `norm(X,2)` is the same as `norm(X)`.
        `norm(X,inf)` is the infinity norm, or largest row sum of X,
            `max(sum(abs(real(X'))+abs(imag(X'))))`.
        `norm(X,'fro')` is the F-norm, `sqrt(sum(diag(X'*X)))`.

    When the argument is a vector, slightly different rules apply:

        `norm(V,p) = sum(abs(V).^p)^(1/p)`
        `norm(V) = norm(V,2)`
        `norm(V)/sqrt(n)` is the root-mean-square (RMS) value.
        `norm(V,inf) = max(abs(V))`
        `norm(V,-inf) = min(abs(V))`

**See also**

    `cond, rcond, svd, min, max`

## Purpose

Number to string conversion.
Formatted output to screen or file.

## Synopsis

```
num2str(x), int2str(x)
sprintf('format',x), sprintf('format',x,y,z)
fprintf('format',x), fprintf('format',x,y,z)
fprintf('filename','format',x,...)
```

Legal in *format* specifiers are `%e`, `%f`, and `%g`.

## Description

`num2str`, `int2str`, and `sprintf` convert numbers to their MATLAB string representations and are useful for labeling and titling plots with numeric values. `fprintf` converts numbers and writes them to the screen or to a file.

`s = num2str(x)` converts the scalar number `x` into a string representation `s` with roughly 4 digits of precision and an exponent if required.

`s = int2str(x)` converts an integer to a string with integer format.

`s = sprintf('format',x)` gives more control over the format by converting the value of `x` to string representation `s`, according to control string *format*. The control string is comprised of ordinary characters, which are simply copied to the output string, and conversion specifiers, each of which causes conversion of the next successive argument to `sprintf`. There can be from zero to three arguments after the control string. Legal conversion specifiers are `%e`, for exponential notation, `%f`, for fixed point notation, and `%g` which uses `%e` or `%f`, whichever is shorter; nonsignificant zeros are not printed. Between the `%` and the conversion character there may be [1]:

> A minus sign, which specifies left adjustment of the converted argument in its field.
>
> A digit string specifying a minimum field width.
>
> A period, which separates the field width from the next digit string.
>
> A digit string specifying the precision (number of digits to the right of the decimal point).

The character string \n signifies *newline* within a control string. For more information, see the C language *stdio* routine *sprintf*.

fprintf does output conversion like sprintf except that it sends the results to the screen, or to a file if a *filename* is given. If a file already exists, the output is appended.

On MS-DOS computers, COM1, PRN, and other devices can be used as *filenames*, so fprintf can be used for some fairly sophisticated effects like sending characters to modems.

## Examples

Here are some examples of fprintf:

```
fprintf('A unit circle has circumference %g\n\n',2*pi)

A unit circle has circumference 6.283186

fprintf('X is %6.2f meters\n or %8.3g millimeters\n',9.9,9900)

X is  9.900 meters
 or 9900.000 millimeters
```

## Algorithm

num2str and int2str are M-files in the *MATLAB Toolbox* that use sprintf.

sprintf and fprintf access low-level C routines directly, with no input checking. It may be possible to wreak havoc if they are used incorrectly.

## Limitations

Only the newline C escape sequence \n is implemented. If others are required, they can be built up in a MATLAB string. For example, the format string

```
s = ['It is %g o''clock',7,13];
```

uses two quotes to indicate a single quote, and includes a bell (ASCII 7) and a carriage return (ASCII 13).

## See also
```
setstr, hex2num
```

## References
Any C language reference. The original is:

B.W. Kernighan and D.M. Ritchie, *The C Programming Language*, Prentice Hall, 1978.

---

**Purpose**

Nyquist frequency response plots.

**Synopsis**

```
[re,im,w] = nyquist(a,b,c,d)
[re,im,w] = nyquist(a,b,c,d,iu)
[re,im,w] = nyquist(a,b,c,d,iu,w)

[re,im,w] = nyquist(num,den)
[re,im,w] = nyquist(num,den,w)
```

**Description**

nyquist calculates the Nyquist frequency response of continuous-time LTI systems. Nyquist plots are used to analyze system properties including gain margin, phase margin, and stability. When invoked without left-hand arguments, nyquist produces a Nyquist plot on the screen.

nyquist can be used to determine the stability of a unity feedback system. Given the Nyquist plot of the open loop transfer function G(s), the closed loop transfer function:

$$G_{cl}(s) = \frac{G(s)}{1 + G(s)}$$

will be stable if the Nyquist plot encircles the -1 + j0 point exactly $P$ times in the counterclockwise direction, where $P$ is the number of unstable open loop poles.

nyquist(A,B,C,D) produces a series of Nyquist plots, one for each input and output combination of the continuous state-space system:

$$\dot{x} = Ax + Bu$$
$$y = Cx + Du$$

with the frequency range automatically determined. More points are used where the response is changing rapidly.

nyquist(A,B,C,D,iu) produces a Nyquist plot from the single input iu to all the outputs of the system with the frequency range determined automatically. The scalar, iu, is an index into the inputs of the system and specifies which input to be used for the Nyquist response.

nyquist(num,den) draws the Nyquist plot of the continuous polynomial transfer function G(s) = num(s)/den(s) where num and den contain the polynomial coefficients in descending powers of $s$.

nyquist(A,B,C,D,iu,w) or nyquist(num,den,w) uses the user-supplied frequency vector w. The vector w specifies the frequencies in radians/sec at which the Nyquist response will be calculated. See logspace to generate frequency vectors that are equally spaced logarithmically in frequency.

When invoked with left-hand arguments:

```
[re,im,w] = nyquist(A,B,C,D,iu)
[re,im,w] = nyquist(A,B,C,D,iu,w)
[re,im,w] = nyquist(num,den)
[re,im,w] = nyquist(num,den,w)
```

returns the frequency response of the system in the matrices re, im and w. No plot is drawn on the screen. The matrices re and im contain the real and imaginary parts of the frequency response of the system evaluated at the frequency values w. re and im have as many columns as outputs and one row for each element in w.

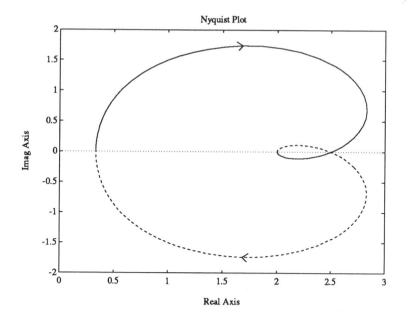

Nyquist Plot

Reference

## Examples

Plot the Nyquist response of the system:

$$H(s) = \frac{2s^2 + 5s + 1}{s^2 + 2s + 3}$$

```
num = [2 5 1];
den = [1 2 3];
nyquist(num,den);
title('Nyquist Plot')
```

Since there are no encirclements of the -1 + $j$0 point, the closed loop system associated with $H(s)$ will be stable.

## Algorithm

nyquist is an M-file in the *Signals and Systems Toolbox*. See bode for a description of the algorithm used.

## See also

bode, logspace

## Diagnostics

If there is a system pole on the $j\omega$ axis and the w vector happens to contain this frequency point, the gain is infinite, $(j\omega I\text{-}A)$ is singular, and nyquist produces the warning message:

```
Matrix is singular to working precision.
```

## References

Laub, A.J., *Efficient Multivariable Frequency Response Computations*, IEEE Transactions on Automatic Control, Vol. AC-26, No. 2, April 1981, pp. 407-408.

## Purpose

Ordinary differential equation solution.

## Synopsis

```
[t,x] = ode23('xprime', t0, tf, x0)
[t,x] = ode45('xprime', t0, tf, x0)
[t,x] = ode23('xprime', t0, tf, x0, tol, trace)
[t,x] = ode45('xprime', t0, tf, x0, tol, trace)
```

## Description

`ode23` and `ode45` are functions for the numerical solution of ordinary differential equations. They can solve simple differential equations, or simulate complex dynamical systems.

A system of nonlinear differential equations can always be expressed as a set of first order differential equations

$$\frac{dx}{dt} = f(x,t)$$

where $x$ is the state vector, $t$ is (usually) time, and $f$ is a function that returns the state derivatives as a function of $x$ and $t$.

`[t,x] = ode23(xprime, t0, tfinal, x0)` integrates a system of ordinary differential equations using second and third order Runge-Kutta formulas.

`[t,y] = ode45(xprime, t0, tfinal, y0)` uses fourth and fifth order Runge-Kutta formulas.

The input arguments to `ode23` and `ode45` are:

xprime     A string variable with the name of the M-file that contains the differential equations to be integrated. The function needs to compute the state derivative vector, given the current time and state vector. It must take two input arguments, scalar `t` (time) and column vector `x` (state), and return output argument `xdot`, a column vector of state derivatives $\dot{x}(t_i) = \dfrac{dx}{dt}(t_i)$.

t0         The starting time for the integration (initial value of `t`).

tf         The ending time for the integration (final value of `t`).

x0              A column vector of initial conditions.

tol             Optional - the desired accuracy of the solution; the default value is 1.e-3 for ode23, 1.e-6 for ode45.

trace           Optional - flag to print intermediate results; the default value is 0 (don't trace).

**Examples**

Consider the second order differential equation known as the Van der Pol equation

$$\ddot{x} + (x^2 - 1)\dot{x} + x = 0$$

We can rewrite this as a system of coupled first order differential equations

$$\dot{x}_1 = x_1(1 - x_2^2) - x_2$$
$$\dot{x}_2 = x_1$$

The first step towards simulating this system is to create a function M-file containing these differential equations. We can call it vdpol.m:

```
function xdot = vdpol(t,x)
xdot(1) = x(1) .* (1 - x(2).^2) - x(2);
xdot(2) = x(1);
```

To simulate the differential equation defined in vdpol over the interval $0 \le t \le 20$, invoke ode23

```
t0 = 0; tf = 20;
x0 = [0  0.25]';    % Initial conditions
[t,x] = ode23('vdpol',t0,tf,x0);
plot(t,x)
```

The general equations for a dynamical system are sometimes written as

$$\frac{dx}{dt} = f(x,t) + u(t), \quad y = g(x,t)$$

where $u$ is a time dependent vector of external inputs and $y$ is a vector of final measured outputs of the system. Simulation of equations of this form can be accomplished in the current framework by recognizing that $u(t)$ can be formed within the `xdot` function, possibly using a global variable to hold a table of input values, and that $y = g(x,t)$ is simply a final function application to the simulation results.

## Algorithm

`ode23` and `ode45` are M-files in the *MATLAB Toolbox* that implement algorithms from [1]. On many systems, MEX-file versions are provided for speed.

`ode23` and `ode45` are automatic step size Runge-Kutta-Fehlberg integration methods. `ode23` uses a simple 2nd and 3rd order pair of formulas for medium accuracy and `ode45` uses a 4th and 5th order pair for higher accuracy.

Automatic step size Runge-Kutta algorithms take larger steps where the solution is more slowly changing. Since `ode45` uses higher order formulas, it usually takes fewer integration steps and gives a solution more rapidly. Interpolation (using `spline`) can be used to give a smoother time history plot.

## Diagnostics

If `ode23` or `ode45` cannot perform the integration over the full time range requested:

```
Singularity likely.
```

## See also

`odedemo`, an M-file in the *MATLAB Toolbox*.

## References

G.E. Forsythe, M.A. Malcolm and C.B. Moler, *Computer Methods for Mathematical Computations*, Prentice Hall, 1977.

## Purpose

Handy utility matrices.

## Synopsis

```
ones(n)
ones(m,n)
ones(A)
zeros, eye
```

## Description

These functions generate special matrices:

ones    All ones. `ones(n)` is an *n*-by-*n* matrix of ones. `ones(m,n)` is an *m*-by-*n* matrix of ones. `ones(A)` is the same size as A and all ones.

zeros    All zeros. `zeros(n)` is an *n*-by-*n* matrix of zeros. `zeros(m,n)` is an *m*-by-*n* matrix of zeros. `zeros(A)` is the same size as A and all zeros.

eye    Identity matrix. `eye(n)` is the *n*-by-*n* identity matrix. `eye(m,n)` is an *m*-by-*n* matrix with ones on the diagonal and zeros elsewhere. `eye(A)` is the same size as A.

## Limitations

There is a syntactic difficulty with these functions that can bite you. Suppose A is a scalar with value 4. What size, then, is `ones(A)`? Using the definitions above, it could be either 4-by-4 or 1-by-1. The answer is 4-by-4, of course, but the point is that `ones(A)` is the same size as A, *except* when A is a scalar. The implication is that if you are writing a general matrix algorithm, and you want it to work for the scalar case as well, use `ones(n)` preceded by a call to `size(A)` to find n explicitly. The functions `zeros` and `eye` should be treated similarly.

## See also

rand

## Purpose

Orthogonalization and null space.

## Synopsis

```
orth(X)
null(X)
```

## Description

orth finds the range space of a matrix. The statement

```
Q = orth(X)
```

returns an orthonormal basis for the range of X. The columns of Q span the same space as the columns of X, matrix Q is orthogonal, so that

```
Q'*Q = eye(X)
```

and the number of columns of Q is the rank of X.

null finds the null space of a matrix. The statement

```
Q = null(X)
```

returns an orthonormal basis for the null space of X, so that

```
Q'*Q = eye(X)
X*Q = 0
```

and the number of columns of Q is the nullity of X.

## Algorithm

orth and null are M-files in the *MATLAB Toolbox.*

## See also

```
qr
```

Reference

## Purpose

Memory garbage collection and compaction.

## Synopsis

```
pack
pack filename
```

## Description

If you get the `Out of memory` message from MATLAB, the `pack` command may find you some free memory, without forcing you to delete variables.

`pack` performs memory garbage collection. Since MATLAB uses a heap method of memory management, extended MATLAB sessions may cause memory to become fragmented. When memory is fragmented, there may be plenty of free space, but not enough contiguous memory to store that large variable you want to create.

The `pack` command:

1.      Saves all variables on disk in a temporary file called `pack.tmp`,

2.      Clears all variables and functions from memory,

3.      Reloads the variables back from `pack.tmp`, and

4.      Deletes the temporary file `pack.tmp`.

This results in your workspace having the variables packed or compressed into the minimum memory required, with no wasted space.

`pack` accepts an optional filename for the temporary file used to hold the variables. Otherwise it uses the file named `pack.tmp`.

If you `pack` and there is still not enough free memory to proceed, you must clear some variables.

If you run out of memory often, here are some system specific tips:

*MS-DOS*

a) Using PC-MATLAB: install a full 640K.
b) Switch to AT-MATLAB and add extended memory.
c) Switch to 386-MATLAB and add extended memory.

*Macintosh*

> Under Multi-Finder, change the application memory size by using 'Get Info' on the program icon. Under Single-Finder, install more memory.

*VAX/VMS*

Ask your system manager to increase your Working Set.

*Unix*

Ask your system manager to increase your Swap Space.

**See also**

```
clear
```

## Purpose

Pause until a key is pressed.

## Synopsis

```
pause
pause(n)
```

## Description

`pause` causes M-files to stop and wait for the user to press any key before continuing.

`pause(n)` pauses for n seconds before continuing.

`pause(-2)` disables subsequent pauses. A second `pause(-2)` turns them back on again.

## Examples

An important use of `pause` is to halt M-files temporarily when graphics commands are encountered. If `pause` is not used, the graphics are visible only momentarily. An example of this is:

```
t = -300:300;
plot(t.*sin(t),t.*cos(t)), pause
plot(rand(1,2000),rand(1,2000),'.'), ...
title('Starry night'), pause
```

# pinv                                                           pinv

**Purpose**

Pseudoinverse.

**Synopsis**

```
pinv(X)
pinv(X,tol)
```

**Description**

X = pinv(A) produces the Moore-Penrose pseudoinverse, which is a matrix X of the same
dimensions as A' so that,

```
A*X*A = A
X*A*X = X
```

and A*X and X*A are Hermitian. The computation is based on svd(A) and any singular values
less than a tolerance are treated as zero. The default tolerance is

```
tol = max(size(A)) * norm(A) * eps
```

This tolerance may be overridden with X = pinv(A,tol).

**Algorithm**

pinv is an M-file in the *MATLAB Toolbox.*

**See also**

```
rank, inv, svd, qr
```

Reference

## Purpose

Linear, logarithmic, and polar engineering graph paper.

## Synopsis

```
plot(y)
plot(x,y)
plot(x,y,'line-type')
plot(x1,y1,x2,y2, ...)
loglog(x,y), semilogx(x,y), semilogy(x,y)
polar(theta,rho)
```

## Description

`plot` makes linear plots of vectors and matrices.

`plot(X,Y)` plots vector X versus vector Y. If X or Y is a matrix, then the vector is plotted versus the rows or columns of the matrix, whichever lines up. If both X and Y are matrices of the same size, the columns of X are plotted versus the columns of Y.

`plot(X1,Y1,X2,Y2)` is another way of producing multiple lines on the plot.

`plot(X1,Y1,':',X2,Y2,'+')` uses a dotted line for the first curve and the point symbol + for the second curve.

`plot(X1,Y1,'r',X2,Y2,'+g')` uses a red line for the first curve and a green + symbol for the second curve, if the system supports color. Other line, point, and color types are:

| Line-Types | | Point-Types | | Colors | |
|---|---|---|---|---|---|
| solid | – | point | . | red | r |
| dashed | – – | plus | + | green | g |
| dotted | : | star | * | blue | b |
| dashdot | – . | circle | o | white | w |
| | | x-mark | x | invisible | i |

`plot(Y)` plots the columns of Y versus their index. If Y has a nonzero imaginary part, `plot(Y)` is equivalent to `plot(real(Y),imag(Y))`. For other uses of `plot`, the imaginary part is ignored.

The commands `loglog`, `semilogx`, `semilogy`, and `polar` are used exactly the same as `plot`, but they result in graphs on different scales.

`polar(theta, rho)` makes a polar coordinate plot of the angle `theta`, in radians, versus the radius `rho.grid` will draw polar grid lines.

`loglog(x,y)` makes a plot using log-log scales.

`semilogx(x,y)` makes a plot using semi-log scales. The $x$-axis is $\log_{10}$ while the $y$-axis is linear.

`semilogy(x,y)` makes a plot using semi-log scales. The $y$-axis is $\log_{10}$ while the $x$-axis is linear.

**See also**

```
bar, title, xlabel, ylabel, text, gtext, grid, shg, clg, hold,
axis, mesh, subplot, stairs.
```

## Purpose

Polynomial fitting.

## Synopsis

```
p = polyfit(x,y,n)
```

## Description

Given data in a vector x, polyfit finds a polynomial $p$ such that $p(x)$ fits the data in a vector y in a least squares sense.

polyfit(x,y,n) returns the coefficients, in descending powers of x, of the $n$-th order polynomial that fits vector y to x.

## Examples

Select a polynomial and generate some noisy data:

```
p = [1, -6, 11, -6];
x = 0:.25:4;   rand('normal')
y = polyval(p,x) + rand(x);
```

Now fit a polynomial and plot the actual data and fitted result:

```
c = polyfit(x,y,3);
fit = polyval(c,x);
plot(x,fit,x,y,'o')
```

## Algorithm

In general, a polynomial fit to data in vectors x and y is a function $p$ of the form:

$$p(x) = c_1 x^n + c_2 x^{n-1} + \cdots + c_d$$

The degree is $n$ and the number of coefficients is $d = n+1$. The coefficients $c_1, c_2, \cdots c_d$ are determined by solving a system of simultaneous linear equations, $Ac = y$, where the columns of $A$ are successive powers of the x vector, also called the Vandermonde matrix. The solution to the equations $Ac = y$ is obtained using the MATLAB "matrix division" operator, c = A\y.

This algorithm is implemented in the M-file `polyfit` in the *MATLAB Toolbox*.

In the *regression* problem, other functions, usually multivariate functions of the columns of the data matrix, are fit to the data by forming the appropriate *A* matrix. For example, if X is a matrix whose rows are observations,

```
A = [X(:,1), X(:,2).^2, sin(X(:,3)), ones(m,1)];
coef = A\y
```

finds the regression coefficients for the indicated function.

### See also

```
poly, roots, roots1, conv, polyval, vander
```

## Purpose

Polynomial stabilization.

## Synopsis

```
b = polystab(a)
```

## Description

`polystab` stabilizes a polynomial with respect to the unit circle; roots whose magnitudes are greater than one are reflected inside the unit circle.

`b = polystab(a)`, where `a` is a vector of polynomial coefficients, normally in the *z*-domain,

$$a(z) = a(1) + a(2)z^{-1} + \cdots + a(na+1)z^{-na}$$

returns a row vector containing the stabilized polynomial.

## Algorithm

`polystab` is an M-file in the *Signal Processing Toolbox* that finds the roots of the polynomial and maps to the inside of the unit circle those roots found to be outside:

```
v = roots(a);
vs = 0.5*(sign(abs(v)-1)+1);
v = (1-vs).*v + vs./conj(v);
b = a(1)*poly(v);
```

## Purpose

Polynomial evaluation.

## Synopsis

```
polyval(p,s)
polyvalm(p,S)
```

## Description

If p is a vector whose elements are the coefficients of a polynomial in descending powers, then polyval(p,s) is the value of the polynomial evaluated at s. If s is a matrix or vector, the polynomial is evaluated at each of the elements.

polyvalm(p,S), with S a matrix, evaluates the polynomial in a matrix sense.

## Examples

The polynomial $p(s) = 3s^2 + 2s + 1$ is evaluated at $s = 5$ with

```
p = [3 2 1];
polyval(p,5)
```

which results in

```
ans =
      86
```

The *Cayley-Hamilton theorem* states that every square matrix satisfies its own characteristic equation. We can show this by forming the quantity polyvalm(poly(A),A), which is zero (within roundoff error), for any matrix A.

## Algorithm

polyval and polyvalm use Horner's method and are M-files in the *MATLAB Toolbox*.

## See also

```
conv, roots, roots1, poly, residue
```

## Purpose

Graphics hardcopy.

## Synopsis

```
prtsc
print
*meta file
*meta
```

## Description

Three commands, `prtsc`, `print`, and `meta`, provide general hard copy capabilities.

• `prtsc` initiates a *print screen*. The graph window screen is dumped to the printer on a pixel-by-pixel basis, resulting in hard copy with the same resolution as the computer screen. On most personal computers, holding the `Shift` key down and pressing the `prtSc` key also dumps the screen to a printer.

• `meta` *file* opens a high resolution graphics metafile, using the specified filename, and writes the current graph to it for later processing. Subsequent `meta` commands append to the previously specified filename. The metafile may be processed later using the graphics postprocessor (GPP) program.

• `print` sends a high resolution copy of the current plot to the printer. On some machines with limited memory, this feature may not be available.

## Algorithm

`print` is an M-file that saves the graph using `meta` and invokes the graphics postprocessor. You may modify `print.m` to select your target hard copy device.

## Limitations

*Note: These functions are not available with *The Student Edition of MATLAB*.

## See also

These three functions vary from machine to machine. See the machine specific section 1 of this guide.

## Purpose

QR decomposition.

## Synopsis

```
[Q,R] = qr(X)
[Q,R,E] = qr(X)
qr(X)
```

## Description

qr performs the orthogonal-triangular decomposition of a matrix. The "QR" factorization is useful for both square and rectangular matrices. It expresses the matrix as the product of a real orthonormal matrix or a complex unitary matrix and an upper triangular matrix.

[Q,R] = qr(X) produces an upper triangular matrix R of the same dimension as X and a unitary matrix Q so that X = Q*R.

[Q,R,E] = qr(X) produces a permutation matrix E, an upper triangular matrix R with decreasing diagonal elements, and a unitary matrix Q so that X*E = Q*R.

By itself, qr(X) returns the output of ZQRDC. triu(qr(X)) is R.

## Examples

Start with

```
A =

        1        2        3
        4        5        6
        7        8        9
       10       11       12
```

We have chosen a rank-deficient matrix; the middle column is the average of the other two columns. The rank deficiency is revealed by the factorization

```
[Q,R] = qr(A)

Q =
    -0.0776    -0.8331     0.5444     0.0605
    -0.3105    -0.4512    -0.7709     0.3251
    -0.5433    -0.0694    -0.0913    -0.8317
    -0.7762     0.3124     0.3178     0.4461

R =
   -12.8841   -14.5916   -16.2992
         0     -1.0413    -2.0826
         0          0      0.0000
         0          0          0
```

The triangular structure of R gives it zeros below the diagonal; the zero on the diagonal in R(3,3) implies that R, and consequently A, do not have full rank.

The QR factorization is used to solve linear systems with more equations than unknowns. For example

```
b =
     1
     3
     5
     7
```

The linear system $Ax = b$ is four equations in only three unknowns. The best solution in a least squares sense is computed by

```
x = A\b
```

which produces

```
Warning: Rank deficient, rank = 2, tol = 1.4594E-014

x =
    0.5000
    0.0000
    0.1667
```

We are warned about the rank deficiency. The quantity `tol` is a tolerance used in deciding that a diagonal element of R is negligible. If `[Q,R,E] = qr(A)`, then `tol = max(size(A))*eps*abs(R(1,1))`.

The solution $x$ was computed using the factorization and the two steps

```
y = Q'*b;
x = R\y
```

If we were to check the computed solution by forming A*x, we would find that it equals `b` to within roundoff error. This tells us that even though the simultaneous equations $Ax = b$ are over-determined and rank deficient, they happen to be consistent. There are infinitely many solution vectors $x$; the QR factorization has found just one of them.

## Algorithm

`qr` uses the LINPACK routines ZQRDC and ZQRSL. ZQRDC computes the QR decomposition, while ZQRSL applies the decomposition.

## See also

`orth, null`

## References

J.J. Dongarra, J.R. Bunch, C.B. Moler, and G.W. Stewart, *LINPACK User's Guide*, SIAM, Philadelphia, 1979.

Reference

**Purpose**

Numerical function integration (quadrature).

**Synopsis**

```
quad('fname', a, b)
quad('fname', a, b, tol)
quad('fname', a, b, tol, trace)
quad8(...)
```

**Description**

*Quadrature* is a numerical method of finding the area beneath a function, i.e., computing a definite integral. *quad* and *quad8* implement two different quadrature algorithms.

`q = quad('fun', a, b)` returns the result of numerically integrating the function `fun(x)` between the limits a and b. The function `fun` must return a vector of output values when given a vector of input values.

$$q = \int_a^b fun(x) \ dx$$

`q = quad('fun', a, b, tol)` iterates until the relative error is less than `tol`. The default value for `tol` is 1e-3.

If the final argument `trace` is nonzero, quad plots a graph showing the progress of the integration.

`quad8` has the same calling format as `quad`.

**Examples**

Integrate the sine function from 0 to $\pi$:

```
a = quad('sin',0,pi)

a =
    2.0000
```

## Algorithm

Both quad and quad8 are M-files in the *MATLAB Toolbox*. quad uses an adaptive recursive Simpson's rule. quad8 uses an adaptive recursive Newton Cotes 8 panel rule. Of the two, quad8 is better at handling functions with "soft" singularities, like $\int_0^1 \sqrt{x}\,dx$.

## Diagnostics

quad and quad8 have recursion level limits of 10 to prevent infinite recursion for a singular integral. Hitting this limit in one of the integration intervals produces the warning message:

```
Recursion level limit reached in quad.  Singularity likely.
```

The computation continues, using the best value available in that interval.

## Limitations

Neither quad nor quad8 is set up to handle integrable singularities like $\int_0^1 \dfrac{1}{\sqrt{x}}\,dx$. If you need to evaluate an integral with such a singularity, recast the problem by transforming the problem into one in which you can explicitly evaluate the integrable singularities and let quad or quad8 take care of the remainder.

## See also

quaddemo

## References

G.E. Forsythe, M.A. Malcolm, and C.B. Moler, *Computer Methods for Mathematical Computations*, Prentice Hall, 1977.

Reference

**Purpose**

    QZ algorithm.

**Synopsis**

    [AA, BB, Q, Z, V] = qz(A,B)

**Description**

The qz function gives access to what are normally only intermediate results in the computation of generalized eigenvalues. For square matrices A and B, the function

    [AA, BB, Q, Z, V] = qz(A,B)

produces upper triangular matrices AA and BB, and matrices Q and Z containing the products of the left and right transformations, such that

    Q*A*Z = AA
    Q*B*Z = BB

qz also returns the generalized eigenvector matrix V.

The $\alpha$'s and $\beta$'s comprising the generalized eigenvalues are the diagonal elements of AA and BB so that

    A*V*diag(BB) = B*V*diag(AA)

**Algorithm**

Complex generalizations of the EISPACK routines QZHES, QZIT, QZVAL, and QZVEC implement the QZ algorithm.

**See also**

    eig

**References**

C.B. Moler and G.W. Stewart, "An Algorithm for Generalized Matrix Eigenvalue Problems," *SIAM J. Numer. Anal.*, Vol. 10, No. 2, April 1973.

## Purpose

Random numbers and matrices.

## Synopsis

```
rand(n)
rand(m,n)
rand('distribution'), rand('dist')
rand('seed',n), rand('seed')
```

The *distribution* can be either uniform or normal.

## Description

rand generates random numbers and matrices. rand(n) is an *n*-by-*n* matrix with random entries. rand(m,n) is an *m*-by-*n* matrix with random entries. rand(A) is the same size as A. rand with no arguments is a scalar whose value changes each time it is referenced.

Ordinarily, random numbers are uniformly distributed in the interval (0.0,1.0). rand('normal') switches to a normal distribution with mean 0.0 and variance 1.0. rand('uniform') switches back to the uniform distribution. rand('dist') returns the current distribution in a string, either 'uniform' or 'normal'.

rand('seed') returns the current value of the seed for the generator. rand('seed',n) sets the seed to *n*. rand('seed',0) resets the seed to 0, its value when MATLAB is started.

## Algorithm

rand is a uniform random number generator based on the linear congruential method. It implements the proposed standard random number generator described in [1]. The basic algorithm is:

$$seed = (7^5 seed) mod(2^{31} - 1)$$

The normally distributed numbers are obtained with the transformation described in [2].

## References

1.   S.K. Park and K.W. Miller, "Random Number Generators: Good ones are hard to find," *Comm. A.C.M.*, vol. 32, n. 10, Oct. 1988, pg. 1192-1201.

2.   G.E. Forsythe, M.A. Malcolm, and C.B. Moler, *Computer Methods for Mathematical Computations*, Prentice Hall, 1977.

Reference

## Purpose

Rank of a matrix.

## Synopsis

```
rank(X)
rank(X,tol)
```

## Description

rank calculates the rank of a matrix.

k = rank(X) is the number of singular values of X that is larger than max(size(X)) * norm(X) * eps.

k = rank(X,tol) is the number of singular values of X that are larger than tol.

## Algorithm

There are a number of ways to compute the rank of a matrix. MATLAB uses the method based on the singular value decomposition described in chapter 11 of the LINPACK guide. The SVD algorithm is the most time-consuming, but also the most reliable.

The rank algorithm, as implemented in an M-file in the *MATLAB Toolbox*, is:

```
s = svd(x);
tol = max(size(x)) * s(1) * eps;
r = sum(s > tol);
```

## References

J.J. Dongarra, J.R. Bunch, C.B. Moler, and G.W. Stewart, *LINPACK User's Guide*, SIAM, Philadelphia, 1979.

## Purpose

Rational approximation.

## Synopsis

```
rat(x)
rat(x,'s')
rat(x,len,max)
rat(x,len,max,'s')
[a,b] = rat(x)
[a,b] = rat(x,len,max)
```

## Description

rat is a function that attempts to remove the roundoff error from results that should be "simple" rational numbers.

rat(x) approximates each element of x by a continued fraction of the form

$$\frac{a}{b} = d_1 + \cfrac{1}{(d_2 + \cfrac{1}{(d_3 + \cdots + \cfrac{1}{d_k})})}$$

The expansion is carried out while $k \leq$ len and $abs(d_i) \leq$ max. The default values of the parameters are

```
len = 13,    max = 10000
```

[A,B] = rat(X) produces integer matrices A and B so that

```
A ./ B  =  rat(X)
```

Invoking rat with the input argument 's' causes rat to display the result symbolically in a string matrix.

## Examples

A rational fraction approximation to $\pi$ is:

```
[a,b] = rat(pi)

a =
   355

b =
   113
```

Some other interesting examples to try are:

```
T = hilb(6), X = inv(T)
[A,B] = rat(X)
H = A ./ B, S = inv(H)

d = 1:8,  e = ones(d),  A = abs(d'*e - e'*d)
X = inv(A)
Y = rat(X)
disp(Y)
```

## Purpose

Parks-McClellan optimal FIR filter design.

## Synopsis

```
b = remez(n,f,m)
b = remez(n,f,m,'ftype')
b = remez(n,f,m,w)
b = remez(n,f,m,w,'ftype')
```

*ftype* can be `hilbert` or `differentiator`.

## Description

`remez` is a function to design linear-phase FIR filters using the Parks-McClellan algorithm. The Parks-McClellan algorithm [1] uses the Remez exchange algorithm and Chebyshev approximation theory to design filters with an optimal fit between the desired and actual frequency responses. The filters are optimal in the sense that the maximum error between the desired frequency response and the actual frequency response is minimized. Filters designed this way exhibit an equiripple behavior in their frequency responses, and hence are sometimes called *equiripple* filters.

`b = remez(n,f,m)` returns row vector `b` containing the `n+1` coefficients of the order `n` FIR filter whose frequency-magnitude characteristics match those given by vectors `f` and `m`.

The output filter coefficients are ordered in descending powers of $z$:

$$b(z) = b(1) + b(2)z^{-1} + \cdots + b(n+1)z^{-n}$$

Vectors `f` and `m` specify the frequency-magnitude characteristics of the filter:

- `f` is a vector of frequency points, specified in the range between 0 and 1, where 1.0 corresponds to half the sample frequency (the Nyquist frequency).

- `m` is a vector containing the desired magnitude response at the points specified in `f`. The elements of `m` must appear in equal-valued pairs.

- `f` and `m` must be the same length. The length must be an even number.

- The first point of `f` must be 0 and the last point 1.

- The frequencies must be in increasing order.

- Duplicate frequency points are allowed, but `remez` will separate them by 0.1 if they are exactly coincident. Note that frequency transitions much faster than 0.1 can cause large amounts of ripple in the magnitude response.

- `plot(f,m)` can be used to display the filter shape.

`remez(n,f,m,w)` uses the weights in vector `w` to weight the fit in each frequency band. The length of `w` is half the length of `f` and `m`.

`remez(n,f,m,ftype)` or `remez(n,f,m,w,ftype)` where `ftype` is the string `'Hilbert'` or `'differentiator'`, designs Hilbert transformers or differentiators, respectively. For the Hilbert case, the lowest frequency should not be 0.

The group delay of the FIR filter designed by `remez` is $-n/2$.

## Examples

Graph the desired and actual frequency responses of a seventeenth order Parks-McClellan bandpass filter:

```
f = [0 0.3 0.4 0.6 0.7 1];
m = [0 0 1 1 0 0];
b = remez(17,f,m);
[h,w] = freqz(b,1,128);
plot(f,m,w/pi,abs(h))
```

## Algorithm

`remez` is an M-file version of the algorithm from [1]. It can take a considerable amount of time to execute, particularly for higher order filters.

## Diagnostics

There are quite a few diagnostic messages that could arise from incorrect usage of `remez`. Here is a list of them; most are self-explanatory.

```
Filter order must be 3 or more.
There should be one weight per band.
Frequency and amplitude vectors must be the same length.
```

```
The number of frequency points must be even.
The first frequency must be 0 and the last 1.
The first frequency for a Hilbert transformer cannot be 0.
Frequencies must be nondecreasing.
```

A more worrisome message that could occur is

```
-- Failure to Converge --
Probable cause is machine rounding error.
```

In the rare event that this message is seen, it is possible that the filter design may still be correct. The filter design can be verified by checking its frequency response.

## See also
```
butter, cheby1, cheby2, ellip, yulewalk
```

## References
1.  *Programs for Digital Signal Processing*, IEEE Press, John Wiley & Sons, 1979, algorithm 5.1.

2.  *Selected Papers in Digital Signal Processing, II*, IEEE Press, 1976, pg. 97.

3.  T.W. Parks and C.S. Burrus, *Digital Filter Design*, John Wiley and Sons, 1987, pg. 83.

4.  L.R. Rabiner, J.H. McClellan, and T.W. Parks, "FIR Digital Filter Design Techniques Using Weighted Chebyshev Approximations," *Proc. IEEE 63*, 595-610, 1975.

Reference

## Purpose

Reshape a matrix.

## Synopsis

```
reshape(A,m,n)
```

## Description

`reshape(A,m,n)` returns the m-by-n matrix whose elements are taken columnwise from A. An error results if A does not have m*n elements.

Reshape a 3-by-4 matrix into a 2-by-6 matrix:

```
a =
     1    4    7   10
     2    5    8   11
     3    6    9   12

b = reshape(a,2,6)
b =
     1    3    5    7    9   11
     2    4    6    8   10   12
```

## Algorithm

MATLAB's colon notation can achieve the same effect, but `reshape` is less cryptic. `reshape` is an M-file in the *MATLAB Toolbox* that uses the equivalent colon notation:

```
B = zeros(m,n);
B(:) = A;
```

## Diagnostics

If `prod(size(A))` is not equal to m*n, `reshape` generates the error:

```
Matrix must have M*N elements.
```

**See also**

     `:, fliplr, flipud, rot90`

---

## Purpose

Partial-fraction expansion or residue computation.

## Synopsis

```
[r,p,k] = residue(b,a)
```

## Description

`[r,p,k] = residue(b,a)` finds the residues, poles, and direct term of a partial-fraction expansion of the ratio of two polynomials $B$ and $A$:

$$\frac{B(s)}{A(s)} = \frac{r(1)}{s-p(1)} + \frac{r(2)}{s-p(2)} + \cdots + \frac{r(n)}{s-p(n)} + k(s)$$

Vectors `b` and `a` specify the coefficients of the polynomials in descending powers of $s$. The residues are returned in column vector `r`, the pole locations in column vector `p`, and the direct terms in row vector `k`.

`[b,a] = residue(r,p,k)` converts the partial-fraction expansion back to the polynomials $B/A$.

## Algorithm

`residue` is an M-file in the *MATLAB Toolbox*. First the poles are found with `roots`. Next, if the fraction is nonproper, the direct term `k` is found using `deconv`, which performs polynomial long division. Finally, the residues are determined by evaluating the polynomial with individual roots removed. For repeated roots, the M-file `resi2` computes the residues at the repeated root locations.

## Limitations

Polynomials are very sensitive to roundoff error, especially if they have repeated roots. Caution is advised for high order polynomials.

## See also

`deconv, poly, roots, roots1`

## References

A.V. Oppenheim and R.W. Schafer, *Digital Signal Processing*, Prentice Hall, 1975, p. 56.

## Purpose

Evans root-locus.

## Synopsis

```
r = rlocus(num,den)
r = rlocus(num,den,k)
r = rlocus(a,b,c,d)
r = rlocus(a,b,c,d,k)
```

## Description

rlocus calculates the Evans root-locus of a SISO system. Root-loci are used to study the effects of varying feedback gain on system pole locations, indirectly providing information on time and frequency responses. For a plant with transfer function $g(s)$ and feedback compensator $k*f(s)$, the closed-loop transfer function is:

$$h(s) = \frac{g(s)}{1 + kg(s)f(s)} = \frac{g(s)}{q(s)}$$

When invoked without left-hand arguments, the root locus plot is drawn on the screen.

rlocus works for both continuous- and discrete-time systems. rlocus(num,den) plots the locus of the roots of:

$$q(s) = 1 + k\frac{num(s)}{den(s)} = 0$$

with the gain vector, $k$, automatically determined. Vectors num and den specify the numerator and denominator coefficients in descending powers of $s$:

$$\frac{num(s)}{den(s)} = \frac{num(1)s^{nn-1} + num(2)s^{nn-2} + \cdots + num(nn)}{den(1)s^{nd-1} + den(2)s^{nd-2} + \cdots + den(nd)}$$

rlocus(A,B,C,D) plots the root locus of the continuous-time or discrete-time SISO state-space system (A,B,C,D) with the gain vector automatically determined.

rlocus(num,den,k) or rlocus(A,B,C,D,k) uses the user supplied gain vector k. The vector k contains the gain for which the closed loop roots are to be computed.

Invoked with left-hand arguments:

```
[r,k] = rlocus(num,den)
[r,k] = rlocus(num,den,k)
[r,k] = rlocus(A,B,C,D)
[r,k] = rlocus(A,B,C,D,k)
```

returns the matrix r and the gain vector k. r has `length(k)` rows and `(length(den)-1)` columns containing the complex root locations. Each row of the matrix corresponds to a gain from vector k. The root-locus may be plotted with `plot(r,'x')`.

## Examples

Find and plot the root-locus of the system:

$$H(s) = \frac{2s^2 + 5s + 1}{s^2 + 2s + 3}$$

```
num = [2 5 1];
den = [1 2 3];
rlocus(num,den);
title('Root Locus')
```

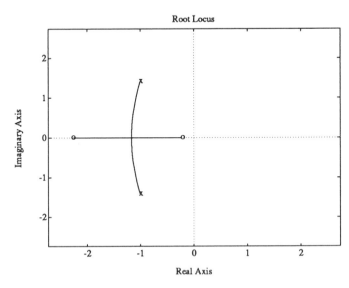

The `rlocus` function solves the most commonly posed special case of the general root-locus problem. MATLAB can also be used to find the root-loci as a function of any parameter in a system. For example, here is a symmetric root-locus, found with repeated applications of `lqr`:

```
i = 1;
for R = 0:1:10
        [K,S,E] = lqr(A,B,Q,R);
        r(i,:) = E.';
        i = i + 1;
end
plot(r,'x')
```

## Algorithm

`rlocus` is an M-file in the *Signals and Systems Toolbox*. It uses repetitive application of the `roots` function.

## See also

`lqr`

## Purpose

Polynomial roots.
Characteristic polynomial.

## Synopsis

```
poly(A)
poly(r)
roots(p)
```

## Description

If A is an $n$-by-$n$ matrix, `poly(A)` is an $n+1$ element row vector whose elements are the coefficients of the characteristic polynomial, $det(sI - A)$. The coefficients are ordered in descending powers: If a vector c has $n+1$ components, the polynomial it represents is:

$$c_1 s^n + \cdots + c_n s + c_{n+1}$$

If r is a column vector containing the *roots* of a polynomial, `poly(r)` returns a row vector whose elements are the *coefficients* of the polynomial.

If c is a row vector containing the *coefficients* of a polynomial, `roots(c)` is a column vector whose elements are the *roots* of the polynomial.

For vectors, `roots` and `poly` are inverse functions of each other, up to ordering, scaling, and roundoff error.

## Examples

Polynomials are represented in MATLAB as row vectors containing the coefficients ordered by descending powers. The characteristic equation of the matrix

```
A   =
        1       2       3
        4       5       6
        7       8       0
```

is returned in a row vector by `poly`:

```
p = poly(A)

p   =
    1     -6     -72     -27
```

The roots of this equation (eigenvalues of matrix A) are returned in a column vector by `roots`:

```
r = roots(p)

r   =
    12.1229
    -5.7345
    -0.3884
```

These may be reassembled into a polynomial with `poly`:

```
p2 = poly(r)

p2  =
    1     -6     -72     -27
```

`roots(poly(1:17))` generates the largest instance of Wilkinson's famous example that can be handled with IEEE precision arithmetic.

### Algorithm

`roots` and `poly` are M-files in the *MATLAB Toolbox*. `roots` solves for the roots of the polynomial by finding the eigenvalues of an associated companion matrix.

The algorithms employed for `poly` and `roots` illustrate an interesting aspect of the modern approach to eigenvalue computation. `poly(A)` generates the characteristic polynomial of A and `roots(poly(A))` finds the roots of that polynomial, which are, of course, the eigenvalues of A. But both `poly` and `roots` use EISPACK eigenvalue subroutines, which are based on similarity transformations. The classical approach which characterizes eigenvalues as roots of the characteristic polynomial is actually reversed.

Reference

If A is an $n$-by-$n$ matrix, $\mathrm{poly}(A)$ produces the coefficients $c(1)$ through $c(n+1)$, with $c(1) = 1$, in

$$det(\lambda I - A) = c_1\lambda^n + \cdots + c_n\lambda + c_{n+1}$$

The algorithm is expressed compactly in an M-file:

```
z = eig(A);
c = zeros(n+1,1);   c(1) = 1;
for j = 1:n
      c(2:j+1) = c(2:j+1) - z(j)*c(1:j);
end
```

This recursion is easily derived by expanding the product

$$(\lambda - \lambda_1)(\lambda - \lambda_2)...(\lambda - \lambda_n)$$

It is possible to prove that $\mathrm{poly}(A)$ produces the coefficients in the characteristic polynomial of a matrix within roundoff error of A. This is true even if the eigenvalues of A are badly conditioned. The traditional algorithms for obtaining the characteristic polynomial that do not use the eigenvalues do not have such satisfactory numerical properties.

If c is a vector with $n+1$ components, $\mathrm{roots}(c)$ finds the roots of the polynomial of degree $n$,

$$p(\lambda) = c_1\lambda^n + \cdots + c_n\lambda + c_{n+1}$$

The algorithm simply involves computing the eigenvalues of the companion matrix:

```
A = diag(ones(n-1,1)),-1);
A(1,:) = -c(2:n-1)/c(1);
eig(A)
```

It is possible to prove that the results produced are the exact eigenvalues of a matrix within round-off error of the companion matrix A, but this does not mean that they are the exact roots of a polynomial with coefficients within roundoff error of those in c.

**See also**
```
polyval, conv, residue
```

## Purpose

Rotate a matrix through 90 degrees.

## Synopsis

```
rot90(A)
rot90(A,k)
```

## Description

rot90(A) rotates the matrix A counterclockwise by 90°.

rot90(A,k) rotates the matrix A counterclockwise by k*90°.   k must be an integer.

## Examples

The matrix

```
x =
        1       2       3
        4       5       6
        7       8       9
```

is rotated by 90°:

```
y  =  rot90(x)

y =
        3       6       9
        2       5       8
        1       4       7
```

## Algorithm

rot90 is an M-file in the *MATLAB Toolbox*.

## See also

```
fliplr, flipud, reshape
```

## Purpose

Rounding, signum, and remainder elementary functions.

## Synopsis

```
round(X), fix(X), ceil(X), floor(X)
sign(X)
rem(X,Y)
```

## Description

These elementary functions operate element-wise on matrices.

round(X)   Round the elements of X to the nearest integers.

fix(X)     Round the elements of X to the nearest integers towards zero.

ceil(X)    Round the elements of X to the nearest integers towards $+\infty$.

floor(X)   Round the elements of X to the nearest integers towards $-\infty$.

sign(X)    The *signum* function. For each element of X, sign(X) returns 1 if the element is greater than zero, 0 if it equals zero and $-1$ if it is less than zero. For complex X, sign(X) = X ./ abs(X).

rem(X,Y)   Calculate remainders. If n = fix(x/y) is the integer nearest the exact value x/y, the remainder, rem(x,y), is x - y * n.

## See also

trig, exp, log

---

### Purpose

Reduced row echelon form.

### Synopsis

```
rref(A)
rref(A,tol)
rrefmovie(A)
```

### Description

`rref(A)` produces the reduced row echelon form of `A` using Gauss-Jordan elimination with partial pivoting. A default tolerance of

```
tol = max(size(A))*eps*norm(A,inf)
```

is used to test for negligible column elements.

`rref(A,tol)` uses `tol` for the tolerance.

`rrefmovie(A)` shows a "movie" of the algorithm working.

### Examples

Use `rref` on a rank-deficient magic square,

```
A = magic(4),  R = rref(A)
A =
      16     2     3    13
       5    11    10     8
       9     7     6    12
       4    14    15     1
R =
       1     0     0     1
       0     1     0     3
       0     0     1    -3
       0     0     0     0
```

## Algorithm

rref is an M-file in the *MATLAB Toolbox*.

## See also

rank, lu, inv

## Purpose

String handling.

## Synopsis

```
setstr(t)
isstr(t)
```

## Description

The statement t = 'Hello, World.' creates a vector whose components are the ASCII codes for the characters. The column dimension of t is the number of characters. It is no different than other MATLAB vectors, except that when displayed, text is shown instead of the decimal ASCII codes:

```
t =
    Hello, World.
```

Associated with each MATLAB variable is a flag that, if set, tells the MATLAB output routines that the variable should be displayed as text.

t = abs(t) is one way of clearing the flag so the vector is displayed in its decimal ASCII representation.

t = setstr(t) sets the flag back to text display.

isstr(t) returns 1 if t is a string, and 0 otherwise.

Strange behavior may be encountered if setstr is used on vectors that contain numbers outside of 0 to 255, or nonintegers.

A quote within a string is indicated by two quotes.

## Examples

The string

```
s = ['It is 1 o''clock',7,13,'It is 2']
```

uses two quotes to indicate a single quote, and includes a bell (ASCII 7) and a carriage return (ASCII 13).

## See also

strcmp

## Purpose

Size of variables, length of vectors.

## Synopsis

```
size(X)
[m,n] = size(X)
length(X)
```

## Description

If X is an *m*-by-*n* matrix, then `size(X)` returns the two-element row vector `[m n]`.

`size` can also be used with a multiple assignment,

```
[m,n] = size(X)
```

in which case m and n are returned separately.

`length(X)` returns the length of vector X. It is equivalent to `max(size(X))`.

## Purpose

Sorting.

## Synopsis

```
sort(X)
[Y,I] = sort(X)
```

## Description

sort(X) sorts each column of X in ascending order.

[Y,I] = sort(X) also returns matrix I containing the indices used in the sort. If X is a vector, Y = X(I).

If elements in the sort are repeated (have equal value), the indices of the repeated values are returned in a manner that preserves the original relative ordering.

When X is complex, the elements are sorted by abs(X).

## Examples

To sort the eigenvalues and eigenvectors of a matrix:

```
[V,D] = eig(A);
[lambda,k] = sort(diag(D));
V = V(:,k);
```

**Purpose**

Cubic spline data interpolation.

**Synopsis**

```
yi = spline(x,y,xi)
pp = spline(x,y)
```

**Description**

spline interpolates between data points using cubic spline fits.

If x and y are vectors containing coarsely spaced data, and xi contains a new, more finely spaced abscissa vector, then

```
yi = spline(x,y,xi)
```

uses cubic spline interpolation to find a vector yi corresponding to xi.

pp = spline(x,y) returns the *pp*-form of the cubic spline interpolant, for later use with ppval, etc.

**Examples**

Here's an example that generates a coarse sine curve, then interpolates over a finer abscissa:

```
x = 0:10;  y = sin(x);
xi = 0:.25:10;
yi = spline(x,y,xi);
plot(x,y,'o',xi,yi)
```

**Algorithm**

spline is an M-file in the *MATLAB Toolbox*. It uses the M-files ppval, mkpp, and unmkpp. These routines form a small suite of functions for working with piecewise polynomials. spline uses them in a fairly simple fashion to perform cubic spline interpolation. For access to the more advanced features, see the M-files.

## See also
```
table1, polyfit
```

## References
C. de Boor, *A Practical Guide to Splines*, Springer-Verlag, 1978.

## Purpose

State-space to transfer function conversion.

## Synopsis

```
[num,den] = ss2tf(a,b,c,d,iu)
```

## Description

`ss2tf` converts state-space systems to transfer function form.

`[NUM,den] = ss2tf(A,B,C,D,iu)` calculates the transfer function:

$$H(s) = \frac{NUM(s)}{den(s)} = C(sI - A)^{-1}B + D$$

of the system:

$$\dot{x} = Ax + Bu$$
$$y = Cx + Du$$

from the $iu$'th input. Vector `den` contains the coefficients of the denominator in descending powers of $s$. The numerator coefficients are returned in matrix NUM with as many rows as there are outputs $y$. The function `tf2ss` is the inverse of `ss2tf`. `ss2tf` also works with systems in discrete-time, in which case the z- transform representation is returned.

## Examples

The function:

```
[a,b,c,d] = ord2(1,.2);
```

returns a second-order system with $\omega_n = 1$ and damping factor $\zeta = .2$. The transfer function of this system is:

```
[num,den] = ss2tf(a,b,c,d,1)

num =
        0            0        1.0000
den =
     1.0000       0.4000      1.0000
```

## Algorithm

ss2tf is an M-file in the *Signals and Systems Toolbox.* It uses poly to find the characteristic polynomial *det(sI-A)*, and the equality:

$$H(s) \ = \ c(sI - A)^{-1}b \ = \ \frac{det(sI - A + bc) - det(sI - A)}{det(sI - A)}$$

## See also

ss2zp, tf2ss, tf2zp, zp2ss, zp2tf

## Purpose

State-space to zero-pole-gain conversion.

## Synopsis

```
[z,p,k] = ss2zp(a,b,c,d,iu)
```

## Description

`ss2zp` finds the zeros, poles, and gains of state-space systems (the transfer function in factored form).

`[z,p,k] = ss2tf(A,B,C,D,iu)` calculates the transfer function in factored form

$$H(s) = \frac{Z(s)}{p(s)} = k\frac{(s - Z(1))(s - Z(2))...(s - Z(nz))}{(s - p(1))(s - p(2))...(s - p(np))}$$

of the system:

$$\dot{x} = Ax + Bu$$
$$y = Cx + Du$$

from the `iu`'th input. Column vector `p` returns the pole locations of the denominator of the transfer function. The numerator zeros are returned in the columns of matrix `Z` with as many columns as there are outputs $y$. The gains for each numerator transfer function are returned in column vector `k`.

The function `zp2ss` is the inverse of `ss2zp`. `ss2zp` also works with systems in discrete-time, in which case the $z$-transform representation is returned.

## Examples

Consider the system

$$H(s) = \frac{2s + 3}{s^2 + 0.4s + 1}$$

Here are two ways of finding the zeros, poles, and gains of this system:

```
num = [2 3];
den = [1 0.4 1];
[z,p,k] = tf2zp(num,den)

z =
   -1.5000
p =
  -0.2000 + 0.9798i
  -0.2000 - 0.9798i
k =
     2

or
[a,b,c,d] = tf2ss9num,den);
[z,p,k] = ss2zp(a,b,c,d,1)

z =
   -1.5000
        Inf
p =
  -0.2000 + 0.9798i
  -0.2000 + 0.9798i
k =
     2
```

### Algorithm

ss2zp is an M-function in the *Signal Processing Toolbox*. The poles are found from the eigenvalues of the *A* matrix. The zeros are found as the finite solutions to a generalized eigenvalue problem:

```
z = eig([a b;c d], diag([ones(1,n) 0]);
```

In many situations this algorithm will produce spurious large, but finite, zeros. Attention is required, using physical insight, to interpret these large zeros as infinite.

The gains are found by solving for the first nonzero Markov parameters.

## See also

```
tf2ss, zp2ss
```

## References

A.J. Laub and B.C. Moore, *Calculation of Transmission Zeros Using QZ Techniques*, Automatica, 14, 1978, p.557.

## Purpose

Starting and ending.

## Synopsis

```
matlab.m
startup.m
quit, exit
```

## Description

The M-scripts `matlab.m` and `startup.m` are executed automatically when MATLAB is invoked. Physical constants, engineering conversion factors, or anything else you would like predefined in your workspace may be put in these files. On multi-user or networked systems, `matlab.m` is reserved for use by the system manager. It can be used to implement systemwide definitions and messages.

`quit` terminates MATLAB. The workspace is not saved. See `save`.

`exit` is a synonym for `quit`.

Typing CTRL-Z, the end-of-file character, will also terminate MATLAB.

## Algorithm

Only `matlab.m` is actually invoked by MATLAB at startup. However, `matlab.m` contains the statements

```
if exist('startup')==2
        startup
end
```

that invoke `startup.m`. This process may be extended to create additional startup M-files, if required.

## See also

```
!, exist
```

Reference

## Purpose

Unit step response.

## Synopsis

```
[y,x,t] = step(a,b,c,d)
[y,x,t] = step(a,b,c,d,iu)
[y,x,t] = step(a,b,c,d,iu,t)
[y,x,t] = step(num,den)
[y,x,t] = step(num,den,t)
```

## Description

`step` calculates the unit step response of a linear system. Invoked without left-hand arguments, `step` plots the impulse response on the screen.

`step(A,B,C,D)` produces a series of step response plots, one for each input and output combination of the continuous LTI system:

$$\dot{x} = Ax + Bu$$
$$y = Cx + Du$$

with the time vector automatically determined.

`step(A,B,C,D,iu)` produces a step response plot from the single input `iu` to all the outputs of the system with the time vector automatically determined. The scalar, `iu`, is an index into the inputs of the system and specifies which input to be used for the impulse response.

`step(num,den)` produces the impulse response plot of the polynomial transfer function $G(s)$ = `num(s)/den(s)` where `num` and `den` contain the polynomial coefficients in descending powers of $s$.

`step(A,B,C,D,iu,t)` or `step(num,den,t)` uses the user-supplied time vector $t$. The vector $t$ specifies the times at which the step response will be computed and must be regularly spaced.

Invoked with lefthand arguments:

```
[y,x,t] = step(A,B,C,D,iu)
[y,x,t] = step(A,B,C,D,iu,t)
[y,x,t] = step(num,den)
[y,x,t] = step(num,den,t)
```

returns the output and state responses of the system and the time vector, $t$. No plot is drawn on the screen. The matrices $y$ and $x$ contain the output and state response of the system respectively evaluated at the time points $t$. $y$ has as many columns as outputs and one row for each element in $t$. $x$ as as many columns as states and one row for each element in $t$.

### Examples

Plot the step response of the second order state-space system:

$$\begin{bmatrix} \dot{x}_1 \\ \dot{x}_2 \end{bmatrix} = \begin{bmatrix} -0.5572 & -0.7814 \\ 0.7814 & 0 \end{bmatrix} \begin{bmatrix} \dot{x}_1 \\ \dot{x}_2 \end{bmatrix} + \begin{bmatrix} 1 \\ 0 \end{bmatrix} u$$

$$y = [1.9691 \ 6.4493] \begin{bmatrix} \dot{x}_1 \\ \dot{x}_2 \end{bmatrix} + [0] u$$

```
a =[-0.5572    -0.7814;  0.7814     0];
b =[1;0];
c =[1.9691      6.4493];
d =[0];
step(a,b,c,d);
title('Step Response')
```

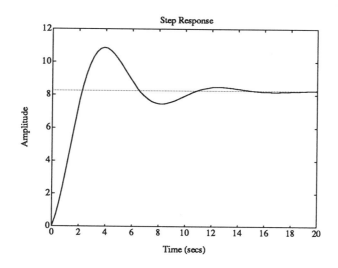

## Algorithm

`step` is an M-file in the *Signals and Systems Toolbox*. `step` converts the continuous system to a discrete one using matrix exponentials and the interval between the time points in vector `t`. The discrete system is then propagated over the number of points in `t`.

---

## Purpose

String comparison.

## Synopsis

```
strcmp(s1, s2)
```

## Description

`strcmp(s1,s2)` compares the strings `s1` and `s2` and returns 1 if the two are identical, and 0 otherwise. Note that the value returned by `strcmp` is *not* the same as the C language convention.

`strcmp` is case sensitive; any leading and trailing blanks in either of the strings are explicitly included in the comparison.

## Examples

```
strcmp('Yes','No') =

        0

strcmp('Yes','Yes') =

        1
```

## Algorithm

`strcmp` is an M-file in the *MATLAB Toolbox*.

## See also

```
isstr, setstr
```

Reference

## Purpose

Split the graph window into subwindows.

## Synopsis

```
subplot(mnp)
subplot
```

## Description

subplot(*mnp*), where *mnp* is a three-digit number, breaks the graph window into an *m*-by-*n* grid of small subwindows, and selects the *p*-th window for the current plot. Windows are numbered from left to right, top to bottom.

subplot(111) returns to the default single-window configuration.

## Examples

The statements

```
t = -20:.2:20;  y = sin(t)./t;
subplot(211), plot(y)
subplot(212), plot(diff(y)/.2)
```

plot the *sinc* function on the top half of the screen and its derivative on the bottom half.

subplot(121) and subplot(122) split the display into left and right halves. subplot(221), 222, 223, and 224 break the display into four small plotting boxes.

## Limitations

The graph window can be split into four windows, at most. The limits are $m \leq 2$ and $n \leq 2$. If $m > 2$ or $n > 2$ or $p > mn$, the value is out of range and subplot will print the error message:

```
Command option is unknown.
```

## See also

```
plot, clg, hold
```

## Purpose

Sums and products.

## Synopsis

```
sum(X), prod(X), cumsum(X), cumprod(X)
```

## Description

sum  For vectors, `sum(X)` is the sum of the elements of X. For matrices, `sum(X)` is a row vector with the sum over each column.

prod  For vectors, `prod(X)` is the product of the elements of X. For matrices, `prod(X)` is a row vector with the product over each column.

cumsum  For vectors, `cumsum(X)` is the cumulative sum of the elements of X. For matrices, `cumsum(X)` is a matrix containing the cumulative sums over each column.

cumprod  For vectors, `cumprod(X)` is the cumulative product of the elements of X. For matrices, `cumprod(X)` is a matrix containing the cumulative products over each column.

## Examples

`sum(diag(X))` is the *trace* of X.

## See also

```
diff, trace
```

Reference

**Purpose**

Singular value decomposition.

**Synopsis**

```
svd(X)
[U,S,V] = svd(X)
[U,S,V] = svd(X,0)
```

**Description**

svd computes the matrix singular value decomposition.

[U,S,V] = svd(X) produces a diagonal matrix S of the same dimension as X, with nonnegative diagonal elements in decreasing order, and unitary matrices U and V so that

```
X = U*S*V'
```

By itself, svd(X) returns a vector containing the singular values.

[U,S,V] = svd(X,0) produces the "economy size" decomposition. If X is *m*-by-*n* with $m > n$, then only the first *n* columns of U are computed and S is *n*-by-*n*.

**Algorithm**

svd uses the LINPACK routine ZSVDC.

**Diagnostics**

If the limit of 75 QR step iterations is exhausted while seeking a singular value:

```
Solution will not converge.
```

**References**

J.J. Dongarra, J.R. Bunch, C.B. Moler, and G.W. Stewart, *LINPACK User's Guide*, SIAM, Philadelphia, 1979.

## Purpose

One- and two-dimensional table look-up.

## Synopsis

```
table1(tab,x)
table2(tab, x, y)
```

## Description

`table1` performs a one-dimensional table look-up using a linear interpolation. If `tab` is a table of numbers, with each column containing a different variable, the function

```
y = table1(tab,x)
```

returns a linearly interpolated row from `tab`, looking up x in the first column of `tab`. The row vector is returned with a length one less than the width of the table. (For example, if `tab` has dimensions *n*-by-2, `table1` returns a scalar.)

`table2(tab,x,y)` performs a 2-dimensional table lookup, returning a linearly interpolated intersection from the table `tab` by looking up x in the first column of `tab` and y in the first row.

## Algorithm

`table1` and `table2` are M-files in the *MATLAB Toolbox*.

## Limitations

For `table1`, the table's first column must be monotonic. The value of x must lie between the first and last values in the first column of `tab`.

For `table2`, the first row and column of the table must be monotonic. The value used for x must lie between the first and last values in the first column of `tab`. The value used for y must lie between the first and last values in the first row of `tab`.

## See also

```
spline, polyfit
```

## Purpose

Transfer function to state-space conversion.

## Synopsis

```
[a,b,c,d] = tf2ss(num,den)
```

## Description

tf2ss converts systems in transfer function form to state-space.

[A,B,C,D] = tf2ss(num,den) finds a state-space representation

$$\dot{x} = Ax + Bu$$
$$y = Cx + Du$$

given a system in transfer function form

$$H(s) = \frac{num(s)}{den(s)} = C(sI-A)^{-1}B + D$$

from a single input. Vector den specifies the coefficients of the denominator in descending powers of $s$. Matrix num indicates the numerator coefficients with as many rows as there are outputs $y$. The A,B,C,D matrices are returned in controller canonical form.

tf2ss also works for discrete systems but the numerator must be padded with trailing zeros to make it the same length as the denominator.

The function ss2tf (not included in *The Student Edition*) does the inverse of tf2ss.

## Examples

Consider the system

$$H(s) = \frac{\left[\dfrac{2s + 3}{s^2 + 2s + 1}\right]}{s^2 + 0.4s + 1}$$

To convert this system to state-space:

```
num = [0 2 3
       1 2 1];
den = [1 0.4 1]

[a,b,c,d] = tf2ss(num,den)

a =
   -0.4000    -1.0000
    1.0000          0
b =
     1
     0
c =
    2.0000     3.0000
    1.6000          0
d =
     0
     1
```

There is disagreement in the literature on naming conventions for the "canonical forms." It is easy, however, to generate similarity transformations that convert to other, perhaps more familiar, forms. For example, here is one such transformation:

```
T = fliplr(eye(n));
A = T\A*T;
```

## Algorithm

tf2ss is an M-function in the *Signal Processing Toolbox*. The *A, B, C, D* matrices are written in controller canonical form "by inspection."

## See also

ss2zp, zp2ss

Reference

## Purpose

Transfer function to zero-pole-gain conversion.

## Synopsis

```
[z,p,k] = tf2zp(num,den)
```

## Description

tf2ss finds the zeros, poles, and gains of systems in polynomial transfer function form.

`[Z,p,k] = tf2zp(NUM,den)` finds the SIMO factored transfer function form:

$$H(s) = \frac{Z(s)}{p(s)} = k\frac{(s - Z(1))(s - Z(2)) \cdots (s - Z(m))}{(s - p(1))(s - p(2)) \cdots (s - p(n))}$$

given a SIMO system in polynomial transfer function form:

$$\frac{NUM(s)}{den(s)} = \frac{NUM(1)s^{nn-1} + \cdots + NUM(nn-1)s + NUM(nn)}{den(1)s^{nd-1} + \cdots + den(nd-1)s + den(nd)}$$

Vector den specifies the coefficients of the denominator in descending powers of s. Matrix NUM indicates the numerator coefficients with as many rows as there are outputs. The zero locations are returned in the columns of matrix Z, with as many columns as there are rows in NUM. The pole locations are returned in column vector p, and the gains for each numerator transfer function in vector k.

tf2zp also works for discrete systems. The function zp2tf does the inverse of tf2zp.

## Examples

Find the zeros, poles, and gains of the system:

$$H(s) = \frac{2s^2 + 5s + 1}{s^2 + 2s + 3}$$

```
num = [2 3];
den = [1 0.4 1];
[z,p,k] = tf2zp(num,den)
```

z =
  -1.5000
p =
  -0.2000 + 0.9798i
  -0.2000 - 0.9798i
k = 2

## Algorithm

tf2zp is an M-file in the *Signals and Systems Toolbox*. The system is converted to state-space using tf2ss and then to zeros, poles, and gains using ss2zp.

## See also

ss2tf, ss2zp, tf2ss, zp2ss, zp2tf

## Purpose

Graph labels, titles, and grid lines.

## Synopsis

```
title('text')
xlabel('text')
ylabel('text')
text(x,y,'text')
grid
```

## Description

`title('text')` writes the text as a title at the top of the current plot.

`xlabel('text')` writes the text on the current plot beneath the x-axis.

`ylabel('text')` writes the text on the current plot beside the y-axis.

`text(X,Y,'text')` writes *text* at (X,Y) on the graphics screen, where (X,Y) are in units from the last plot. If X and Y are vectors, `text` writes the text at all locations given. If *text* is an array the same length as X and Y, `text` marks each point with the corresponding row of the *text* array.

`text(X,Y,'text','sc')` interprets the (X,Y) points in *screen coordinates* where (0.0,0.0) is the lower left corner of the screen, and (1.0,1.0) is the upper right.

`grid` draws grid lines on the current plot.

## Examples

The statements

```
plot([1 5 10],[1 10 20],'x')
text(5,10,' Action point')
```

annotate the point at (5,10) with the text, while

```
plot(x1,y1,x2,y2)
text(x1,y1,'1'), text(x2,y2,'2')
```

marks two curves so they can be distinguished easily.

To include a variable's value in a title:

```
f = 70; c = (f-32)/1.8;
title(['Room temperature is ',num2str(c),'degrees C'])
```

**See also**

```
gtext, plot, num2str, int2str
```

Reference

**Purpose**

Form Toeplitz matrices.

**Synopsis**

```
toeplitz(c,r)
toeplitz(c)
```

**Description**

A *Toeplitz* matrix is defined by one row and one column. A *symmetric Toeplitz* matrix is defined by just one vector. `toeplitz` generates Toeplitz matrices given just the row or column description.

`toeplitz(c,r)` is a nonsymmetric Toeplitz matrix having `c` as its first column and `r` as its first row. If the first elements of `c` and `r` are different, a message is printed and the column wins the disagreement.

`toeplitz(c)` is the symmetric or Hermitian Toeplitz matrix formed from vector `c`.

**Examples**

A Toeplitz matrix with diagonal disagreement is:

```
c = [1     2     3     4     5];
r = [1.5   2.5   3.5   4.5   5.5];
toeplitz(c,r)

Column wins diagonal conflict.

ans =
    1.000   2.500   3.500   4.500   5.500
    2.000   1.000   2.500   3.500   4.500
    3.000   2.000   1.000   2.500   3.500
    4.000   3.000   2.000   1.000   2.500
    5.000   4.000   3.000   2.000   1.000
```

**Algorithm**

toeplitz is an M-file in the *MATLAB Toolbox.*

**See also**

hankel, vander

## Purpose

Matrix trace.

## Synopsis

```
trace(a)
```

## Description

`trace(A)` returns the trace of matrix A.

## Algorithm

`trace` is a single-statement M-file in the *MATLAB Toolbox*:

```
t = sum(diag(a));
```

## Purpose

Trigonometric functions.

## Synopsis

```
sin(x),   cos(x),   tan(x)
asin(x),  acos(x),  atan(x),  atan2(y,x)
sinh(x),  cosh(x),  tanh(x)
asinh(x), acosh(x), atanh(x)
```

## Description

The trigonometric functions operate elementwise on matrices. Their domains and ranges include complex numbers, which can lead to unexpected results if used unintentionally.

`sin`, `cos`, and `tan` return trigonometric functions of radian arguments:

`sin(X)` is the *sine* of the elements of `X`. For complex $z = x + iy$, the complex *sine* is returned:

$$sin(z) = sin(x)\,cosh(y) + i\ cos(x)\,sinh(y)$$

`cos(X)` is the *cosine* of the elements of `X`. For complex $z = x + iy$, the complex *sine* is returned:

$$cos(z) = cos(x)\,cosh(y) - i\ sin(x)\,sinh(y)$$

`tan(X)` is the *tangent* of the elements of `X`. For complex `z`, the complex *tangent* `sin(z)/cos(z)` is returned.

Reference

acos, asin, atan, and atan2 return inverse trigonometric functions in radians:

acos(X) is the *arccosine* of the elements of X. For real x, such that $abs(x) \leq 1.0$, the result is in the range 0 to $\pi$. Complex results are obtained if $abs(x) > 1.0$ for some element, or if x is complex. The complex *arccosine* is defined as:

$$\cos^{-1}(z) = -i \ log(z + i \ sqrt(1-z^2))$$

asin(X) is the *arcsine* of the elements of X. For real x, such that $abs(x) \leq 1.0$, the result is in the range $-\pi/2$ to $+\pi/2$. Complex results are obtained if $abs(x) > 1.0$ for some element, or if x is complex. The complex *arcsine* is defined as:

$$\sin^{-1}(z) = -i \ log(iz + sqrt(1-z^2))$$

atan(X) is the *arctangent* of the elements of X. For real x, the result is in the range $-\pi/2$ to $+\pi/2$. If x is complex, the complex *arctangent* is returned:

$$\tan^{-1}(z) = \frac{i}{2} \log \frac{(i + z)}{(i - z)}$$

atan2(Y,X) is the four-quadrant *arctangent* of the real elements of Y./X. The imaginary part is ignored. The result is in the range $-\pi$ to $+\pi$.

The hyperbolic functions sinh, cosh and tanh and their inverses asinh, acosh and atanh are available too, implemented as M-files in the *MATLAB Toolbox*.

**See also**

exp, log, log10, expm, funm

**References**

Churchhill, R.V., Brown, J.W., and Verhey, R.F., *Complex Variables and Applications*, McGraw-Hill, 1974.

## Purpose

Vandermonde matrix.

## Synopsis

```
vander(c)
```

## Description

`vander(c)` returns the Vandermonde matrix whose next to last column is `c`. The `j`-th column of a Vandermonde matrix is the `(n-j)`-th power of vector `c`, where `n` is the length of `c` (the size of the Vandermonde matrix). The elements of a Vandermonde matrix are:

$$vander(i,j) = c(i)^{(n-j)}$$

Vandermonde matrices arise in connection with fitting polynomials to data.

## Examples

Create a small Vandermonde matrix from a vector `c`:

```
c =
      2      3      4      5

a = vander(c)

a =
        8      4      2      1
       27      9      3      1
       64     16      4      1
      125     25      5      1
```

## Algorithm

`vander` is an M-file in the *MATLAB Toolbox*.

## See also

```
polyfit, hankel, toeplitz
```

## Purpose

Repeat statements an indefinite number of times.

## Synopsis

```
while s
  statements
end
```

## Description

`while` repeats statements an indefinite number of times. The general format is:

```
while expression
  statements
end
```

The statements are executed while the *expression* has all nonzero elements. The *expression* is usually of the form

```
expression rop expression
```

where *rop* is `==`, `<`, `>`, `<=`, `>=`, or `~=`.

## Examples

The variable `eps` is a tolerance used to determine such things as near singularity and rank. Its initial value is the *machine epsilon*, the distance from 1.0 to the next largest floating point number on your machine. Its calculation demonstrates `while` loops:

```
eps = 1;
while (1+eps) > 1
      eps = eps/2;
end
eps = eps*2
```

## See also

```
for, if, end, break, return, any, all
```

## Purpose

Directory of the variables in memory.
Directory of the M-files in the current disk directory.
Check if a variable or file *exists*.

## Synopsis

```
who, whos
what
exist('item')
```

The *item* can be either a variable or a file.

## Description

`who` lists the variables currently in memory.

`whos` lists the current variables, their sizes, and whether they have nonzero imaginary parts.

`what` shows a directory listing of the M-files and MAT-files on the disk in the current directory. Files with other file-types are not shown.

`exist('A')` returns 1 if A exists as a variable in the workspace, 2 if A.m is a file on disk, and 0 if A doesn't exist. Note that the variable name must be in quotes.

`exist('filename.ext')` tests for the existence of the specified filename and returns 2 if found.

## See also

`dir, help`

## Purpose

Zero-pole-gain to state-space conversion.

## Synopsis

```
[a,b,c,d] = zp2ss(z,p,k)
```

## Description

zp2ss forms state-space models from the zeros, poles, and gains of systems in transfer function form.

[A,B,C,D] = zp2ss(z,p,k) finds a single input, multiple output state-space representation

$$\dot{x} = Ax + Bu$$
$$y = Cx + Du$$

given a system in factored transfer function form

$$H(s) = \frac{z(s)}{p(s)} = k\frac{(s + z(1))(s + z(2))...(s + z(n))}{(s + p(1))(s + p(2))...(s + p(n))}$$

Column vector p specifies the pole locations and matrix z the zero locations with as many columns as there are outputs. The gains for each numerator transfer function are in vector k. The A,B,C,D matrices are returned in controller canonical form.

Infs can be used as place holders in z if some columns have fewer zeros.

## Algorithm

zp2ss is an M-file in the *Signal Processing Toolbox* that, for single-input systems, groups complex pairs together into two-by-two blocks down the diagonal of the A-matrix.

## See also

ss2zp, tf2ss

## Purpose

Zero-pole-gain to transfer function conversion.

## Synopsis

```
[num,den] = zp2tf(z,p,k)
```

## Description

zp2tf forms transfer function polynomials from the zeros, poles, and gains of systems in factored form.

[NUM,den] = zp2tf(Z,p,k) finds a rational transfer function:

$$\frac{NUM(s)}{den(s)} = \frac{NUM(1)s^{nn-1} + \cdots + NUM(nn-1)s + NUM(nn)}{den(1)s^{nd-1} + \cdots + den(nd-1)s + den(nd)}$$

given a system in factored transfer function form:

$$H(s) = \frac{Z(s)}{p(s)} = k\frac{(s-Z(1))(s-Z(2)) \cdots (s-Z(m))}{(s-p(1))(s-p(2)) \cdots (s-p(n))}$$

Column vector p specifies the pole locations and matrix Z the zero locations with as many columns as there are outputs. The gains for each numerator transfer function are in vector k. The polynomial coefficients are returned in vectors, the denominator coefficients in row vector den, and the numerator coefficients in matrix NUM with as many rows as there are columns of Z.

Inf's can be used as place holders in Z if some columns have fewer zeros. See the *Tutorial* section.

## Algorithm

zp2tf is an M-file in the *Signals and Systems Toolbox*. The system is converted to transfer function form using poly on p and the columns of Z.

## See also

```
ss2tf, ss2zp, tf2ss, zp2ss
```

---

## Purpose

Matrix and array arithmetic.

## Synopsis

```
                    X  +  Y
                    X  -  Y
     X  *  Y            X  .*  Y
     X  /  Y            X  ./  Y
     X  \  Y            X  .\  Y
     X  ^  Y            X  .^  Y
     X '                 X .'
```

## Description

Matrix arithmetic operations are obtained with +, −, ∗, /, \, ^. Element-by-element array arithmetic operations are indicated by preceding the operator with a period "." resulting in .∗, .^, ./, and .\.

+      Addition.    X + Y adds matrices X and Y. X and Y must have the same dimensions unless one is a scalar. A scalar can be added to anything.

−      Subtraction.    X − Y subtracts matrix X from Y. X and Y must have the same dimensions unless one is a scalar. A scalar can be subtracted from anything.

∗      Multiplication.    X∗Y is the matrix product of X and Y. A scalar (1-by-1 matrix) may multiply anything. Otherwise, the number of columns of X must equal the number of rows of Y.

        X.∗Y denotes element-by-element multiplication. X and Y must have the same dimensions unless one is a scalar. A scalar may multiply anything.

\      Backslash or matrix left division. If A is a square matrix, A\B is roughly the same as inv(A)∗B, except it is computed in a different way. If A is an $n$-by-$n$ matrix and B is a column vector with $n$ components, or a matrix with several such columns, then X = A\B is the solution to the equation $AX = B$ computed by Gaussian elimination. A warning message is printed if A is badly scaled or nearly singular.

If A is an $m$-by-$n$ matrix with $m \neq n$ and B is a column vector with $m$ components, or a matrix with several such columns, then X = A\B is the solution in the least squares sense to the under- or overdetermined system of equations $AX = B$. The effective rank, $k$, of A, is determined from the QR decomposition with pivoting. A solution X is computed which has at most $k$ nonzero components per column. If $k < n$ this will usually not be the same solution as pinv(A)\*B, which is the least squares solution with the smallest norm(A\*X−B).

If A and B have the same dimensions, then A.\B has elements $a(i,j)\backslash b(i,j)$ denoting element-by-element division. For example, C = A .\ B is the matrix with elements $c(i,j) = b(i,j)/a(i,j)$.

Slash or matrix right division. B/A is roughly the same as B\*inv(A). More precisely, B/A = (A'\B')'. See \.

B./A denotes element-by-element division. A and B must have the same dimensions unless one is a scalar. A scalar can be divided with anything. *Caution:* 3./A is NOT the same as 3 ./A because in the first case the dot is picked up by the 3 as a decimal point causing matrix division, while in the second case the dot is associated with the / for element-wise division.

Powers. X^p is X to the power p, if p is a scalar. If p is an integer, the power is computed by repeated multiplication. If the integer is negative, X is inverted first. For other values of p, the calculation involves eigenvalues and eigenvectors, such that if [V,D] = eig(X), then X^p = V\*D.^p/V.

If P is a matrix, x^P is x raised to the matrix power P using eigenvalues and eigenvectors. X^P, where X and P are matrices, is an error.

Z = X.^Y denotes element-by-element powers. X and Y must have the same dimensions unless one is a scalar. A scalar can operate into anything.

The quote symbol ' indicates transposition. X' is the matrix, or complex conjugate transpose. X.' is the array, or nonconjugate transpose.

## Examples

A\eye(A) is one way to find the inverse of A.

For the nonsquare case, the statement A\eye(A) produces a generalized inverse of A.

Reference

## Algorithm

If A is square, the LINPACK routines ZGECO and ZGESL solve the general nonsymmetric simultaneous linear equation problems B/A, and A\B. ZGECO uses Gaussian elimination with partial pivoting to compute the LU factorization of A and then estimates its condition. ZGESL uses the LU factorization of matrix A to solve the linear system $AX = B$, or $A'X = B$.

If A is not square, the LINPACK routines ZQRDC and ZQRSL solve the over- or under-constrained least squares problem. ZQRDC computes the QR decomposition of matrix A, while ZQRSL applies the decomposition to B.

For more information, see the *LINPACK User's Guide*.

## Diagnostics

From matrix division, if a square A is singular:

```
Matrix is singular to working precision.
```

From element-wise division, if the divisor has zero elements:

```
Division by zero is a no-no.
```

On machines without IEEE arithmetic, like the VAX, the above two operations generate the error messages shown. On machines with IEEE arithmetic, only warning messages are generated. The matrix division returns a matrix with each element set to Inf; the element-wise division produces NaNs or infinities where appropriate.

If the inverse was found, but is not reliable:

```
Warning: Matrix is close to singular or badly scaled.
         Results may be inaccurate. RCOND = xxx
```

From matrix division, if a nonsquare A is rank deficient:

```
Warning: Rank deficient, rank = xxx  tol = xxx
```

## See also

```
inv, qr, det, lu, rcond, orth, rref
<   <=   >   >=   ==   ~=
&  |  ~
```

## References

J.J. Dongarra, J.R. Bunch, C.B. Moler, and G.W. Stewart, *LINPACK User's Guide*, SIAM, Philadelphia, 1979.

## Purpose

Relational operations.

## Synopsis

$<$   $<=$   $>$   $>=$   $==$   $\tilde{}=$

## Description

The relational operators are $<$, $<=$, $>$, $>=$, $==$, and $\tilde{}=$. Relational operators perform element-by-element comparisons between two matrices. They return a matrix of the same size, with elements set to one where the relation is true, and elements set to zero where it is not.

The operators $<$, $<=$, $>$, and $>=$ use only the real part of their operands for the comparison if the operands are complex. Operators $==$ and $\tilde{}=$ test both real and imaginary parts.

The relational operators have precedence midway between the logical operators and the arithmetic operators.

To test if two strings are equivalent, use strcmp, which allows vectors of dissimilar length to be compared.

## Examples

If one of the operands is a scalar and the other a matrix, the scalar "expands" to the size of the matrix. For example, the two statements

```
X = 5 >= [1 2 3;4 5 6;7 8 10]
X = 5*ones(3,3) >= [1 2 3;4 5 6;7 8 10]
```

produce the same result,

```
X =

    1     1     1
    1     1     0
    0     0     0
```

## See also

find, any, all, strcmp, &, |, ~

## Purpose

Logical operations.

## Synopsis

```
&  |  ~
```

## Description

The symbols `&`, `|`, and `~` are the logical operators AND, OR, and NOT. They work element-wise on matrices, with 0 representing FALSE and anything nonzero regarded as TRUE. `A & B` logically ANDs the elements, `A | B` does a logical OR, and `~A` complements the elements of `A`.

The logical operators have the lowest precedence, with relational operators and arithmetic operators being higher.

## Examples

Here are two scalar expressions that illustrate precedence relationships:

```
1 & 0 + 3
3 >.4 & 1
```

They evaluate to 1 and 0 respectively, and are equivalent to

```
1 & (0 + 3)
(3 > 4) & 1
```

## See also

```
find, any, all, <, <=, >, >=, ==, ~=
```

Reference

## Purpose

Special characters.

## Synopsis

[ ] ( ) , . ´ ; % !

## Description

[ ]  Brackets are used to form vectors and matrices.

[6.9  9.64  sqrt(-1)] is a vector with three elements separated by blanks.
[6.9,  9.64,  i] is the same thing.
[1+j 2-j 3] and [1 +j 2 -j 3] are not the same. The first has three elements, the second has five.
[11 12 13; 21 22 23] is a 2-by-3 matrix. The semicolon ends the first row.

Vectors and matrices can be used inside [  ] brackets. [A B;C] is allowed if the number of rows of A equals the number of rows of B and the number of columns of A plus the number of columns of B equals the number of columns of C. This rule generalizes in a hopefully obvious way to allow fairly complicated constructions.

A = [  ] stores an empty matrix in A.

For the use of [ and ] on the left of an "=" in multiple assignment statements, see lu, eig, svd, and so on.

( )  Parentheses are used to indicate precedence in arithmetic expressions in the usual way. They are used to enclose arguments of functions in the usual way. They are also used to enclose subscripts of vectors and matrices in a manner somewhat more general than the usual way. If X and V are vectors, then X(V) is [X(V(1)),  X(V(2)),  ..., X(V(n))]. The components of V are rounded to nearest integers and used as subscripts. An error occurs if any such subscript is less than 1 or greater than the dimension of X. Some examples:

X(3) is the third element of X.
X([1 2 3]) is the first three elements of X. So is
X([sqrt(2), sqrt(3), 4*atan(1)]).

If X has n components, X(n:-1:1) reverses them. The same indirect subscripting works in matrices. If V has m components and W has n components, then A(V,W) is the m-by-n matrix formed from the elements of A whose subscripts are the elements of V and W. For example A([1,5],:) = A([5,1],:) interchanges rows 1 and 5 of A.

=  Used in assignment statements. == is the relational EQUALS operator. See <   <=   > >=   ==   ~=.

´  Matrix transpose. X´ is the complex conjugate transpose of X.   X.´ is the nonconjugate transpose.

Quote. 'any text' is a vector whose components are the ASCII codes for the characters. A quote within the text is indicated by two quotes.

.  Decimal point. 314/100, 3.14 and .314e1 are all the same.

Element-by-element operations are obtained using .*  ,   .^  ,  ./  , or .\. See + - * / \ ^ '.

Three or more points at the end of a line indicate continuation.

,  Comma. Used to separate matrix subscripts and function arguments. Used to separate statements in multi-statement lines. For multi-statement lines, it may be replaced by a semicolon to suppress printing.

;  Semicolon. Used inside brackets to end rows. Used after an expression or statement to suppress printing or separate statements.

%  Percent. The percent symbol denotes a comment; it indicates a logical end of line. Any following text is ignored.

!  Exclamation point. Indicates that the rest of the input line should be issued as a command to the operating system.

**See also**

Arithmetic, relational, and logical operators.

---

## Purpose

Creating vectors, matrix subscripting, and `for` iterations.

## Description

The colon is one of the most useful operators in MATLAB. It can create vectors, subscript matrices, and specify `for` iterations.

The rules the colon operator uses to create regularly spaced vectors are:

```
j:k   is the same as [j, j+1, ..., k].
j:k   is empty if j > k.
j:i:k is the same as [j, j+i, j+2i, ..., k].
j:i:k is empty if i > 0 and j > k or if i < 0 and j < k.
```

Here are definitions that govern the use of the colon to pick out selected rows, columns, and elements of vectors and matrices:

```
A(:,j)  is the j-th column of A.
A(i,:)  is the i-th row of A.
A(:,:)  is the same as A.
A(j:k)  is A(j),A(j+1),...,A(k).
A(:,j:k) is A(:,j),A(:,j+1),...,A(:,k)  and so on.
A(:)  is all the elements of A, regarded as a single
column.  On the left side of an assignment statement, A(:)
fills A, preserving its shape from before.
```

If you are new to MATLAB, spend some time learning about the colon because once you master the colon, you've mastered MATLAB.

## Examples

Using the colon with integers:

```
D = 1:4
```

results in

```
D =
      1     2     3     4
```

Using two colons to create a vector with arbitrary real increments between the elements:

```
E = 0:.1:.5
```

results in

```
E =
   0.000   0.100   0.200   0.300   0.400   0.500
```

## See also

```
for, logspace, linspace, reshape
```

Reference

# Appendices

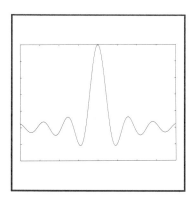

# A
# MATLAB
# on the Macintosh

---

## A.1  MATLAB Window Types

MATLAB has four different types of windows:

**Command**    The input/output display window

**Graph**      The window for displaying plots and graphs

**Edit**       The window for creating and modifying M-files

**Help**       The online Help and Demo facility window

If there are several windows open on the Macintosh screen, you can activate a particular window by clicking anywhere within the window. Since the menu bar across the top of the screen is context-sensitive, it changes to reflect the menu choices applicable to the newly selected window after you click in the window.

Except for the Help window, you can grow or shrink all windows using the grow boxes in the lower right-hand corners or zoom boxes in the upper right-hand corners of the windows.

## A.1.1 Command Window

The Command window allows you to enter commands and MATLAB to display its numerical output. Most mathematical operations with MATLAB are performed by issuing commands at the command prompt, or by running scripts, which are stored lists of commands. A few operations, like file management and editing, can be done only from the menus. Other operations can be done from the menu bar or by entering a command in the Command window.

MATLAB keeps a history of your session. You can scroll back through the session history using the scroll bars. To make scrolling through your session history easier, MATLAB automatically positions the insertion point at the end of the command line if you have moved away from the command prompt and pressed a key. If the character that you type is displayable (such as a letter or digit), the character is added to the command line.

Memory for the history is quite large - about 32K bytes. If you exceed this limit, by producing a large amount of output, the beginning of the history is truncated.

To delete the session history, thereby freeing the memory it uses, click on the close box in the upper-left corner of the Command window. Select **New** from the **File** menu. A dialog box appears. Click on the **Command** radio button, and then on the **OK** button to open a new Command window.

## A.1.2 Graph Window

The Graph window is where plots appear when graph-producing commands are issued. For example, from the Command window, enter

```
x = .1:.5:4*pi;
y = x.*(sin(x)+2);
plot(y *y)
```

If your Graph window is obscured by other windows, it pops automatically to the top and displays a family of growing sine curves.

## A.1.3 Edit Window

MATLAB has its own built-in editor for creating and modifying M-files, which can be scripts or functions:

- *Scripts* are files containing stored sequences of MATLAB commands.

- *Functions* are like scripts, but allow you to pass arguments and have local internal variables.

For detailed information on M-files, see the *Tutorial* section of this guide.

As you become more experienced with MATLAB, you may find that instead of entering commands in the Command window, you prefer the "what if" capabilities afforded by entering commands into an Edit window, as a script, where they can be changed and re-executed easily. Suppose you've been entering statements into the Command window to plot Bessel functions of different orders:

```
n = 0;
x = 0:.5:20;
y = bessel(n,x);
plot(x,y)
```

Rather than typing the same command sequence repetitively for different values of n, you can

1. Select **New** from the **File** menu.

2. Enter the commands into the Edit window.

3. Select **Save And Go** from the **File** menu.

4. Enter a filename, perhaps `Bess`, and click on the **Save** button.

This executes the commands and plots the Bessel function of order zero. To plot the Bessel function of order one

1. Click on the Edit window to make it active.

2. Change `n=0` to `n=1` in the Edit window.

3. Select **Save And Go** from the **File** menu to rerun the script.

## A.1.4 Help Window

MATLAB has a Help system that gives you immediate online assistance if you've forgotten how to use a command, or if you need a quick overview of a function that's unfamiliar to you. Online Help is brief; detailed descriptions of all functions and commands are found in the *Reference* section of this guide.

To use Help

1.  Select **About MATLAB** from the  menu. A Help window appears.

2.  Double-click on the category of interest. Except for **Built-in commands**, the categories correspond to the folders that lie in the MATLAB search path, which by default, includes all the folders beneath the directory in which MATLAB resides. Another list of items appears in the Help window. If you have chosen the **Built-in commands** category, the items correspond to built-in MATLAB commands. Otherwise, the items correspond to M-files on disk.

3.  Scroll to the item of interest and double-click on it with the mouse. A description of the item appears in the Help window.

After you're finished reading the Help entry, you can click on the **Topics** button to move back up to the list of Help items. From here, you can choose another item by double-clicking on it or you can click on **Topics** to return you to the list of Help categories. Clicking on the close box in the upper left corner closes the Help window.

The Help system is organized hierarchically, according to the MATLAB search path. The **Help** button and double-clicking on items moves you down the tree out into the folders. The **Topics** button moves you back up towards the root. Within an individual folder, the actual Help text is the first few commented lines of each M-file.

The **Demos** button in the Help window lists a set of demonstration scripts for you to run. It's the same as selecting **Run Script** from the **M-File** menu and moving to the **Demonstrations** folder.

You can have several Help windows open at once. Help windows remain on the screen until you close them. They can be kept on the screen concurrently with other windows for easy reference.

# A.2 MATLAB Menus

## A.2.1 Command Window Menu Bar

When the Command window is active, the menu bar looks like

| &#xF8FF; | File | Edit | Workspace | M-file | Format | Window |

The following menus are available from the command window menu bar. These menus are described on the following pages.

| Menus | Description |
|-------|-------------|
| &#xF8FF; | See the online Help facility. |
| **File** | Edit a script or function M-file. |
| **Edit** | Cut and paste to the Clipboard. |
| **Workspace** | Load or save data from disk (MAT-files). |
| **M-File** | Execute script M-files, including demonstrations. |
| **Format** | Set the numeric display format. |
| **Window** | Bring a hidden window to the front. |

## File Menu

The **File** menu provides choices for managing files and printing.

| File | | |
|------|------|------|
| **New...** | ⌘N | Create a new M-file. |
| **Open...** | ⌘O | Open an existing M-file. |
| **Close** | ⌘W | Close currently active window. |
| 𝕾𝖆𝖛𝖊 | ⌘𝕾 | |
| 𝕾𝖆𝖛𝖊 𝕬𝖘... | | |
| 𝕾𝖆𝖛𝖊 𝕬𝖓𝖉 𝕲𝖔 | ⌘𝕲 | |
| 𝕽𝖊𝖛𝖊𝖗𝖙 𝖙𝖔 𝕾𝖆𝖛𝖊𝖉 | | |
| **Delete...** | | Delete a file. |
| **Page Setup...** | | Setup for printing. |
| **Print...** | ⌘P | Print contents of the selected window. |
| **M-File To TEXT...** | | Convert an M-file to a text file. |
| **TEXT To M-File...** | | Convert a text file to an M-file. |
| **Quit** | ⌘Q | Exit from MATLAB |

The **New** and **Open** items open Edit windows on new or selected files, respectively. Edit windows allow you to create and modify M-file scripts and functions. Refer to the *Edit Windows* section for details.

If you have closed the existing Command and Graph window pair, the **New** item creates a new Command and Graph window pair. After selecting **New**, a dialog box appears. Click on the **Command** radio button, and then on the **OK** button to create a new pair.

The **Page Setup** and **Print** items allow you to print the contents of the Command window. Refer to the *Printing* section for details.

The **M-File to TEXT** and **TEXT to M-File** items convert M-files from the special MATLAB file type with icon to standard text files that can be transferred to other programs or computers.

## Edit Menu

The **Edit** menu provides the standard Macintosh editing commands.

| | | |
|---|---|---|
| **Edit** | | |
| Undo | ⌘Z | |
| **Cut** | ⌘H | Move selected text to the Clipboard. |
| **Copy** | ⌘C | Copy selected text to the Clipboard. |
| **Paste** | ⌘U | Copy contents of the Clipboard to the selected location. |
| **Clear** | | Delete selected text. |
| Cmds Only | | |
| **Show Clipboard** | | Display contents of the Clipboard in a window. |

---

**Hint: Repeating Commands and Last Line Editing**

If you scroll back through the session history, you can select any previous text with the mouse and copy it to the Clipboard. This allows you to copy a selected command line, and then paste it in order to re-execute it. The **Paste** command automatically positions the blinking insertion point at the end of the Command window before doing the paste.

---

## Workspace Menu

The **Workspace** menu provides choices for managing MATLAB's workspace:

Display a list of the variables in the workspace.

Display a list of variables and their sizes.

Load data from a MAT- or ASCII file on disk.

Save the workspace to a MAT-file on disk.

Clear all variables from the workspace.

Experienced users can execute these operations by typing them at the command prompt.

## M-File Menu

The **M-File** menu groups commands relating to M-files:

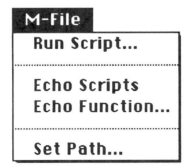

Run a script M-file.

Control whether scripts echo as they execute.

Control function echoing.

Specifying folders in which to look for M-files.

Script M-files are sequences of MATLAB commands that are saved in files on disk. There are several ways you can run a script:

- By selecting **Run Script** from the **M-File** menu when the Command window is active.

- By typing the command's name to the command prompt when the Command window is active.

- By selecting **Save And Go** from the **File** menu when the file is open in the active window.

If you need to interrupt an executing M-file before it is finished, type either Command-Period by holding down the **Command** key and pressing a Period, or Control-C by holding down the **Control** key (if your keyboard has one) and pressing C. Command-Period is to the Macintosh what Control-C is to other computers.

## Format Menu

The result of any MATLAB assignment statement not terminated by a semicolon is displayed on the screen, as well as assigned to the specific variable, or to `ans` if no variable is given. The **Format** menu controls the numeric format in which the output is displayed.

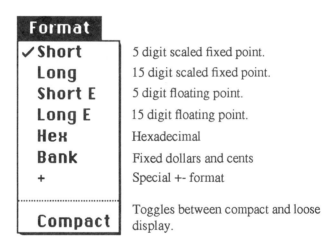

| Format | |
|---|---|
| ✓ **Short** | 5 digit scaled fixed point. |
| **Long** | 15 digit scaled fixed point. |
| **Short E** | 5 digit floating point. |
| **Long E** | 15 digit floating point. |
| **Hex** | Hexadecimal |
| **Bank** | Fixed dollars and cents |
| **+** | Special +- format |
| **Compact** | Toggles between compact and loose display. |

The output format does not affect how output is computed or saved - all computation is in double precision. For more information, see the format command in the *Reference* section for a table containing examples of each of the various formats.

## Window Menu

The **Window** menu is always the rightmost item on the menu bar. If you pull down the **Window** menu, a list of the currently open windows appears. Select one and release the mouse button to make the selected window the active window. With the **Window** menu pulled down, a list of command key equivalents for each of the windows is displayed.

For example, if you create a new Edit window (using the **New** command from the **File** menu), the **Window** menu appears.

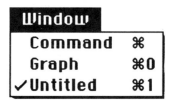

The **Command** key equivalent for the Command window is **Command-Space**. The checkmark next to **Untitled** indicates that this is the active window.

## A.2.2  Graph Window Menu Bar

When the Graph window is active, the menu bar looks like

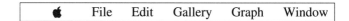

Only two of these menus are different than the command Window menu and are available while the Graph window is active; they are

**Gallery**   Select the type of graph paper.

**Graph**   Control the appearance of a graph.

---

**Hint: Special Menu Actions**

When the Graph window is active, **Print** from the **File** menu sends a copy of the current graph to the printer. **Copy** from the **Edit** menu saves a copy of the graph on the Clipboard in PICT format. **Save As** from the **File** menu saves the file on disk in either PICT or Encapsulated PostScript File (EPSF) format.

---

## Gallery Menu

The **Gallery** menu provides different types of graph paper for the plot displayed in the Graph window on your screen. MATLAB redraws the graph using the new graph type you select.

| **Gallery** | |
|---|---|
| **Linear Plot** | Linear X-Y |
| **Log-log** | Logarithmic |
| **Semi-log X** | Logarithmic X, linear Y |
| **Semi-log Y** | Logarithmic Y, linear X |
| **Polar** | Polar coordinates |
| **3-D Mesh** | 3-D perspective mesh plot |
| **Contour** | Contour plot |

## Graph Menu

The **Graph** menu provides the tools for controlling the appearance of the graph:

| **Graph** | |
|---|---|
| **Labels...** | Add labels and titles to the graph. |
| **Text...** | |
| **Grid** | Draw grid lines. |
| **Axis Limits...** | Set axis ranges for next graph. |
| **Hold Graph** | Toggle option to erase screen between plots. |
| **Clear Graph** | Clear the graph. |
| **Black Background** | Toggle background color between white and black. |

To return from the Command window to the Graph window,

- Press any key, or

- Click on the desired window with the mouse, or

- Select the desired window from the **Window** menu.

## A.2.3 Edit Window Menu Bar

When an Edit window is active, the menu bar looks like

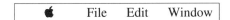

Only the **File** menu is different on this menu while the Edit window is active. It is explained in the next section.

### File Menu

The **File** menu provides selections for working with M-files:

| **File** | | |
|---|---|---|
| **New...** | ⌘N | Create a new M-file. |
| **Open...** | ⌘O | Open an existing M-file for editing. |
| **Close** | ⌘W | Close currently active window. |
| **Save** | ⌘S | Save M-file. |
| **Save As...** | | Save M-file with a different name. |
| **Save And Go** | ⌘G | Save M-file and execute it. |
| **Revert to Saved** | | Revert to last saved copy of file. |
| **Delete...** | | Delete a file. |
| **Page Setup...** | | Setup for printing |
| **Print...** | ⌘P | Print contents of the active window. |
| **M-File To TEXT...** | | Convert an M-file to a text file. |
| **TEXT To M-File...** | | Convert a text file to an M-file. |
| **Quit** | ⌘Q | Exit from MATLAB. |

To edit an existing M-file, select **Open** from the **File** menu. It displays a list of the M-files on disk to choose from. To create a new M-file, select **New** from the **File** menu. You can have as many Edit windows open as you like.

The **M-File to TEXT** and **TEXT to M-File** items convert M-files from the special MATLAB file type to standard text files that can be transferred to other programs or computers. MATLAB can edit and run M-files created by your favorite editor or word processing program, as long as the M-file is a standard text file with a .m extension.

## A.2.4  Help Window Menu Bar

The following is a view of the menu bar when the Help window is active:

Only the **File** menu is different on this menu while the Help window is active. It is explained in the next section.

### File Menu

The **File** menu provides selections for managing files.

| File | | |
|---|---|---|
| **New...** | ⌘N | Create a new M-file. |
| **Open...** | ⌘O | Open an existing M-file for editing. |
| **Close** | ⌘W | Close currently active window. |
| Save | ⌘S | |
| Save As... | | |
| Save And Go | ⌘G | |
| Revert to Saved | | |
| **Delete...** | | Delete a file. |
| Page Setup... | | |
| Print... | ⌘P | |
| **M-File To TEXT...** | | Convert an M-file to a text file. |
| **TEXT To M-File...** | | Convert a text file to an M-file. |
| **Quit** | ⌘Q | Exit from MATLAB. |

The **New** command creates an untitled Edit window. The **Open** command allows you to edit an existing M-file on disk. The **Close** command closes the Help window. The **Delete** command deletes a file on disk. The **M-File to TEXT** and **TEXT to M-File** commands convert M-files between the special MATLAB file type and standard text files.

## A.3  Using the Clipboard

You can move information within MATLAB and between MATLAB and other applications using the Macintosh Clipboard. The **Cut**, **Copy**, **Paste**, and **Clear** commands under the **Edit** menu let you move information between the active window and the Clipboard. **Show Clipboard** shows you the current contents of the Clipboard.

In the Command and Edit windows, the **Cut**, **Copy**, **Paste**, and **Clear** commands work in the normal Macintosh style on text that is selected (highlighted). In the Graph window, the only valid Edit operation is **Copy**, which copies the plot in the Graph window onto the Clipboard. Internally, the plot is saved in PICT format, and you can paste it into applications that work with PICT files, including PageMaker and MacDraw. Pasting your graph into MacDraw allows you to rearrange it, add text, change fonts, etc.

### A.3.1  Using the Clipboard to Import Data

You can use the Clipboard to import data from other applications. Suppose you have several columns of data saved to the Clipboard from a spreadsheet application. To import this data into a MATLAB variable named $Q$:

1. Select **New** from the **File** menu.

2. Enter **Q=[ ]**; into the Edit window.

3. Position the insertion point between the two brackets.

4. Select **Paste** from the **Edit** menu.

5. Select **Save And Go** from the **File** menu.

6. Enter a filename, perhaps $Q$, and click on the **Save** button.

Your data is now stored in the MATLAB workspace with the name $Q$.

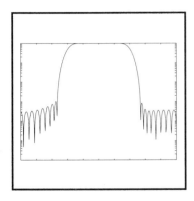

# B
# Reading
# and Writing
# MAT-Files

---

## B.1 MS-DOS Subroutines

The `save` command in MATLAB saves the variables currently in memory into a binary disk file called a "MAT-file" (it is called a MAT-file because the filename extension is `.MAT`). The `load` command is the inverse - it reads the MAT-file on disk into MATLAB's memory. There are occasions in which you may find it desirable to directly read and write MAT-files from your own Fortran, C, or Pascal programs. To help you with this task, there is a collection of subroutines for this purpose in the \MATLAB\LOADSAVE directory on your disk. In addition, the structure of a MAT-file is documented fully under `load` in the *Reference* section of this guide.

### B.1.1 C Programs

There are three files in \MATLAB\LOADSAVE directory associated with reading and writing MAT-files from C programs. These routines are machine-independent and portable to all different platforms on which MATLAB is currently available.

LOADMAT.C     C routines to read MAT-files

SAVEMAT.C     C routines to write MAT-files

TESTLS.C     A main program illustrating the use of LOADMAT.C and SAVEMAT.C

## B.1.2 Pascal Programs

There is one file in `\MATLAB\LOADSAVE` that gives an example of reading and writing MAT-files from Pascal. It is tested with Turbo Pascal.

`TESTLS.PAS`    Pascal program and subprocedures showing how to read and write MAT-files


## B.1.3 Fortran Programs

Fortran poses interesting challenges with respect to reading and writing MAT-files. MAT-files are arbitrary byte streams, which Fortran does not provide a convenient way of writing. Some Fortrans on some platforms do provide extensions that allow them to be written, but often only in a very inefficient manner.

There are two distinct sets of files in `\MATLAB\LOADSAVE` for reading and writing MAT-files from Fortran programs. The first, and preferred, set implements a machine-independent set of subroutines for working with MAT-files. It does this, however, by coding the subroutines in C. This means that you *must* have access to the object libraries of a C compiler in order to link your Fortran program. If you do have a C compiler, these routines are machine-independent and available on all different platforms on which MATLAB is currently running.

The files in `\MATLAB\LOADSAVE` associated with the preferred set are:

| | |
|---|---|
| `FLOADSAV.C` | A C module containing the functions `MOPEN`, `MCLOSE`, `MLOAD`, and `MSAVE` which open and close MAT-files and do buffered file `I/O` |
| `FLOADSAV.OBJ` | Compiled version of `FLOADSAV.C` (small memory model) |
| `FLOADXX.F` | An example of a Fortran program using the `MLOAD` function |
| `FSAVXX.F` | An example of a Fortran program using the `MSAVE` function |
| `FLOADSAV.BAT` | A batch file showing how to compile and link the above files |

The `FLOADSAV.C` routines are implemented to support Microsoft Fortran V5.0 and Microsoft C 6.0. You must have the small memory model object code libraries from Microsoft C 6.0 in order to use these files. It should be possible to modify `FLOADSAV.C` to support other Fortran compilers, if desired.

Near to the top of `FLOADSAV.C` is the line:

```
#define PC
```

Change this line to port `FLOADSAV.C` to other platforms.

If you do not have access to a C compiler, the other files in the \MATLAB\LOADSAVE directory for reading and writing MAT-files from Fortran programs are:

LOADMAT.FOR          Fortran subroutines to read MAT-files.

SAVEMAT.FOR          Fortran subroutines to write MAT-files.

TESTLS1.FOR          A main program illustrating the use of SAVEMAT.FOR.

TESTLS2.FOR          A main program illustrating the use of SAVEMAT.FOR and LOADMAT.FOR.

These files require Microsoft Fortran, are inefficient because they use single-byte file direct access input/output, and are not portable to other computers. But if you do not have access to a C compiler, and you are not worried about porting your Fortran programs to other computers, they will get the job done.

# B.2 Macintosh Subroutines

The save command in MATLAB saves the variables currently in memory into a binary disk file called a *MAT-file*. (It is called a MAT-file because the filename extension is .mat.) The load command is the inverse; it reads the MAT-file on disk into MATLAB's memory. Sometimes you may want to read and write MAT-files directly from your own programs. To help you with this task, there is a collection of subroutines in the LOAD SAVE folder on your disk. In addition, the structure of a MAT-file is documented fully under load in the *Reference* section.

## B.2.1 C Language Programs

There are four files in the LOAD SAVE:C folder associated with reading and writing MAT-files from C programs. These routines are compiler-independent on the Macintosh.

loadmat.c  C routines to read MAT-files

savemat.c  C routines to write MAT-files

setmat.c   C routines to set MAT-file icon

testls.c   A main program illustrating the use of loadmat.c, savamat.c, and setmat.c

## B.2.2 Fortran Programs

Fortran poses interesting challenges with respect to reading and writing MAT-files. MAT-files are arbitrary byte streams, for which Fortran does not provide a convenient way of writing. Furthermore, different techniques for accessing the Macintosh Toolbox (routines that require you to change a file's creator and type) make it impossible to have compiler-independent routines. As a result, the following folders are in the `LOAD SAVE` folder:

`Absoft MF`  Contains `matfile.for` and `testls.for` for Absoft's compiler.

`Absoft MF II` Contains `matfile.f` and `testls.f` for Absoft's MacFortran II compiler.

`LS`  Contains `matfile.f` and `testls.f` for Language Systems FORTRAN compiler.

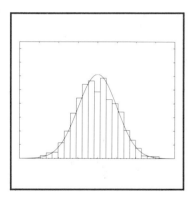

# C
# Printing with Professional MATLAB on the PC

Professional versions of MATLAB provide graphics hard copy through both a screen dump facility and graphics *metafiles* and a *graphics postprocessor* program (GPP); the *Student Edition of MATLAB* allows only for screen dumps. The quality of the screen dump hard copy is limited by the resolution of the PC graphics screen while hard copy from GPP uses the full resolution of the output device itself.

Three MATLAB commands, `prtsc`, `meta`, and `print`, are associated with hard copy operations:

- `prtsc` initiates a *print screen*. The graphics screen is dumped to the printer on a pixel-by-pixel basis, resulting in hard copy with the same resolution as the computer screen. Pressing the **Shift-PrtSc** keys on the keyboard does the same operation.

- `meta` *file* opens a high-resolution graphics metafile using the specified filename, and writes the current graph to it for later processing. Subsequent `meta` commands that do not specify a file append to the previously specified file. The metafile may be processed later using the graphics postprocessor (GPP) program. Metafiles use a default filetype of `.MET`.

- `print` immediately spools a copy of the graph on the screen to the printer, if you've configured `PRINT.M` correctly and if you've got enough free memory. `print` is an M-file that uses the metafile facility.

One DOS command provided with the MATLAB system, GPP, is associated with hard copy operations:

- GPP *file /options* invokes the Graphics Postprocessor program directly.

We'll discuss each of the four commands in the next sections.

## C.1 Using GPP

The professional version of MATLAB includes a special graphics printing facility. The graphics postprocessor, GPP, operates on device-independent MET-files (files with a filename extension of .MET produced by the meta command) to produce device-specific plot files that can be spooled to a particular hard copy device. The GPP program is invoked at the MS-DOS operating system level with a command of the form:

GPP *filename /Ddevice* [/F /P /OP /OL /CS /CC]

where spaces are used between arguments, the brackets indicate optional arguments, and *device* can be one of the following:

| GPP Devices | |
|---|---|
| epsd | Epson printer, draft quality |
| epsf | Epson printer, final quality |
| lqd | Epson LQ printer, draft quality |
| lqf | Epson LQ printer, final quality |
| jet | HP LaserJet Plus (300 dpi) |
| jet150 | HP LaserJet Plus (150 dpi) |
| desk | HP DeskJet (300 dpi) |
| hpgl | HPGL (HP compatible plotters) |
| ps | PostScript (Apple LaserWriter) |
| eps | Encapsulated PostScript (EPSF) |
| pic | pic format (troff) |
| cgi | A GSS CGI device driver |
| pen | Simple ASCII pen movements |
| tek | Tektronix 4010/4014 output |
| img | Imagen Laserprinter |
| vga | VGA graphics display |
| ega | EGA graphics display |
| cga | CGA graphics display |
| hgc | Hercules graphics display |
| att | AT&T 6300 graphics display |

GPP takes the specified MET-file and creates a new file containing device-specific control sequences for the requested device. The filename extension on the new file is the same as the first three letters of the device type specifier in the table. For example, the MATLAB commands:

```
t = -50:.3:50;
y = sin(t)./t;
plot(t,y)
meta sincplot
plot(diff(y)./diff(t))
meta
```

create a metafile called SINCPLOT.MET containing two graphs, one of a sinc function and a second of its derivative. From MS-DOS, after quitting from MATLAB, the commands:

```
GPP SINCPLOT /DEPSD
COPY SINCPLOT.EPS PRN /B
```

convert the metafile to Epson printer output, place it in a new file called SINCPLOT.EPS, and send it to an Epson printer for final output.

To send output to a serial device like a plotter, use:

```
GPP SINCPLOT /DHPGL
SPR SINCPLOT.HPG
```

where SPR is a utility that sends files to serial devices.

*Optional Arguments for GPP:*

/F          Optional argument /F selects a name for the output file created by GPP. If an MS-DOS device name is used, the output of GPP is sent directly to the device, without creating a file. For example, if we have an Epson printer connected to a parallel port:

```
GPP SINCPLOT /DEPSD /FPRN
```

sends Epson format output directly to the printer port PRN, without creating what otherwise is a very large file. Other legal output specifiers are the usual DOS device names:

| DOS Devices | |
|---|---|
| PRN | First parallel printer |
| LPT1 | Same as PRN |
| LPT2 | Second parallel printer |
| COM1 | First serial port |
| COM2 | Second serial port |

Appendices

The /F option does not work reliably with serial devices unless the handshaking wires are connected and the communication parameters are set exactly right on the printer. Use the SPR utility instead.

/P
Optional argument /P tells GPP to pause between plots if there are several on the metafile. This can be useful if GPP is being used with an interactive display device to preview graphs. GPP will pause until any key is pressed.

/OP /OL /OT
These three arguments select whether hard copy is made in *portrait*, *landscape*, or *tall* orientation. The *tall* option produces portrait-oriented output filling a whole page. Different hard copy devices have different defaults, and some do not offer both options. In general, the higher-resolution devices default to portrait orientation, which is the best for inclusion into books and reports.

/CS /CC
These two optional arguments select the text character quality used on devices whose characters are stroke-generated. /CS uses a simplex or single-line character set, while /CC uses a higher quality complex or multi-line character set. Devices that use stroke characters include the HPGL, *pic*, pen, and CGI drivers. The complex font is the default.

If there is enough free memory, GPP can be run without quitting from MATLAB using the (!) operator. In PC-MATLAB, more often than not you'll get out of memory messages from GPP, in which case you'll have to exit from MATLAB before running GPP. In AT-MATLAB there should not be a problem, unless you have only a small amount of memory installed.

New output devices will be added to GPP over time. If you invoke GPP with no arguments, you'll see a usage summary and a list of the currently available devices.

MET-files, the metafiles produced by MATLAB, can be sent directly to VAX, Sun, Apollo, and other implementations of MATLAB that you may have access to. This can be useful if the big machines have laser printers or other high-quality hard copy devices that you would like to use.

MET-files are not actually representations of the saved graph. MET-files are composed of actual data used to generate the graph, along with the graphing commands used. GPP regenerates the graph for the output device you specify. Since the graphs are optimized to the output device (either your screen or the printer) printed graphs may vary in some details from your screen representation but the content will remain the same.

## C.2  Configuring GPP.BAT

The GPP command invokes a batch file GPP.BAT that is initially configured to produce Epson printer output.  For example, from MS-DOS, the command:

```
GPP SINCPLOT
```

processes the metafile described in the previous section and sends the output to an Epson printer connected to the PRN port.

You can configure GPP.BAT with your favorite printer and GPP options. Here is one line from the GPP.BAT file that is distributed:

```
GPP386 %1.MET /DEPSD /FPRN
```

The options are set to send pictures directly to an Epson compatible printer in draft-quality mode.  The %1 is an MS-DOS replaceable parameter that allows GPP to be used with arguments.

You should edit GPP.BAT to configure it for your printer.  Once you've set up GPP, you won't have to remember all the complicated GPP options each time you want hard copy.

## C.3  Configuring PRINT.M

If you have enough memory the MATLAB print command immediately spools a copy of the graph on the screen to the printer.  print is really an M-file that saves the graph using meta and invokes the graphics postprocessor.  Here is what PRINT.M looks like as distributed:

```
meta metatmp
!gpp metatmp /depsd /fprn
delete metatmp.met
```

To see what's inside PRINT.M, execute the MATLAB command type print. You'll want to modify PRINT.M to reflect your own hard copy equipment.

print works best when used from AT-MATLAB and 386-MATLAB.  If you are running PC-MATLAB, print is not very useful - it will usually give out-of-memory messages because of the 640K byte memory limitation.  In this case, you will have to use the meta command inside MATLAB, quit out of MATLAB, and execute GPP directly.

Appendices

# C.4 SPR - Printing Out the Serial Port

If your printer or plotter is connected to a serial port, there are, in principle, two different methods of transmitting the graphics file produced by GPP to the device:

- Hardware handshaking.

- XON/XOFF software handshaking using SPR.EXE.

In practice, hardware handshaking is difficult to set up, so we recommend using the software handshaking method. Both methods are discussed in this section.

*Software Handshaking:*

SPR.EXE is a program provided with MATLAB that sends a file out the serial port using XON/XOFF software handshaking. SPR has a number of options, but usually it just needs to be given the name of the file to transfer. For example, to send a PostScript file out the COM1 communication port to an Apple LaserWriter, use:

```
SPR SINCPLOT.PS
```

The SPR program is invoked at the MS-DOS operating system level with a command of the form:

```
SPR filename [Line Settings] [Trigger Characters] [Options]
```

where spaces are used between arguments and the brackets indicate optional arguments.

*Line Settings* can be:

| | |
|---|---|
| port | - COM1 or COM2 (default = COM1) |
| baud rate | - any standard baud rate (default = 9600) |
| parity | - ODD, EVEN, or NONE (default = NONE) |
| data bits | - 7 or 8 (default = 8) |
| stop bits | - 1 or 2 (default = 1) |

Trigger Characters, set by xon=number or xoff=number, can be:

| | |
|---|---|
| xon | - decimal number (default = 17, DC1) |
| xoff | - decimal number (default = 19, DC3) |

*Options* can be hpgl. This causes SPR to scan the output stream for HPGL page eject requests, which occur on files with multiple graphs. When found, SPR pauses and displays a message asking for a new piece of paper to be inserted.

Here are some examples of legal SPR invocations:

```
SPR SINCPLOT.PS
SPR SINCPLOT.PS COM2 2400
SPR SINCPLOT.HPG COM2 HPGL
```

Entering just SPR will list the command syntax used by SPR as well as the output devices supported by SPR.

*Hardware Handshaking:*

Although we recommend the software handshaking method, it is possible to use hardware handshaking, which allows files to be sent using the DOS COPY command and using the /F option of GPP. To make hardware handshaking work, the RS-232 wires must be connected correctly between the computer and the printer, and communication parameters must be set properly on both ends. On the PC end, the communication parameters are set using the DOS MODE command. For example, if you have a plotter connected to COM1 at 9600 baud, you should use:

```
MODE COM1:9600,n,8,1,p
```

Consult a DOS manual for further details.

On the plotter end, you should consult the plotter documentation. If configured successfully, a graphics file can be transferred using the DOS COPY command:

```
GPP SINCPLOT /DHGPL
COPY SINCPLOT.HPG COM1
```

or directly from GPP using the /F option:

```
GPP SINCPLOT /DHGPL /FCOM1
```

If the handshaking is not configured correctly, the result is usually a fragmented graph, or no graph at all.

## C.5 Output Devices

The subsections that follow discuss the individual output hard copy devices supported by GPP. In general, there are two classes of devices: Vector devices and raster devices. For most MATLAB applications, vector devices are less demanding on available computational and storage resources.

Appendices

## C.5.1 Epson Printers

GPP can drive Epson and compatible dot-matrix printers in two modes: draft and final.

The option /depsd creates a draft mode 72 dpi (dots per inch) portrait orientation graph that occupies half the page. If there are two or more graphs, they are printed two per page.

The option /depsd works only on Epson 9-pin (and compatible) printers, not on LQ-compatible printers.

The option /depsf works on Epson 9-pin and LQ-compatible printers. It creates a final mode high-quality 240 x 216 dpi portrait orientation graph. The resulting plots emerge slightly elongated on LQ-compatible printers.

Epson files are quite large. To save disk space, it is usually best to send them directly to the printer using the /FPRN option of GPP:

```
GPP SINCPLOT /depsd /FPRN
```

If you don't use the FPRN option, you can send them to the printer manually, using the DOS COPY command.

```
GPP SINCPLOT /depsd
COPY SINCPLOT.EPS PRN /B
```

Don't forget to use the /B binary option.


## C.5.2 Epson LQ 24-Pin Printers

GPP can drive Epson LQ and compatible 24-pin dot-matrix printers in two modes: draft and final.

The option /dlqd creates a draft mode 90 dpi (dots per inch) portrait orientation graph that occupies half the page. If there are two or more graphs, they are printed two per page.

The option /dlqf creates a final mode high-quality 180 dpi portrait orientation graph.

Epson LQ files are quite large. To save disk space, it is usually best to send them directly to the printer using the /FPRN option of GPP:

```
GPP SINCPLOT /dlqd /FPRN
```

If you don't use the /FPRN option you can send them to the printer manually, using the DOS COPY command.

```
GPP SINCPLOT /dlqd
COPY SINCPLOT.LQD PRN /B
```

Don't forget to use the /B binary option.

## C.5.3 Hewlett-Packard LaserJet Printers

GPP can generate output on the LaserJet Plus, LaserJet II, and LaserJet III printers. GPP does not support the original LaserJet printer because it has so little memory (64K) that only postage-stamp sized graphics would be possible. The output file is in Hewlett-Packard PCL (Printer Control Language) format.

The command:

```
GPP SINCPLOT /djet
```

generates a LaserJet file called `SINCPLOT.JET` that contains a 300 dpi graph in portrait orientation that occupies half the page. If there are two or more graphs, they are printed two per page.

The command:

```
GPP SINCPLOT /djet150
```

generates a file with a 150 dpi graph at half the resolution and half the file size of `djet`. This graph is a portrait orientation occupying half the page like the output from `djet`.

It may take as long as one minute per page to send the data over a parallel connection. If you are unlucky enough to be using a serial connection, it takes eight times longer. If printing speed is critical, use the `/djet150` option to halve the printing time.

Ordinary text on the graph uses a 12-point font read from the file `JET.FNT`. Exponent text uses an 8-point font obtained from the file `JETEXP.FNT`. Fonts can be changed by substituting for these files any valid HP Soft Font file. Some things to keep in mind if you substitute your own font files:

- If you replace the font files with your own, be sure to save the original font files in a safe place.

- The file `JETEXP.FNT` must contain the marker characters "+ * o x" or GPP will exit with an error message.

- The font files should be portrait fonts; GPP will rotate these as needed for landscape plots.

- GPP only downloads to the printer the characters it needs to avoid wasting memory.

- The larger the font, the smaller the area remaining for the contents of the plot. In addition, larger size fonts use more printer memory than smaller ones.

There are two common errors that may occur when printing to an HP LaserJet. The error status is shown by a flashing error code on the LaserJet front panel. The first is "20 ERROR" . This error indicates that the printer has run out of memory. This may be due to using an overly large font file or attempting to draw a very complex graph. This error can be corrected either by using the /djet150 option, by adding additional memory to your printer, or by using a smaller point size for your soft font file. This error will occur most often in *tall* and *landscape* orientations, so using /op is also a possible solution.

The second common error is "21 ERROR". This error indicates that the graph is too complicated. Usually this happens if the plot contains a large number of vertical lines. To correct this problem, use the GPP /ol option to turn the graph on its side, use the /ddesk device driver, or remove some of the lines from the plot. The /ddesk option produces a significantly larger output file (it is a complete bitmap), but it should not produce a 21 ERROR. Note that graphs that cause 21 ERRORs an HP LaserJet II or Plus are less likely to cause these errors on an HP LaserJet IIP since that model has a faster processor and a slower paper feed mechanism. The HP Laserjet III has a patch that also eliminates this problem.

LaserJet files are quite large. To save disk space, it is usually best to send them directly to the printer using the /FPRN option of GPP:

```
GPP SINCPLOT /djet /FPRN
```

If you don't use the /FPRN option, you can send them to the printer manually, using the DOS COPY command:

```
GPP SINCPLOT /djet
COPY SINCPLOT.JET PRN /B
```

Don't forget to use the /B binary option.


## C.5.4 Hewlett-Packard DeskJet Printers

GPP can drive HP DeskJet printers. The option /ddesk creates a 300 dpi portrait orientation graph that occupies half the page. If there are two or more graphs, they are printed two per page.

The DeskJet driver, like the LaserJet driver, uses the Soft Font files JET.FNT and JETEXP.FNT, but it does not download these to the printer.

DeskJet files are Hewlett-Packard PCL files and may work on other PCL compatible printers. For example, HP LaserJets can print them.

DeskJet files are quite large. To save disk space, it is usually best to send them directly to the printer using the /FPRN option of GPP:

```
GPP SINCPLOT /ddesk /FPRN
```

If you don't use the /FPRN option, you can send them to the printer manually, using the DOS COPY command:

```
GPP SINCPLOT /ddesk
COPY SINCPLOT.DES PRN /B
```

Don't forget to use the /B binary option.


## C.5.5  HPGL Plotters

GPP can generate Hewlett-Packard Graphics Language (HPGL) output for HP 7470, HP 7475, HP 7550, and other HPGL-compatible plotters. GPP uses a subset of the full HPGL command set that is universally supported by all HPGL plotters. The graph will be drawn in color if color pens are available on the plotter.

The command:

```
GPP SINCPLOT /dhpgl
```

generates an HPGL file called SINCPLOT.HPG that contains a landscape orientation picture that occupies the whole page. The orientation options of GPP have no effect in the current implementation.

HPGL files are ASCII files whose length is dependent on the complexity of the graph. *They cannot reliably be sent to a plotter using the* /f *option of GPP.* See *Configuring SPR - Printing Out the Serial Port* on serial communication. Instead, use SPR, the serial print program, to send HPGL files to the plotter:

```
SPR SINCPLOT.HPG HPGL
```

If you use the HPGL option, SPR will pause between graphs on multipicture files and give you a chance to insert a new piece of paper.


## C.5.6  PostScript (Apple LaserWriter)

GPP can generate normal and Encapsulated PostScript files for the Apple LaserWriter and compatible PostScript laser printers. PostScript is a page description language (PDL) that has become a de facto standard for desktop publishing. PostScript laser printer output is the fastest and best-looking output available from GPP. Since PostScript is a language, PostScript files consist of human readable statements that may be edited to scale picture sizes, change fonts, etc.

The command:

```
GPP SINCPLOT /dps
```

generates a PostScript file called SINCPLOT.PS that contains a portrait orientation picture occupying the upper half of the page. If there is more than one plot in the metafile, the second plot will appear on the bottom half of the page, the third plot will start at the top of the second page, etc.

Text is written in a 12-point Times Roman font. The orientation option /ol selects landscape orientation and one graph per page.

The command:

```
GPP SINCPLOT /deps
```

generates an Encapsulated PostScript file (EPSF) called SINCPLOT.EPS containing a portrait orientation picture. EPSF files can be read by many desktop publishing packages. They are normal PostScript files with the PostScript commands initgraphics, erasepage, and copypage removed. There should be only one plot per GPP metafile. PostScript files are ASCII files, whose length is dependent on the complexity of the graph. *They cannot reliably be sent to a printer using the* /f *option of GPP.* See *SPR - Printing Out the Serial Port* on serial communication.

To send PostScript files to an Apple LaserWriter, connect a serial cable between the serial port on your PC and the RS-232 connection on the LaserWriter. Set the LaserWriter switches for 9600 baud serial communication and use SPR, the serial print program, to send the PostScript file to the printer:

```
SPR SINCPLOT.PS
```

At *The MathWorks, Inc.*, we use TOPS FlashCards and TOPS DOS on our PCs. This low-cost hardware and software allows us to share a LaserWriter with Macintoshes in an AppleTalk network, and to print files at up to 230K baud, which is considerably faster than a 9600 baud serial connection. For more information call TOPS at 415-769-8808.

## C.5.7  pic (for troff)

GPP can generate *pic* format output for use with the *troff* document processing system found on UNIX-based machines.

The command:

```
GPP SINCPLOT /dpic
```

generates an ASCII pic file named SINCPLOT.PIC that contains a picture in portrait orientation.

The command:

```
GPP SINCPLOT /dpic /OL
```

generates a `pic` file in landscape orientation.

In both modes, text is written in a Hershey stroke-generated font. Multiple pictures may be included in the GPP metafile. Because the first line of a *pic* file contains parameters that determine the size (in inches) of the picture being generated, *pic* files can be edited to change the final size of the figure.

To include `SINCPLOT.PIC` into a *troff* document, include the *pic* preprocessor command:

```
.PS <SINCPLOT.PIC
```

in the document where you want the picture placed. To use the preprocessor in conjunction with *troff*, execute a command like:

```
pic example.doc | troff -ps >matlab.ps
```

See your *troff* user's guide and the documentation for the *pic* preprocessor for more information.


## C.5.8  Pen File

The `/dpen` device option creates a simple ASCII "pen" movement file. If you have an unusual hard copy device that is not supported directly by GPP, nor through the CGI option, it is possible to write your own translation program to convert the pen-file to the output commands for your own device. The pen-file is an ASCII file where each carriage-return separated line contains three fields: X-position, Y-position, and Pen-flag. Here is a short excerpt from a typical pen-file:

```
   0       0   0
 231     235   1
1543    5031   1
1873    1236   1
```

The X- and Y-positions are 4-digit integers where (0,0) corresponds to the lower-left corner of the plotting area and (9999,9999) is the upper right. The Pen-flag is 0 if the pen is up, 1 if the pen is down, 2 to signal end-of- picture, and 3 to signal the end-of-file.

## C.5.9 The GSS/CGI Drivers

PCGPP has an interface to the Computer Graphics Interface (CGI) system from Graphics Software Systems (GSS). The main feature of the CGI system is a huge library of device drivers spanning almost every available hard copy device. If you don't find your hard copy device listed in the table of GPP devices that are supported directly, you can use the /dcgi option of GPP to drive your hard copy device through the CGI.

The CGI system is not included with the main MATLAB system. It can be ordered directly from Graphics Software Systems at 503-641-2200. Depending on which version of CGI you use, the following instructions may differ slightly from those you receive from GSS. If that is the case, please follow the directions below for the best results with the MATLAB system.

In order to use the CGI option of GPP, you need to install the appropriate device drivers and then specify their locations along with the main GSS CGI-driver file, GSSCGI.SYS, in your CONFIG.SYS file. For example, if you have LaserJet and Okidata hard-copy devices and have installed the device driver files for them in the C:\DRIVERS directory, you must enter the following in your CONFIG.SYS file:

```
device = c:\drivers\laserjet.sys
device = c:\drivers\okid92.sys
device = c:\drivers\gsscgi.sys /t
```

The device drivers should be listed contiguously with GSSCGI.SYS listed last; in addition, GSSCGI.SYS must include the /t option, which loads the driver in transient mode so that it occupies only 1.5K bytes of memory when it is not in use.

Before GPP can be invoked with the /dcgi option, it must be told which of the available device drivers to use. This is done by setting an environment variable called CGIDEV. For example, to select the Okidata driver from the two that where specified above, enter:

```
SET CGIDEV=OKID92
```

at the MS-DOS prompt; then enter:

```
GPP SINCPLOT /DCGI
```

to run GPP. This procedure sends Okidata device codes directly out the parallel port. If a serial device is specified, the output is sent to COM1. The default output port can be changed by setting the device name to a port name. For example, SET OKID92=COM1 sends the output through COM1.

You'll probably want to set the CGIDEV environment variable in your AUTOEXEC.BAT file. For more information on environment variables, see *Environment Parameters* or an MS-DOS guide.

The GSS CGI system can be controlled by setting a number of DOS environment variables. For example SET ORIENTATION=PORTRAIT tells it to print the plot in portrait orientation. Other options are described in the README files on the CGI distribution disks.

One of the most useful GSS CGI device drivers is the ANSI standard *Computer Graphics Metafile*. Many word processing and desktop publishing programs can accept graphics files in this format.

GPP386, the 80386 version of GPP, does not support the GSS CGI system.

# C.6 Including Graphs in Word Processors

An increasing number of word processing and desktop publishing programs have the ability to import various graphics file formats directly into documents. Here is a brief summary of the file formats accepted by several leading programs:

Word Perfect™

> PostScript EPSF, HPGL, and GSS Computer Graphics Metafiles are advertised to work.

Manuscript™

> Only GSS Computer Graphics Metafile.

PageMaker™

> PostScript EPSF, possibly others.

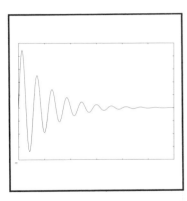

# D

# References Cited
# in this Manual

1. Bryson, A.E. Jr., and Ho, Y.C., *Applied Optimal Control*, Hemisphere Publishing, 1975. pp. 328-338.

2. Dongarra, J.J., Moler, C.B., Bunch, J.R., Stewart, G.W., *LINPACK Users' Guide*, Society for Industrial and Applied Mathematics, Philadelphia, 1979.

3. Franklin, G.F. and J.D. Powell, *Digital Control of Dynamic Systems*, Addison-Wesley, 1980.

4. Garbow, B. S., Boyle, J. M., Dongarra, J. J. Moler, C. B., *Matrix Eigensystem Routines -- EISPACK Guide Extension*, Lecture Notes in Computer Science, volume 51, Springer-Verlag, 1977.

5. Golub, G. H. and Van Loan, C. F., *Matrix Computations*, Johns Hopkins University Press, 1983.

6. Kailath, T., *Linear Systems*, Prentice-Hall, 1980.

7. Laub, A.J., *Efficient Multivariable Frequency Response Computations*, IEEE Transactions on Automatic Control, Vol. AC-26, No. 2, April 1981, pp. 407-408.

8. Laub, A.J., *Numerical Linear Algebra Aspects of Control Design Computations*, IEEE Transactions on Automatic Control, Vol. AC-30, No. 2, February 1985, pp. 97-108.

9. Oppenheim, A. V. and R. W. Schafer, *Digital Signal Processing*, Prentice-Hall, 1975.

10. Parks, T. W. and C. S. Burrus, *Digital Filter Design*, John Wiley & Sons, 1987.

11. *Programs for Digital Signal Processing*, IEEE Press, John Wiley & Sons, 1979.

12.  Rabiner, L. R. and B. Gold, *Theory and Application of Digital Signal Processing*, Prentice-Hall, 1975.

13.  Smith, B. T., Boyle, J. M., Dongarra, J.J., Garbow, B. S., Ikebe, Y., Klema, V. C., Moler, C. B., *Matrix Eigensystem Routines -- EISPACK Guide*, Lecture Notes in Computer Science, Volume 6, Second Edition, Springer-Verlag, 1976.

14.  Wilkinson, J.H., *The Algebraic Eigenvalue Problem*, Oxford University Press, 1965.

15.  Wilkinson, J.H., *Rounding Errors in Algebraic Processes*, Prentice-Hall, 1963.

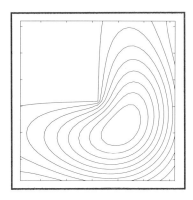

# Index

Note: Entries in boldface are MATLAB keywords and functions

if and **break** statements, 122–23
    **while** loops, 121–22
Control System Toolbox, 8, 141
**conv**, 97, 166, 190, 193, 194, 241–42
**conv2**, 98
Conventions, typographical, 14
Convolution and deconvolution in signal
    processing, 166–67, 241–42
**corrcoef**, 81, 193, 243
Correlation/convolution functions list, 194
**cos**, 67, 189
**cosh**, 67, 189
**cov**, 81, 97, 193, 243
**cplxpair**, 81, 193, 244
Cubic spline data interpolation, 404–5
**cumprod**, 81, 193, 417
**cumsum**, 81, 193, 417
Curve fitting, 85–86

## D

Data
    imaginary and complex, 113
    importing and exporting, 136–38
Data analysis, 79–86
    column-oriented, 79–82, 193
    missing values, 82–83
    outlier removal, 84
    regression and curve fitting, 85–86
**date**, 186, 234–35
Decompositions, 191, 375–77
**deconv**, 97, 166, 190, 193, 241–42
**delete**, 135, 188, 248
**demo**, 185, 306
Design functions, 181
**det**, 60, 74, 88, 192, 317–20
**diag**, 75, 77, 78, 190, 191, 245
Diagonal matrix, 245
**diary**, 136, 188, 246
**diff**, 81, 193, 247
Difference functions, 247
Differential equation solution, 104–5
Digital filters, 289–90
**dir**, 135, 188, 248
Discrete Fourier transform (DFT), 149
Discrete-time LTI systems, 175–77
Discretization, 178
Disk directory, 433
Disk files, 135–38

data importation and exportation,
    136–38
external program execution, 136
functions, 188
manipulation of, 135–36
**disp**, 187, 249
Division
    array, 62, 185
    matrix, 58–59

## E

**echo**, 129, 187, 188, 250
Editing in DOS, 23–25
**eig**, 93, 191, 251–53
Eigenvalues, 92–93, 251–53
Eigenvectors, 251–53
**ellip**, 153–54, 194, 254–56
**ellipap**, 155, 193, 257
**ellipj**, 68, 190, 258–59
**ellipk**, 68, 190, 260–61
Elliptic (Cauer) filters, 153–57, 254–56,
    257
Elliptic functions, Jacobian, 258–59
Elliptic integral, 260–61
**else**, 188, 313–14
**elseif**, 188
Empty matrices, 74
Encapsulated PostScript File (EPSF), 40
**end**, 188, 262
Environment parameters (DOS), 25–27
**eps**, 47–48, 186, 197–98
Equations, 103–5
    differential equation solution, 104–5, 192,
    359–61
    nonlinear, 103–4, 192
**erf**, 68, 190, 263
**error**, 188, 214
**errorbar**, 187, 264
Error functions, 263
Error message display, 214
**etime**, 188, 234–35
**eval**, 130, 186, 188, 265–66
Evans root-locus, 391–93
**exist**, 66, 74, 188, 189, 433
**exit**, 185, 411
**exp**, 67, 189, 267
**expm**, 60, 192, 268–69
Exponential functions, 267, 268

Vectors, 43, 69–77. *See also* Matrix/matrices
  generating, 69–70, 444–45
  logarithmically and linearly spaced, 329
  signals as, 144–47
  subscripting, 71–73, 444–45

**W**

**what**, 128, 185, 188, 433
**while**, 121–22, 132, 188, 432
**who**, 47, 185, 433
Windows, 168–69
  command control, 232
  functions, 187, 194, 304
  graph control, 232
  graphs and, 416
  Macintosh, 449–62
  screen control, 116–17
Workspace
  getting information on, 47–48

quitting and saving, 53

**X**

**xlabel**, 107, 187, 424–25
x-y plots, 108

**Y**

**ylabel**, 107, 187, 424–25
**yulewalk**, 160, 194

**Z**

0–1 Vectors, subscripting, 73
Zero-pole-gain systems, 159, 173–75, 177
  state-space conversion, 434
  transfer function conversion to, 422–23,
    435
**zeros**, 76, 191, 362
**zp2ss**, 157, 178, 194, 434
**zp2tf**, 178, 435